SCOTLAND

NORTHUMBERLAND

TYNE & WEAR

CUMBRIA

DURHAM

CLEVELAND

NORTH YORKSHIRE

LANCASHIRE

WEST YORKSHIRE

HUMBERSIDE

MERSEYSIDE

GREATER MANCHESTER

SOUTH YORKSHIRE

CHESHIRE

DERBY

LINCOLN

NOTTS.

CLWYD

GWYNEDD

STAFFS.

LEICESTER

NORFOLK

SALOP

WEST MIDLANDS

POWYS

HEREFORD & WORCESTER

WARWICK

NORTHAMPTON

CAMBRIDGE

SUFFOLK

DYFED

GWENT

GLOUCESTER

BUCKS.

BEDFORD

HERTFORD

ESSEX

WEST GLAMORGAN

MID GLAMORGAN

SOUTH

OXFORD

GREATER LONDON

AVON

BERKS.

SURREY

KENT

WILTSHIRE

HAMPSHIRE

WEST SUSSEX

EAST SUSSEX

SOMERSET

DEVON

DORSET

CORNWALL

The Beauty of English Churches

By the same author

Observer's Old English Churches (Warne)
What to see in a Country Church
Enjoying Historic Churches (S.P.C.K.)
A County Guide to English Churches (S.P.C.K.)

The Beauty of English Churches

Lawrence E. Jones F.S.A.

Constable London

First published in Great Britain 1978
by Constable and Company Ltd
10 Orange Street London WC2H 7EG
Copyright © 1978 Lawrence E. Jones
Reprinted 1981

ISBN 0 09 461730 9

Filmset in Monophoto Times New Roman 9 pt
and printed in Great Britain by
BAS Printers Limited, Over Wallop, Hampshire

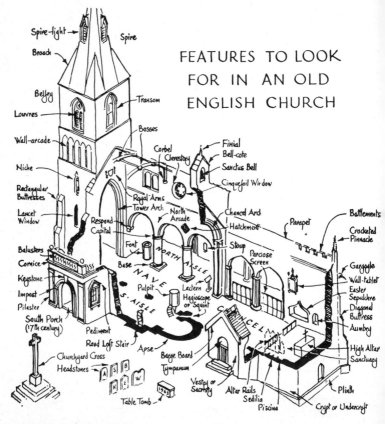

FEATURES TO LOOK FOR IN AN OLD ENGLISH CHURCH

Drawn by Anthony S. B. New and reproduced by
kind permission of Frederick Warne & Co Ltd

Contents

Illustrations 7
County List of Illustrations 9
Acknowledgments 12
The New County Boundaries 13
Introduction 17
Architectural Periods 19
Situation and Prettiest Villages 20
The Churchyard 26
Towers 31
Bells 80
Spires 81
Weather-Vanes 102
Clocks and Clock-jacks 104
Clerestories 105
Porches 108
Holy Water Stoups 114
Doorways 115
Doors 120
Gargoyles 124
Other Exterior Figure Sculpture 126
Mass Dials and Sundials 128
Plan 129
Orientation 131
Crypts/Exterior Roofs 132
Windows 133
Interior Roofs (Wooden) 145
Stone Roofs (or Vaults) 156
Cathedrals 162
Piers and Arches and Complete Churches in one Style 164
Interiors 181
Fonts 186
Font Covers 204
Chests 208
Wall-paintings 209
Benches 218
Lecterns 228
Pulpits 230

Hour-glasses **240**
Rood-screens **242**
Rood-lofts **260**
Stalls **264**
Bishops' Thrones **270**
Misericords **271**
Hatchments **274**
Royal Arms **276**
Monuments **279**
Chantry Chapels **310**
Stained Glass **313**
Low-side Windows **323**
Piscinas **325**
Sedilia **326**
Easter Sepulchres **329**
Squints/Altar Rails **331**
High Altar and Communion Tables **332**
Reredoses **334**
Sanctuary Chairs/Church Plate **337**
Embroidery **340**
Organs **342**
West Galleries/Candelabra or Chandeliers **343**
Family Pews/Libraries and Chained Books **344**
Tiles/Consecration Crosses **345**
Votive Crosses and Graffiti **346**
Aumbries and Banner Stave Lockers **346**
Dole Cupboards **346**
Anchorite Cells/Stations of the Cross/Alms Boxes **347**
The Instruments of the Passion **349**
Emblems of the Twelve Apostles **350**
Symbols of the Four Evangelists **350**
The Four Latin Doctors **350**
Emblems of some other 'popular' saints **351**
Sacred Monograms **351**
Conclusion **352**
Index of Subjects **357**
Index of Places **359**
County Index of Places **375**

Illustrations

Plate numbers in light (59) page numbers in bold (**122**)

Addlethorpe 59, **122**

Adel 55, 60, 86, **117**, **123**, **171**

Amberley 85, **169**

Ashover 99, **196**

Ashton 131, **258**

Bamburgh 7, **27**

Banwell 121, 125, **239**, **246**

Barton-on-Humber 29, **69**

Baunton 108, **211**

Beeston-next-Mileham 68, **141**

Begbroke 18, **49**

Bere Regis 75, **154**

Besthorpe 67, 141, **140**, **291**

Beverley Minster 24, **63**

Beverley St Mary 25, **65**

Binfield 122, **241**

Birdbrook 36, **82**

Bisham 140, **289**

Blakeney 160, **353**

Blythburgh 51, **107**

Boston 20, **56**

Bovey Tracey 115, **229**

Boxgrove 78, **157**

Bradninch 132, **259**

Bramfield 127, 128, **251**, **253**

Braunton 113, **224**

Brent Knoll 114, **227**

Bridekirk 95, **190**

Brookland 40, 100, **87**, **197**

Brympton D'Evercy 4, **21**

Burnham Deepdale 94, **189**

Burnham Norton 116, **231**

Canterbury 1, **14**

Carleton Rode 129, 154, **255**, **333**

Castle Ashby 145, **303**

Castle Eaton 150, **323**

Castle Frome 97, **193**

Chaldon 110, **217**

Chalton 65, **138**

Chester 134, **265**

Chewton Mendip 11, **35**

Compton 39, **86**

Cowlam 93, **187**

Culbone 62, **130**

Cullompton 71, **148**

Dent 8, **29**

Dittisham 119, **237**

Doddiscombsleigh 148, **317**

Dorchester 151, **327**

Dormston 27, **67**

Durham 3, **18**

East Harling 149, **319**

East Hendred 88, **173**

East Markham 146, **307**

Eaton Bray 58, **121**

Elkstone 56, **119**

Elmley Castle 143, **295**

Euston 91, **179**

Evercreech 10, **33**

Exeter St Mary Steps 50, **103**

Flamborough 133, **261**

Forncett St Peter 33, **75**

Friston 37, **84**

Fritton 34, **77**

Gayhurst 32, **73**

Great Bircham 158, **341**

Happisburgh 102, **199**

Harberton 120, **238**

Hawkshead 6, **24**

Hawton 152, **329**

Hedon 26, **66**

Hemingborough 46, **97**

High Halden 54, **113**
Hilborough 57, **119**
Hook Norton 98, **194**
Horsham St Faith 15, **45**
Hoveton St Peter 137, **274**
Huish Episcopi 12, **37**
Iffley 30, **71**
Ivychurch 19, **54**
Knapton 73, **151**
Lapford 124, **245**
Laxfield 103, **202**
Leigh-on-Mendip 9, **30**
London, St Mary-le-Bow 48, **100**
Long Sutton 41, **89**
Long Wittenham 66, **139**
Louth 44, **93**
March 74, **153**
Martock 70, **147**
Marton 28, **68**
Nettleton 23, **61**
Northleach 52, **109**
North Leigh 82, **161**
North Rauceby 43, **91**
Norton Subcourse 138, **277**
Norwich 80, **159**
Ockham 64, **137**
Old Shoreham 31, **72**
Oxford Cathedral 42, **90**
　　Magdalen Tower 21, **59**
　　Merton Tower 22, **60**
　　St Mary's Spire 47, **99**
Patrington 89, **175**
Pickering 109, **213**
Pinhoe 159, **348**
Plymtree 123, **243**
Pulham St Mary Virgin 53, **111**
Ripple 136, **273**
St Anthony-in-Meneage 5, **22**
St Levan 14, **40**

Sall 69, 76, **143, 155**
Scarning 126, **249**
Selworthy 72, **150**
Sharrington 77, **155**
Sherborne 81, **160**
Sheringham 111, **219**
Sloley 104, **203**
Somerleyton 130, **257**
Southrop 96, **191**
Stock 38, **85**
Stoke D'Abernon 142, **293**
Stoke St Gregory 118, **236**
Stowlangtoft 112, **221**
Strelley 139, **282**
Swimbridge 106, **207**
Swinbrook 147, 153, **309, 331**
Tewkesbury 79, **158**
Theberton 35, **79**
Tichborne 63, **134**
Tickencote 84, **167**
Tong 135, **269**
Trull 117, **233**
Truro 49, **101**
Ufford 105, **205**
Walcott 16, **46**
Walsoken 87, **172**
Ware 101, **198**
Wenhaston 107, **210**
Whittlesey 45, **95**
Widecombe 13, **39**
Winchester 155, **335**
Winterborne Tomson 61, 92, **129, 183**
Wittering 83, **165**
Wolborough 90, **175**
Wylye 157, **339**
Wymondham 17, **47**
Yarnton 144, 156, **299, 336**
York 2, **16**

County List of Illustrations

Plate numbers in light (58) page numbers in bold (121)

Bedfordshire
Eaton Bray 58, **121**

Berkshire
Binfield 122, **241**
Bisham 140, **289**
East Hendred 88, **173**
Long Wittenham 66, **139**

Buckinghamshire
Gayhurst 32, **73**

Cambridgeshire
March 74, **153**
Whittlesey 45, **95**

Cheshire
Chester 134, **265**
Marton 28, **68**

Cornwall
St Anthony-in-Meneage 5, **22**
St Levan 14, **40**
Truro 49, **101**

Cumberland
Bridekirk 95, **190**

Devon
Ashton 131, **258**
Bovey Tracey 115, **229**
Bradninch 132, **259**
Braunton 113, **224**
Cullompton 71, **148**
Dittisham 119, **237**
Doddiscombsleigh 148, **317**

Exeter St Mary Steps 50, **103**
Harberton 120, **238**
Lapford 124, **245**
Pinhoe 159, **348**
Plymtree 123, **243**
Swimbridge 106, **207**
Widecombe 13, **39**
Wolborough 90, **175**

Derbyshire
Ashover 99, **196**

Dorset
Bere Regis 75, **154**
Sherborne 81, **160**
Winterborne Tomson 61, 92,
    129, 183

Durham
Durham 3, **18**

Essex
Birdbrook 36, **82**
Stock 38, **85**

Gloucestershire
Baunton 108, **211**
Elkstone 56, **119**
Northleach 52, **109**
Southrop 96, **191**
Tewkesbury 79, **158**

Hampshire
Chalton 65, **138**
Tichborne 63, **134**
Winchester 155, **335**

Herefordshire
Castle Frome 97, **193**

Hertfordshire
Ware 101, **198**

Kent
Brookland 40, 100, **87, 197**
Canterbury 1, **14**
High Halden 54, **113**
Ivychurch 19, **54**

Lancashire
Hawkshead 6, **24**

Lincolnshire
Addlethorpe 59, **122**
Barton-on-Humber 29, **69**
Boston 20, **56**
Long Sutton 41, **89**
Louth 44, **93**
North Rauceby 43, **91**

London
St Mary-le-Bow 48, **100**

Norfolk
Beeston-next-Mileham 68, **141**
Besthorpe 67, 141, **140, 291**
Blakeney 160, **353**
Burnham Deepdale 94, **189**
Burnham Norton 116, **231**
Carleton Rode 129, 154, **255, 333**
East Harling 149, **319**
Forncett St Peter 33, **75**
Great Bircham 158, **341**
Happisburgh 102, **199**

Hilborough 57, **119**
Horsham St Faith 15, **45**
Hoveton St Peter 137, **274**
Knapton 73, **151**
Norton Subcourse 138, **277**
Norwich 80, **159**
Pulham St Mary the Virgin 53, **111**
Sall 69, 76, **143, 155**
Scarning 126, **249**
Sharrington 77, **155**
Sheringham 111, **219**
Sloley 104, **203**
Walcott 16, **46**
Walsoken 87, **172**
Wymondham 17, **47**

Northamptonshire
Castle Ashby 145, **303**
Wittering 83, **165**

Northumberland
Bamburgh 7, **27**

Nottinghamshire
East Markham 146, **307**
Hawton 152, **329**
Strelley 139, **282**

Oxfordshire
Begbroke 18, **49**
Dorchester 151, **327**
Hook Norton 98, **194**
Iffley 30, **71**
North Leigh 82, **161**
Oxford Cathedral 42, **90**
Magdalen Tower 21, **59**
Merton Tower 22, **60**
St Mary's Spire 47, **99**

Swinbrook 147, 153, **309, 331**
Yarnton 144, 156, **299, 336**

Rutland
Tickencote 84, **167**

Shropshire
Tong 135, **269**

Somerset
Banwell 121, 125, **239, 246**
Brent Knoll 114, **227**
Brympton D'Evercy 4, **21**
Chewton Mendip 11, **35**
Culbone 62, **130**
Evercreech 10, **33**
Huish Episcopi 12, **37**
Leigh-on-Mendip 9, **30**
Martock 70, **147**
Selworthy 72, **150**
Stoke St Gregory 118, **236**
Trull 117, **233**

Suffolk
Blythburgh 51, **107**
Bramfield 127, 128, **251, 253**
Euston 91, **179**
Fritton 34, **77**
Laxfield 103, **202**
Somerleyton 130, **257**
Stowlangtoft 112, **221**
Theberton 35, **79**
Ufford 105, **205**
Wenhaston 107, **210**

Surrey
Chaldon 110, **217**
Compton 39, **86**
Ockham 64, **137**
Stoke D'Abernon 142, **293**

Sussex
Amberley 85, **169**
Boxgrove 78, **157**
Friston 37, **84**
Old Shoreham 31, **72**

Wiltshire
Castle Eaton 150, **323**
Nettleton 23, **61**
Wylye 157, **339**

Worcestershire
Dormston 27, **67**
Elmley Castle 143, **295**
Ripple 136, **273**

Yorkshire
Adel 55, 60, 86, **117, 123, 171**
Beverley Minster 24, **63**
Beverley St Mary 25, **65**
Cowlam 93, **187**
Dent 8, **29**
Flamborough 133, **261**
Hedon 26, **66**
Hemingborough 46, **97**
Patrington 89, **175**
Pickering 109, **213**
York 2, **16**

Acknowledgments

The author wishes to thank all those who have kindly given consent for reproduction of their photographs.

Mr. Alfred Proctor is responsible for Plate 5.

Mr. A. F. Kersting's superb photography is well known and he has provided the following plates: 4, 7, 12, 13, 14, 20, 21, 24, 29, 35, 36, 39, 44, 45, 46, 50, 51, 62, 64, 79, 91, 93, 94, 107, 108, 114, 117, 118, 121, 125, 127, 128, 133, 139, 142, 143, and 146.

Plates 18, 59, 60, 71, 81, 82, 86, 88, 89, 90, 103, 106, 115, 120, 123, 124, 131, 135, 144, 147, 153, 156, and 159, are from the excellent collection of the late Mr. F. H. Crossley and are reproduced by kind permission of Canon Maurice H. Ridgway.

Plate 38 is a photograph by Mr. C. J. Bassham, Plate 55 by Mr. J. Morrey, and Plate 8 by Mr. G. N. Wright. Plates 23, 43, and 72, are by the late Dr. F. Butler.

Permission has kindly been given by B. T. Batsford Limited for Plates 26, 52, 58, 95, 100, and 132, the Council for Places of Worship for Plates 40 and 134, the Courtauld Institute for Plate 119, the Hampshire Field Club for Plate 65, and the Oxfordshire County Libraries for Plate 150.

Plate 6 has been included by the kind consent of the Vicar of Hawkshead.

All the remaining photographs have been obtained from the splendid library of the National Monuments Record of 23 Savile Row, London W.1. The writer gladly records not only their generosity, but also the courteous help always given by their staff.

Frederick Warne & Company Limited must also be thanked for allowing the author to refer to his book on *Old English Churches* in their Observer Series.

Finally the Publishers, Constable, must receive most grateful acknowledgment; their kindness and assistance throughout has added greatly to the pleasure of this task. The author is indeed indebted to them for getting into print some of the results of his many happy years spent in visiting churches and cathedrals.

The New County Boundaries

County boundaries were fixed hundreds of years ago mainly by geological strata and by rivers. One could often name the county by looking at the church and houses of any village and by the scenery. The new boundaries ignore such characteristics, and are based on population.

The finest church towers are in the former county of Somerset. The county of Avon has now been formed partly out of Somerset and partly out of Gloucestershire. The reference to the finest towers therefore only applies to a small portion of the new county that was formerly in Somerset.

Then again, if there was a county of East Yorkshire following the former East Riding, all would be well, but it is now included in the new county of Humberside, which extends across the river to include north Lincolnshire, where the churches are quite different to the grand ones of the former East Riding.

Rutland was a most attractive small county with very distinctive churches of its own. It is now swallowed up by Leicestershire. The same applies to Huntingdonshire, now incorporated into Cambridgeshire.

Worcestershire and Herefordshire (again quite different architecturally) are combined and are referred to by both names, so that each former county can still be referred to individually. The same applies to Cumberland and Westmorland, except that the new county is called Cumbria. Parts of Lancashire have been transferred to Cumbria, and this is indeed appropriate with regard to scenery.

The most difficult new boundary is the straight line putting the whole of north Berkshire into Oxfordshire. Rather oddly the converse could almost have been an improvement geologically, as the south of Oxfordshire is typically Berkshire (Oxford being the real boundary).

The tower of Christchurch Priory is of Dorset character and so the transfer from Hampshire is appropriate.

Many people still refer to the old counties, and they have little knowledge about the alterations. It will be a most

difficult task to alter the various County Guides at present in existence.

For all these reasons it has been decided to adhere to the old county names in this book, but the above facts should be borne in mind. In order to reconcile past and present, two maps showing former and present county boundaries have been included.

It is also hoped that young people born in, say, the County of Cleveland, will not think that the book is out of date!

All places in their new counties are however clearly set out in the County Index. This book therefore combines both.

1   Central Tower, Canterbury Cathedral

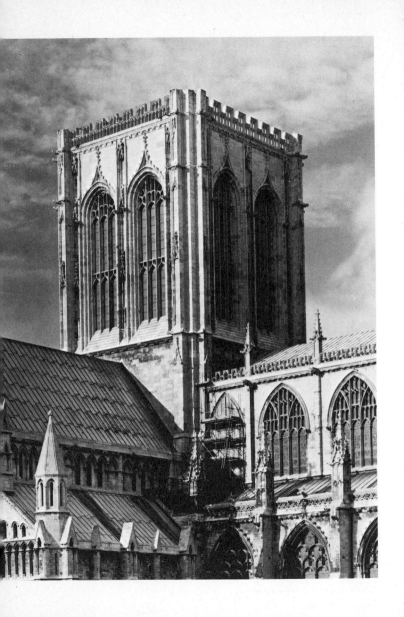

Introduction

This book attempts the impossible. There are 10,000 churches (and 43 cathedrals) in England that are medieval or of medieval foundation. Each is of some interest and to visit them all one must begin in the year that one is born, live to a hundred and visit a hundred a year.

To condense this enormous number into a nutshell is therefore not possible, and should not be allowed for the sake of all the churches omitted, and who will rightly complain bitterly.

Nevertheless not everyone did start in the year in which they were born, and this book is for them, to help them make up for their sad loss.

The object therefore is to list all that is finest in English Ecclesiastical Art, so that a visit to all, or even the majority, will give not only great joy and pleasure, but a very fair knowledge of the subject, and certainly of the English countryside in trying to find them. So often, the more isolated the church, the more of interest and beauty within. The drivers of the writer's coach excursions to country churches refer to them as 'Jones's Jungle Jaunts'.

The index is also under counties for easy reference when in that locality.

With some items, such as the finest Somerset towers and the delightful painted screen panels of East Anglia and Devon, the list is fairly complete, but with some features, owing to sheer numbers, we give excellent or typical examples.

If this book does nothing else, it should at least make one realize how little of England one has seen, and do you also realize that it is all free, which is rather staggering. Moreover studying and visiting churches can be indulged in day and night throughout the year, far more than any sport or other hobby.

Criticism will come from every church not mentioned. It is agreed that every old church should have been mentioned, as each has something of interest, and is well worth a visit, but to bring the book within reasonable bounds the proverbial line had regretfully to be drawn.

2   York Minster, Central Tower

Architectural Periods

Saxon	7th century to 1066	⎫
Norman	1066 to 1189	⎬ Romanesque
Transitional Norman	1145 to 1189	⎭
Early English	1189 to 1280	⎫
Decorated	1280 to 1377	⎬ Gothic
Perpendicular	1377 to 1547	⎬
Early Tudor	1500 to 1547	⎭
Late Tudor	1547 to 1603	⎫ Renaissance
Stuart	1603 to 1689	⎭
(Jacobean 1603 to 1625, Carolean 1625 to 1649)		⎫
		⎬ Classical
Hanoverian (William and Mary, Anne, and Georgian)	1689 to 1837	⎭

3 Superb position, Durham Cathedral

Situation and Prettiest Villages

Frequently one's first joy is finding the church at all! Quite
often it is a long way from the village and possibly in the
middle of a large park. The Lord of the Manor was usually
responsible originally for building the parish church and he
did so on his own land and near his house. Church and
manor-house together make a charming scene as at:

Cornwall	**Boconnoc** and **Lanhydrock**: Beautiful gardens.
Oxfordshire	**Chastleton**
Shropshire	**Pitchford**: Beautiful black-and-white Hall. **Stokesay**: The Castle is notable.
Somerset	**Brympton D'Evercy** (Plate 4): The small church, medieval chantry-house, and Tudor manor-house in delightful gardens make an unforgettable scene. Yet how many visitors to Montacute, nearby, know it? **North Cadbury**: Stately. **St Catherine's**: Much to see in the church.
Wiltshire	**Great Chalfield**
Worcestershire	**Wickhamford**: A typical English scene.

Churches situated in gorgeous scenery, particularly in the
North and West, make a long list:

Cornwall	**Gunwalloe**: On coast. **Mylor**: On estuary. **St Anthony-in-Meneage** (Plate 5): On estuary. **St Enodoc**: On golf links on Atlantic coast. **St Just-in-Roseland**: The beauty of its setting is unrivalled. **St Winnow**: On river.
Cumberland	All these in this county are very beautiful: **Isel**, **Millom**, **Ulpha**, and **Waberthwaite**.
Devon	St Petrock's, **Dartmouth**: On estuary. **Wembury**: On coast.

4 *Church and Manor-House, Brympton D'Evercy, Somerset*

Lancashire	**Cartmel Fell** and **Hawkshead** (Plate 6).
Northumberland	**Bolam** and **Brinkburn**. **Bamburgh** (Plate 7) – the church should be visited in addition to the castle.
Staffordshire	**Ilam**, near Dovedale.
Westmorland	**Brougham** (or **Ninekirk**), **Grasmere.**
Wiltshire	**Stourton**: Adjoining the loveliest National Trust Gardens of Stourhead.
Yorkshire	**Arncliffe**, **Grinton** (in Swaledale) and **Husthwaite**

Churches on hills make imposing landmarks:

| Devon | **Brentor**: Isolated on a steep cliff of volcanic stone |
| Leicestershire | **Breedon-on-the-Hill** |

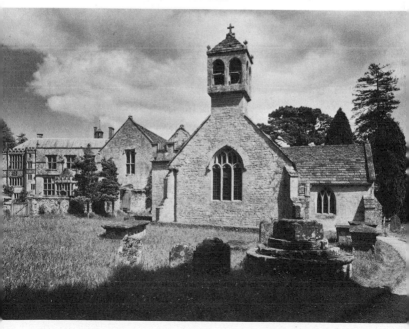

| Somerset | **Dundry**: Built as a landmark for shipping in the Bristol Channel, being on a hill 750 feet above sea-level and seen for miles around. |
| Yorkshire | **Holme-upon-Spalding-Moor** |

Two cathedrals are on hill-top sites, namely **Durham** (Plate 3) and **Lincoln** (and **Ely** is on a hill for those parts).

Views from churches on hills are always rewarding. In addition to the above, must be mentioned:

Northampton-shire	**Rockingham**: Looking across the Welland Valley to Leicestershire and Rutland.
Somerset	**Selworthy**: Superb view to Dunkery Beacon, the highest point on Exmoor.
Suffolk	**Kersey**: Looking down the village street.

There is an even longer list of the typical picture-postcard scene of church and village, but it is nearly always the church

that does make the picture. It is hoped that this list will be useful to the tourist. Each village mentioned is a 'must' for anyone who appreciates the beauty of England:

Buckinghamshire	**Bradenham**: The church, big house, village green and the Chiltern Hills behind make this typical English scene.
Essex	**Finchingfield**: The church dominates the village and pond. **Thaxted**: No one can fail to feel the medieval atmosphere that is still here.
Hampshire, Isle of Wight	**Godshill**: The church behind the thatched cottages is perhaps the most illustrated of all, and rightly so.
Hertfordshire	**Braughing**: Several delightful vistas. **Westmill**: The Herts spike peeps above the village green.
Huntingdonshire	**Kimbolton**: The picturesque street has the castle at one end and the church, with a stone broach spire, at the other.
Kent	**Aylesford**: Church and old houses above the river Medway, crossed here by a fourteenth-century bridge. **Chilham**: Village square with the church, with a Kent tower, peeping through at one corner.
Lincolnshire	**Folkingham**: The fine tower here also peeps through a corner to the large square with old houses.
Northampton-shire	**Geddington**: The tower and stone parapet spire of the church group splendidly with the Eleanor Cross of 1294 and the old bridge of about the same date.
Oxfordshire	**Whitchurch**: It is the view from the Thames that is the delight of any artist.
Somerset	**Luccombe**: The tall tower dominates the pretty village, and the view from the hill is most attractive. **Minehead**: Every visitor here will know (or should know) the

5   *A beautiful Cornish estuary, St Anthony-in-Meneage*

church high up on North Hill, with the old thatched cottages climbing up to it.

Suffolk   **Cavendish**: Again the church with its prominent tower stair turret, village green, and old thatched cottages make the perfect scene. **Kersey**: The village street is the prettiest anywhere and it remains unspoilt. The water-splash is an attraction and the church on the hill above completes the picture.

Surrey   **Shere**: Noted for its beauty. The village square leads on to the church of all dates with its timber spire.

Sussex   **South Harting**: At the foot of the South Downs. The green copper spire and red tiles on the church and old houses make a colourful scene.

Wiltshire   **Aldbourne**: The church stands proudly
                     above its village and green. **Castle Combe**:
                     Another picture-postcard village. Old
                     stone houses, stream, bridge and church –
                     what more could there be? The stair turret
                     has the spirelet of the area. **Steeple Ashton**:
                     The imposing late Perpendicular church
                     and large houses are due to the prosperity
                     of the cloth-weaving industry.

Yorkshire   **Bishop Burton**: In a green hollow are set
                     the church, cottages and pool. **Dent** (Plate
                     8): The illustration shows a typical
                     Northern scene. **Romaldkirk**: The
                     handsome church, village green and old
                     houses blend to make a perfect whole.
                     Thornton-le-Dale: A charming village. **West
                     Tanfield**: The church and the fifteenth-
                     century Marmion's Tower above the river
                     Ure make an unforgettable view.

6   *The mountains of the Lake District, Hawkshead*

The Churchyard

A churchyard must be centred upon the church, which alone gives meaning to Christian burial.

Entry is usually through a lych-gate. A few medieval ones remain, the most notable being at **Boughton Monchelsea**, Kent, and **Anstey**, Herts.

The churchyard cross dominated every churchyard before the Reformation. It was the only memorial to all the departed in the days before gravestones, and a much better idea, too, for belief in eternal life with God is rather more important than the desire to be remembered in the sight of men.

The head of the cross would usually contain a rood (a crucifix) on one side and figures of the Virgin and Child on the other side under a gabled head. Two remain complete, namely at **Ampney Crucis**, Glos., and **Somersby**, Lincs.

Remains of such crosses are common, particularly in stone districts, but usually only the steps and part of the shaft have survived.

In the North and in Cornwall, Saxon crosses in churchyards may still be found. Well-known examples are at **Bewcastle** and **Gosforth**, Cumberland, and **Bakewell** and **Eyam**, Derbyshire.

The tallest monolith in England, 25 feet, is in the churchyard of **Rudston**, Yorkshire. This churchyard is circular. A circular churchyard usually indicates a very ancient site, no doubt that of a heathen temple.

Gravestones are not therefore earlier than the late seventeenth century. Many of the following century remain and they usually have bold lettering and pleasing designs. They are of stone and harmonize with the setting (unlike appalling foreign marble of a later date). Good examples are at **Lyddington**, Rutland, and **Cavendish**, Suffolk. **Bladon** churchyard, Oxfordshire, is filled with very attractive headstones, and now made famous for all time by having the grave of Sir Winston Churchill (the church itself is rebuilt Victorian).

7   A northern scene, Bamburgh church and castle, Northumberland

The beauty and antiquity of trees in an English country churchyard are proverbial. The yew is the pre-eminent tree, and, although it may have provided bows for archers, its main use was to supply the evergreen which was the special emblem of immortality. It would also undoubtedly have afforded some protection to the fabric from our climate.

Many old yew trees, often of immense size, over 30 feet round, and well over a thousand years old, remain, particularly in the south of England, and Hampshire in particular.

Here is a list of some magnificent examples:

Derbyshire	**Darley Dale** and **Doveridge**
Dorset	**Woolland**
Gloucestershire	**Painswick**: Noted for its 99 trimmed yew trees.
Hampshire	**Brockenhurst, Corhampton, Selborne, South Hayling** and **Warblington**.
Kent	**Ulcombe**. Some neighbouring parishes in East Kent are not content with one yew, they must have several: **Stelling** – two, **Elmsted** – four, **Sellindge** – no less than five.
Surrey	**Crowhurst**: Twelve people can sit at a bench inside it. **Hambledon, Tandridge**
Sussex	**Crowhurst**: A rival to its namesake in Surrey, and a further similarity is that both churches are dedicated to St. George.

Two Churches in one Churchyard

This rare feature always arouses interest. Soil is probably the reason. Each church would have been a parish church, and the only hard ground suitable for such a building in each parish was at that particular point.

Reepham, Norfolk, actually had three together. One of the two is usually now in ruins, as at **South Walsham**, Norfolk, but both are in use at **Willingale**, Essex, and **Trimley**, Suffolk. **Swaftham Prior**, Cambridgeshire, is well-known.

English people are very parochially-minded (the reason why there were originally 100 churches in the square mile of the City of London), and the parochial system is still very strong, notwithstanding group and team ministries.

Every little community loves its old church and the congregation do not usually wish to travel to any other.

8   A typical northern scene, Dent, Yorkshire

Towers

The old church tower, sometimes with a spire, is the making of the typically English scene. What would the countryside be like if there were no ancient churches dominating the villages?

We can judge a tower by the belfry windows and by the arrangement of the parapet, whether battlemented and with or without pinnacles. All ornament should be concentrated at the top storey and the middle can be absolutely plain (Magdalen Tower, **Oxford**, shows this).

The arrangement of the buttresses is also important, whether two at right angles at each corner (called rectangular), or one built diagonally at each corner.

A local variation around Northamptonshire clasps the corners, and in the valleys of the Thames and Waveney, octagonal buttresses are found.

On the ground storey, a large west window enhances a tower (if it is a west tower).

Somerset

We begin in Somerset, because the grand Perpendicular towers of that county are unrivalled anywhere in England, and for beauty and perfection we have no hesitation in stating that they have no rivals anywhere in the world. In composition and exquisite detail in the rich golden stone they are unsurpassed. A beautiful local feature is perforation of belfry windows instead of the usual wooden louvre-boards.

As each tower is a gem there can be no omissions in our list and classification, which is reasonably complete and which comprises no less than 63 churches (**Wells** Cathedral and **Bath** Abbey are not included in this section – cathedral towers are discussed on page 74).

The most perfect are marked with an asterisk. Unless otherwise mentioned, the windows below the belfry storey are single ones.

9   *One of the finest Somerset towers: Leigh-on-Mendip*

Three belfry windows abreast (all perforated) and battlements

East Mendip area: ***Bruton, Cranmore, *Ilminster**: Three blank windows below the belfry storey, all square-headed, 12 pinnacles, and spirelet on stair turret. Very lovely. ***Leigh-on-Mendip** (Plate 9): Three blank windows below, and an elaborate parapet with 12 pinnacles. Not very high, but perhaps the most perfect of all. ***Mells**: Three blank windows below. In a beautiful setting.

Three belfry windows abreast, but only the centre one is perforated, the other windows being blank arcading, and a straight parapet (without battlements), but pierced with a beautiful pattern

West Mendip area: **Axbridge, Banwell, Bleadon, Brent Knoll, Cheddar, Mark, Shepton Mallet**: Thought to be the earliest. A stone spire was begun, but not continued, as the tower was seen to be so beautiful as it was. ***Weare**: Eight pinnacles. Small, but most artistic. **Wedmore**: No pinnacles. ***Winscombe**: With its 12 pinnacles, it is very lovely.

The same, but with battlements instead of a straight parapet

Mid-Somerset area: **Langport, Long Sutton, *Weston Zoyland**.

Belfry windows continued into stage below

*Batcombe: Three windows, straight parapet, no pinnacles, and fine figure sculpture. ***Evercreech** (Plate 10): Two windows. A perfect tower. ***Wells**, St Cuthbert: Two windows. The largest and 142 feet high. ***Wrington**: Two windows.

10   Another fine Somerset tower: Evercreech

Two belfry windows abreast

Vale of Taunton: In some of these towers the pinnacles are beautiful and sometimes with slender flying pinnacles attached. **Bishop's Lydeard**: Red Sandstone. **Blagdon**: Spirelet on stair turret. **Chedzoy**, ***Chewton Mendip*** (Plate 11): Two blank windows below, elaborate parapet and pinnacles, and figure sculpture. 126 feet high. Very lovely. **Glastonbury**, St Benign, ***Glastonbury***, St John the Baptist: Blank panelling in stage below, and elaborate parapet and pinnacles. 134 feet high. ***Huish Episcopi*** (Plate 12): Probably illustrated more than any other tower. **Hutton**, ***Ile Abbots***: Original figures in niches. A beautiful composition. ***Kingsbury Episcopi***, ***Kingston St Mary***: A beautiful composition. **Locking**, **Lympsham**, **Lyng**, **Martock**, **Middlezoy**, **Muchelney**, ***North Petherton***: Very lovely. **Ruishton**: No battlements or pinnacles (unfinished). ***Staple Fitzpaine***: A beautiful composition. **Taunton**, St James: Rebuilt. ***Taunton***, St Mary Magdalene: Also rebuilt. Two windows in each of the two stages below, and elaborate parapet and pinnacles. The highest, 163 feet high.

A single belfry window. Spirelet on stair turret

North Somerset area: **Batheaston**, **Brislington**, **Chew Stoke**, **Nailsea**, **Portishead**, **Publow**, **Wraxall**.

A single belfry window

Chew Magna, **Crewkerne**: Octagonal stair turret with pinnacles. **Dundry**: Exceptionally elaborate parapet and pinnacles (see Situation, page 22). **Enmore**: Octagonal stair turret with pinnacles. **Hatch Beauchamp**: A beautiful parapet with eight pinnacles. **Hinton St George**: Octagonal stair turret with pinnacles. **Kilmersdon**, **Mudford**: Octagonal stair turret with battlements. **Norton-sub-Hamdon**, **Othery**, **Winford**, **Yeovil**: Straight parapet. No pinnacles.

11   Another fine Somerset tower: Chewton Mendip

There are only two towers of complete Somerset standard outside that county. They both have double belfry windows and are very beautiful.

Cornwall   **Probus**: 118 feet high
Devon   **Chittlehampton**: 115 feet high

Dorset

This county is included next as the fine Perpendicular towers have certain affinities to Somerset. All have double belfry windows, except **Cerne Abbas** with a single one. **Beaminster**: Figure sculpture. **Bradford Abbas**: Octagonal buttresses, niches. **Cerne Abbas**: Octagonal buttresses. **Charminster**: Square-headed windows. **Dorchester**, **Fordington**, **Milton Abbey**, **Piddletrenthide**: Octagonal stair turret with pinnacles. **Sherborne** Abbey.

Also in the same group: **Christchurch** Priory, Hampshire.

Pinnacles on octagonal stair turrets have been noted. If the stair turret is square, then four pinnacles make a perfect finish, as at:

Cornwall   **Gwinear**
Devon   **Silverton**
Dorset   **Affpuddle** and **Piddlehinton**

The West Country

West Devon and Cornwall have some very attractive tall fifteenth-century towers, often of great blocks of granite, with large octagonal pinnacles having crocketed spirelets. **Widecombe**, Devon (Plate 13), is the well-known picture-postcard scene. Others are:

Cornwall

        Linkinhorne, **Morwenstow**, **North Hill**,
        Pillaton, **Poughill**, **St Cleer**, **St Erme**,
        and **Stoke Climsland**.

12   A grand Somerset tower, Huish Episcopi

| Devon | **Chulmleigh**, **Peter Tavy**, **Plympton St Mary**, **Sheepstor**, **Totnes** and **West Alvington** |

Smaller towers usually have small pinnacles, but of rather crude construction: they are, however, an unmistakable part of the glorious West Country scene. Typical examples are at **St Levan**, Cornwall (Plate 14) (octagonal pinnacles), and **Hennock**, Devon (square pinnacles).

A very local feature in south Devon is that the stair turret is sometimes in the middle of one of the sides of the tower instead of at the corner. Examples are **Ashburton**, **Harberton**, **Ipplepen**, **Little Hempston**, **Torbryan** and **Totnes**.

The last-mentioned is a good example of the warm-looking red sandstone, as are also the notable towers of **Cullompton** (figure sculpture) and **Kenton** (120 feet high). **Exminster** nearby is particularly red, and also **Combe Florey**, Somerset.

Bradninch is a typical example of the Kent tower with projecting stair turret but with pinnacles which are absent in Kent.

East Anglia

Flint is almost the only material. Stone from the Midlands would have to be carried at great cost and was therefore used with strict economy. Combination of the two materials produces the very beautiful ornamentation known as flush-work. To produce the black colour the flints are knapped or split in half. Often a whole wall or tower may be built of knapped flints, occasionally laboriously cut into squares. The surface and cores of flints may be black or grey, and these are therefore the predominant colours in East Anglia.

The Perpendicular towers are tall and on the coast are very tall as landmarks for shipping.

The buttresses (usually diagonal) often stop at the bottom of the belfry stage which give these towers their pleasing outline. In the middle stage of Norfolk towers is often a square aperture filled with elaborate tracery and called a Norfolk air-hole.

13   The beautiful West Country type of tower, Widecombe, Devon

Battlements sometimes take a stepped form. Many towers, however, end in a straight parapet and are probably unfinished, but this entirely suits the very pleasant but flatter East Anglian scene. It is most probable that battlements and pinnacles, or even a spire, were originally intended, but money for the stone had already run out.

Pinnacles, when they do occur, sometimes take the form of figures or animals.

The stairway is often internal, but even if there is a turret it is rarely prominent and it nearly always ends below the top.

The average tower in Norfolk and Suffolk is well above the average anywhere else, both in height and in appearance. Yet even here, as everywhere else in England, it is the innumerable small, simple, unassuming towers that possess an unsurpassed charm, as, for instance, **Burgh-next-Aylsham**, Norfolk, and **Framsden**, Suffolk. There are, indeed, over 1,000 old church towers in those two counties, for there are just on 700 churches in Norfolk and 500 in Suffolk. How, therefore, can one possibly make a list and classification of the finest? (And who in Cornwall is interested anyway?)

The answer is now attempted. The list is fairly complete, and should make one realize our heritage in those two counties alone.

Belaugh church, Norfolk, standing high above the River Bure, gave Sir John Betjeman his love for the subject, and the author was given his (many years ago) by the towers of **Bacton**, **Walcott** (Plate 16) and **Happisburgh**, all seen together on the coast near Mundesley.

In this list all the towers are of flint and have diagonal buttresses and single belfry windows, unless otherwise mentioned.

Ordinary battlements and four pinnacles:

Norfolk	**Aylsham** (rectangular buttresses), **Blakeney**, **Blofield** (a fine tower, with figures for pinnacles), **Brisley**, **Cromer** (rectangular buttresses and double belfry windows; the highest 160 feet), **Ditchingham**, **Fakenham** (rectangular buttresses), **Great Massingham**, **Grimston**, **Norwich**, St John the Baptist Sepulchre, **Pulham St Mary the Virgin**, **Reedham**, **Saham Toney**, **Sall** (rectangular buttresses, 126 feet high), **Sparham**, **Tibenham**, and **Wood Dalling**.
Suffolk	**Bungay**, St Mary (a fine tower, with octagonal buttresses and pinnacles with crocketed spirelets), **Framlingham**, **Laxfield** (octagonal buttresses with slender pinnacles, double belfry windows, and flush-work), and **Ufford**.
Essex	**Brightlingsea** and **Dedham** (octagonal buttresses: seen in Constable's paintings).

14   A Cornish scene, St Levan

Ordinary battlements and eight pinnacles:

| Norfolk | **Terrington St Clement** (tower of stone) |
| Suffolk | **Hessett** |

Ordinary battlements and twelve pinnacles:

Norfolk **Winterton**: Rectangular buttresses. The eight intermediate pinnacles are figures; 130 feet high and a landmark for shipping.

Stepped battlements and four pinnacles:

Norfolk **Filby** (pinnacles are figures), **Foulsham**, **Hilborough**, **Ingham**, **Northrepps**, and **Swaffham** (rectangular buttresses).

Suffolk **Eye** (octagonal buttresses and pinnacles, double belfry windows, and flush-work), **Little Waldingfield**, **Rougham**, **Stoke-by-Nayland** (a massive tower with octagonal buttresses, 120 feet high and situated on a hill), and **Wilby** (a fine tower).

Stepped battlements and eight pinnacles:

Norfolk **Garboldisham** (intermediate pinnacles are figures), **Redenhall** (octagonal buttresses and pinnacles with crocketed spirelets, and flush-work), and **Strumpshaw** (slender, with no horizontal divisions).

Suffolk **Helmingham** (a fine tower), **Little Stonham** (double belfry windows), **Mendlesham** (intermediate pinnacles are crosses, double belfry windows), **Walberswick** and **Woodbridge** (four types of buttresses, double belfry windows, flush-work on

parapet and intermediate pinnacles are
figures).

Ordinary battlements and no pinnacles:

Norfolk	**Bacton**, **Carbrooke**, **Erpingham**, **Happisburgh** (very pleasing, 110 feet high and a landmark for shipping), **Hickling** (rectangular buttresses), **Hindringham**, **Honing**, **Horsham St Faith** (Plate 15), **Marham**, **Narborough**, **Norwich**, St Giles (rectangular buttresses) and St Margaret, **Ranworth**, **Scottow**, **Southrepps** (rectangular buttresses and 114 feet high), **Swanton Morley** (very large belfry windows) and **Worstead** (rectangular buttresses).
Suffolk	**Combs**, **Covehithe** (landmark for shipping), **Great Wenham** and **Mildenhall** (rectangular buttresses).

Stepped battlements and no pinnacles:

Norfolk	**Walcott** (Plate 16) (very pleasing)
Suffolk	**Earl Stonham**, **Falkenham** (double belfry windows), **Great Barton**, **Hollesley** and **Snape**

Straight or flat parapet only:

Although rather austere, the outline against the sky is
distinctly pleasing.

Norfolk	**Bradfield**, **Cawston** (tower of stone with rectangular buttresses: 120 feet high), **East Dereham** (a central tower and a detached one, the former having double belfry windows, and both having straight

	parapets), **Sharrington** (fourteenth century), **Trunch** (picturesque setting), and **Wymondham Abbey** (Plate 17) (the massive West tower has octagonal buttresses and double belfry windows and is 142 feet high).
Suffolk	**Beccles** (a well-known landmark on the River Waveney, the tower is of stone and is detached; it has rectangular buttresses and double belfry windows), **Kessingland** (a landmark for shipping), **Lavenham** (very well-known; a massive tower with rectangular buttresses, and is 141 feet high), and **Southwold** (also very well-known and a landmark for shipping; it has double belfry windows and flush-work).

The Early Tudor Brick Towers of Essex

The early sixteenth-century red brick towers with their warm-looking mellow colouring are as delightful as can be found anywhere. Sometimes there are stepped battlements on a corbel-table, and pinnacles, also of brick, and the stair-turret is often prominent.

Gestingthorpe and **Ingatestone** are outstanding, but the following are all charming – **Castle Hedingham**, **Chignal Smealy** (the church and even the font are of Tudor brick as well), **Downham**, **Epping Upland**, **Fryerning**, **Great Holland**, **Layer Marney** (adjoining the showpiece brick house of the same date), **Liston**, **Nazeing**, **North Weald**, **Rayne**, **Rochford**, **Sandon**, **Theydon Garnon**, **Thorpe-le-Soken**, **Tilbury-juxta-Clare**, **Ugley**, **Weeley**, and **Wickham St Paul**. Suffolk also has two of the same period – at **Hemley** and **Waldringfield**.

(Timber towers are included in the section on Timber spires.)

15   Typically East Anglian, Horsham St Faith, Norfolk

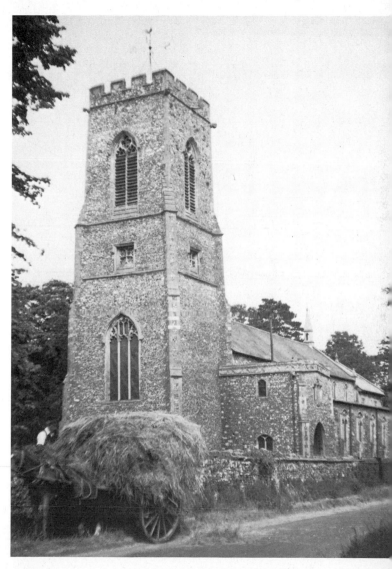

16   Stepped battlements, Walcott, Norfolk

17 Straight parapet towers, Wymondham Abbey, Norfolk

Gabled Towers

Gabled or saddle-back towers are usually of early date and often indicate that the tower is unfinished. Very oddly they occur around the Cotswold area where stone was so plentiful. Such a tower, with its stone-tiled roof, does, however, harmonize with the Cotswold scene.

An example of a tower that was obviously intended to take a gabled form is at **Ickford**, Buckinghamshire.

Other good examples are at **Ardley**, **Begbroke** (Plate 18), **Caversfield** and **Emmington**, Oxfordshire, **Bagendon**, **Duntisbourne Abbots** (and nearby at **Duntisbourne Rous**, very small), and **Eastleach Turville**, Gloucestershire, and **Wadenhoe**, Northamptonshire, and **Tinwell**, Rutland.

If you like this form of tower and also solitary and remote churches, then we can recommend a visit to **Stoke Pero**, Somerset (if you can find it), in the heart of Exmoor.

Detached Towers

Sometimes a tower is detached. It is usually in marshy country, where the tower could not be built in its usual position. **West Walton**, Norfolk, in the Fens, has a notable Early English example, and **Beccles**, Suffolk, on the River Waveney has a huge one of the Perpendicular period, but better known are the timber structure at **Brookland**, Kent, on Romney Marsh (Plate 40) and the bell-cage at **East Bergholt**, Suffolk. In that county is also the round detached tower at **Bramfield**.

Gunwalloe is in a lovely situation on the beach of the west coast of the Lizard peninsula in Cornwall.

Herefordshire has several, as at **Bosbury** and **Pembridge** (with timber belfry and spire), and Bedfordshire has a well-known one at **Elstow**.

18   Gabled tower, Begbroke, Oxfordshire

Round Towers

There are no more charming church towers than the round
towers of East Anglia. They are always very simple and are
therefore so typically English. What a contrast to our great
cathedral towers, yet both are equally beautiful in their own
way and both perform the same function.

It is sometimes said that round towers obviated the
necessity of obtaining stone for buttresses at great expense
from a distance, but a square flint tower can be built without
dressed stone, as at **Beeston Regis**, Norfolk.

The better opinion is that they were built for strength and
for defensive purposes – either as a look-out or to
accommodate the villagers if there was an attack by the
Danes. They are all near the sea or a river, are Saxon in
origin, and originally they never had any opening low down,
access being gained to the upper part by a ladder hauled up
afterwards.

Many still retain their circular double-splayed openings and
triangular-headed belfry windows divided by a baluster shaft
typical of the Saxon period (or very early Norman at the
latest).

Towers round to the top either had battlements, probably
added later, or ended in a flat parapet so characteristic of the
Norfolk scene. The latter type usually had a string-course just
below the top to give a pleasing finish.

Many round towers had an octagonal upper storey added
in the thirteenth, fourteenth, or fifteenth centuries. They can,
of course, be dated by the type of belfry window on the
cardinal sides. Sometimes these octagonal storeys also have
flush-work copies of their windows on the diagonal sides.

Battlements may also have flush-work, either chequer-
board pattern or in vertical strips.

The number of round towers that remain are 111 in
Norfolk, 41 in Suffolk, six in Essex (**Bardfield Saling**,
Broomfield, **Great Leighs**, **Lamarsh**, **Pentlow** and **South
Ockendon**), three in Sussex (all on the River Ouse, St
Michael's, **Lewes**, **Southease**, and **Piddinghoe**), two in
Cambridgeshire (**Bartlow** and **Snailwell**), and rather oddly two

in Berkshire (**Great Shefford** and **Welford**).

The following list of Norfolk and Suffolk is fairly representative, but, as mentioned, all are charming and fascinating.

Norfolk

Completely round towers:

Aslacton, Bawburgh: Picturesque red-tiled conical roof. **Bessingham**: Built mainly of brown carstone. **Forncett St Peter** (Plate 33): A good example. **Framingham Earl, Gissing**: Very attractive. **Haddiscoe**: This is the champion round tower. **Hales**: A charming church. **Roughton, Runhall, Wickmere**: A most attractive tower and church.

Round towers with octagonal upper storeys:

Acle: The pinnacles are figures. **Bedingham, Edingthorpe**: In fields. **Intwood, Matlask, Poringland, Potter Heigham**: Small pinnacles and grotesque heads. **Repps**: Thirteenth-century arcading. **Rushall, Woodton**.

Suffolk

Completely round towers:

Aldham, Fritton (Plate 34): An interesting church. **Herringfleet, Ilketshall St Margaret, Little Saxham**: Norman arcading. **Weybread**.

Round towers with octagonal upper storeys:

Hasketon, Rickinghall Inferior: A charming tower with pinnacles. **Theberton** (Plate 35): Attractive.

The finest towers in England (outside the Somerset group) are the central tower of **Canterbury** Cathedral (Plate 1), Magdalen Tower, **Oxford** (Plate 21), and the two western towers of **Beverley Minster**, Yorkshire (Plate 24).

These are followed very closely by the central tower of **York** Minster (Plate 2), Merton Tower, **Oxford** (Plate 22), **Titchmarsh**, Northants, **Hedon**, Yorkshire (Plate 26), and **Gresford**, Denbigh.

It must, however, again be stressed that it is the unassuming, simple towers, that are never mentioned or illustrated, that are the real charm of England, and fortunately they are innumerable. Here are some typical examples:

Towers with battlements only:

Stanton Harcourt and **Tackley**, Oxfordshire, and **Chirton**, Wiltshire.

Towers with four pinnacles:

Upper Slaughter, Gloucestershire, **Garthorpe**, Leicestershire, and **Bathampton** and **Chelvey** (pierced parapet), Somerset.

Otherwise plain towers can be considerably enhanced by a group of eight pinnacles, as at:

Gloucestershire	**Longborough** and **Winchcombe**
Nottinghamshire	**Averham**, **Gamston** and **Rolleston**
Oxfordshire	**Great Rollright**, **Hook Norton** and **Somerton**
Shropshire	**Shawbury**
Worcestershire	**Badsey**

Outside the West Country and East Anglia, the following are the most notable towers throughout the country (other than cathedrals), all of the Perpendicular period.

Cambridgeshire	**Haslingfield**: Double belfry windows of Northants type, a Norfolk air-hole, crenellated turrets based on Ely Cathedral, and a Herts spike. **Soham**: A very elaborate parapet with flush-work and eight pinnacles.
Cheshire	**Barthomley**: Double belfry windows, band of ornament, and eight pinnacles
Denbighshire (Wales)	**Gresford**: A very beautiful tower with double belfry windows, and a very elaborate parapet with 16 pinnacles, the lesser intermediate ones being figures.
Derbyshire	**Derby**: The second highest tower in England built for a parish church (174 feet). Large single belfry windows with blank panelling below. The church is now the Cathedral. **Tideswell**: Huge octagonal turrets with crocketed spirelets.
Gloucestershire	**Bitton**: Elaborate parapet with pinnacles and spirelet on stair-turret, which became popular in the Bristol area. **Chipping Campden**: A fine tower with an unusual use of pilasters for panelling. **Tortworth**: Very effective owing to its four tall pinnacles; open-work battlements. **Upton St Leonards**: Also very effective owing to its four tall pinnacles. **Wickwar**: A most pleasing tower. Four main pinnacles and two median on each side. **Yate**: A tall tower with elaborate parapet.
Huntingdonshire	**Conington**: Seen well above the flat country. Octagonal buttresses with pinnacles with crocketed spirelets. **Great Staughton**: Double belfry windows, band of ornament and four pinnacles. **Hamerton**: As last, but battlements without pinnacles. **St Neots**: This tower is one of the finest anywhere, particularly when seen from a distance. It has elaborate square pinnacles

Kent

and tall double belfry windows.
Tenterden: This is the finest parish church
tower in the county. It has double belfry
windows and octagonal pinnacles with
crocketed spirelets.

The average tower in Kent has a special beauty of its own.
The typical Kent tower has a prominent octagonal stair turret
at the corner projecting above the tower. There are no
pinnacles and the belfry windows are usually square-headed.
Kentish rag is often the material. Beautiful examples will be
found at **Boughton-under-Blean**, **Charing**, **Hernhill**, **Ivychurch**
(Plate 19), **Newington-on-the-Street** (should be seen when the
blossom is out), **Rodmersham** (flint), and **Seal**. This county
also has some extremely simple towers without any stair-
turret and indeed even without any buttresses. Examples are
at **Monkton** and **Upper Hardres** with a straight parapet and at
Bobbing with battlements. In their way they are just as
attractive as anything grander.

Leicestershire

Sileby: Double belfry windows and band of
ornament

Lincolnshire

Boston (Plate 20): The famous Stump. The
highest tower in England (including
cathedrals) 272½ feet. The top storey is an
octagon supported by flying buttresses
from the pinnacles. The interior of the
tower is open to the height of 137 feet.
Great Ponton: Built by a wealthy wool
merchant in 1519. He realized the source of
his wealth, however, for on the tower are
the words 'Think and Thank God of all'.
There are large single belfry windows (with
the Stamford motif of the bisecting mullion
at the top of the arch) and an effective
parapet and eight pinnacles. The weather-
vane is a violin. **Tetney**: A good example of

19   Typical Kent tower, Ivychurch

double belfry windows under a single ogee hood-mould, as in some North Midland towers. Four pinnacles.

Northampton-shire

Fotheringhay: The rather plain massive tower with local clasping buttresses is surmounted by a beautiful tall octagon with large windows, battlements and pinnacles. **Lowick**: Somewhat similar to the last mentioned, but the octagon is supported by flying buttresses from the pinnacles, as at Boston. **Titchmarsh**: This tower is said to be the best parish church tower in England outside the Somerset group. It stands up very nicely to be admired from the west. In addition to its eight pinnacles are eight pointed battlements. **Warkton**: A tall tower with local clasping buttresses, band of ornament and four pinnacles. **Whiston**: Tall pinnacles. Remarkable colour scheme of yellow-brown ironstone and grey oolite in strips.

Oxfordshire

Oxford: Magdalen College (Plate 21). This is said to be the most successful top stage in England. It was built in 1509 and is 145 feet high. It has the octagonal buttresses of the Thames valley. There are eight fine pinnacles with crocketed spirelets. The stage below is exceedingly rough and plain. **Oxford**, Merton College (Plate 22): It could almost be said to be on a par with its neighbour, Magdalen Tower. However, two such fine towers are not seen together anywhere else in England. Merton Tower has ordinary rectangular buttresses, but particularly beautiful double belfry

20   The highest tower in England, Boston Stump, Lincolnshire

windows and parapet with eight pinnacles.
It is more massive and lower than its rival.

Somerset **Bath** Abbey: The tower belongs to the
octagonal buttress group of towers rather
than to Somerset. It is oblong with square-
headed windows and is one of the latest
Gothic towers. It is 162 feet high. **North
Curry**: Occasionally a tower is octagonal
and there are several central towers of that
form in this county. This is a good example
of the fourteenth century. The pierced
parapet round the church is an attractive
local feature. **Stoke St Gregory**: Nearby
and also an octagonal central tower, but of
the thirteenth and fifteenth centuries with a
small spire of lead.

Wiltshire **Nettleton** (Plate 23): Some towers in this
county continue to have panelling much
favoured on some West Midland towers.
When not overdone and confined to the
top stage, as here, it is attractive.
Westwood: This is similar to the last
named, but it has a prominent stair-turret
capped by an ogee cupola which confirms
its late date of 1530.

Worcestershire **Great Malvern** Priory: A beautiful tower
with panelling, and can be said to be a
reduced edition of the tower of Gloucester
Cathedral. **Evesham** Abbey: Also a
beautiful tower with panelling. It stands
apart between the two parish churches with
their stone spires, making a fine group.

In the north-west Midlands the whole tower is occasionally
constructed of the local black-and-white half timber and
plaster. Three of these 'magpie' towers are in this county with
amazing interior construction of early date somewhat similar
to those of Essex. They are at **Pirton** with a pyramidal cap

21   *Magdalen Tower, Oxford*

22   Merton College Chapel, Oxford

23 *Panelled tower, Nettleton, Wiltshire*

and at **Dormston** (Plate 27) and **Warndon** with gabled roofs
(whole black-and-white churches exist at **Lower Peover** (not
tower) and **Marton**, Cheshire (Plate 28) and **Melverley**,
Shropshire).

Yorkshire

Beeford: The lace-like open-work parapet
of Yorkshire, and eight pinnacles. **Beverley
Minster** (Plate 24): The two west towers are
easily the finest group of west towers in
England. They are Perpendicular
architecture at its best. The proportions are
superb. What might not be realized is that
they are oblong. There are 14 pinnacles on
each tower. **Beverley St Mary** (Plate 25):
Also one of our finest towers. It is massive
with large single belfry windows and 16
pinnacles. **Great Driffield**: A most
handsome tower with large single belfry
windows and effective pinnacles. **Hedon**
(Plate 26): One of the grandest towers in
England. It is 128 feet high with fine double
belfry windows (and two blank ones
below), pierced parapet and 16 pinnacles.
Preston: Much plainer, but it can hold its
own with its top storey of double belfry
windows, pierced parapet and eight
pinnacles. **Tickhill**: A beautiful tower, 124
feet high. Well-proportioned double belfry
windows and eight pinnacles and a good
example of the Yorkshire lace-like open-
work parapet.

There are two towers of note, and being
octagonal from the ground are rare,
Coxwold and **Sancton**, each having eight
well-proportioned belfry windows and
pinnacles, the parapet of the former being
of the lace-like open-work type and of the
latter being straight.

24   Our finest West towers, Beverley Minster, Yorkshire

Towers of the Different Building Periods

Almost all of the above-mentioned towers are of the Perpendicular period, but towers of all periods can be found almost anywhere, and they can, of course, be dated by their details.

Saxon

In this period the belfry windows were never recessed. They usually consist of round-headed openings divided by a mid-wall shaft usually baluster-shaped. A common and easy feature to detect is long-and-short work at the corners of the tower, the corner stones being alternately horizontal and vertical.

Sometimes the surface of a tower is covered with pilaster strips, obviously copied from ornamental work on the wooden buildings of the time.

Northampton- shire	All these features can be seen on our most famous Saxon tower, **Earls Barton**.
Lincolnshire	Very similar (but a central tower which is unusual at this time) is St Peter's, **Barton-on-Humber**, Lincolnshire (Plate 29), a county that has more Saxon towers than any other. All the following are excellent examples with baluster-shaft belfry windows – **Bracebridge**, **Clee** (with Perpendicular battlements and pinnacles), **Glentworth**, **Lincoln**, St Mary-le-Wigford and St Peter-at-Gowts, **Marton**, **Rothwell** and **Scartho**.
Northumberland	**Bolam**, **Bywell St Andrew**, and **Ovingham**
Yorkshire	**Appleton-le-Street** (exceptional with two tiers of Saxon belfry windows), **Kirk Hammerton** and **Wharram-le-Street**.
Oxfordshire and Cambridgeshire	Each have well-known examples – St Michael's, at **Oxford**, and St Bene'ts, at **Cambridge**, the oldest church towers, of course, in those two cities.
Sussex	**Sompting**: On the coast near Worthing and therefore also well-known. Its gabled top is unique, although the type is common in the Rhineland.

The majority of the round towers of East Anglia are also Saxon.

Norman

The usual arrangement of belfry windows now is two round-headed arches divided by an ordinary shaft or column and recessed within a large round-headed containing arch. A

25   East Riding splendour, St Mary's, Beverley

circular opening is also quite usual. All the following are
central towers:

Buckinghamshire	**Stewkley**:	Arcade of intersecting round arches.
Gloucestershire	**Tewkesbury** Abbey:	Very massive and the largest Norman tower in England.
Hampshire	**East Meon**:	An attractive tower with an overlapping lead spire. Three round-headed windows and three circular openings above on each side of the tower.
Hertfordshire	**St Albans** Abbey (now the Cathedral):	Another very massive Norman tower. Built of red Roman bricks. Two large round-arched belfry windows above four smaller

	ones on each side of the tower.
Kent	St Clement's, **Sandwich**: Three tiers of round-arched arcading on each side. Later battlements.
Northampton-shire	**Castor**: The most elaborate. Three round-arched double openings below and five in the stage above on each side. Fourteenth-century stone parapet spire.
Oxfordshire	**Iffley** (Plate 30): Very simple, but as attractive as any. Each side has two single round-arched openings divided by a pilaster strip, and with a corbel-table and later battlements above.
Sussex	**Old Shoreham** (Plate 31): Three round-headed openings and two circular openings above on each side. Pyramidal cap.
Wiltshire	St John's, **Devizes**: Oblong, with later parapet and pinnacles. Two tiers of round-arched openings on each side. Large circular stair turret.

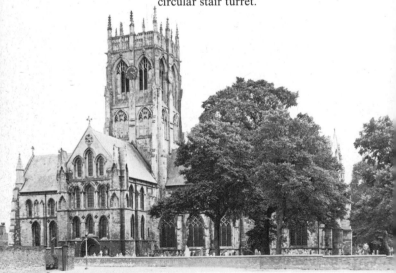

26   *A superb tower and the three styles of Gothic, Hedon, Yorkshire*

27 *Half-timbered tower, Dormston, Worcestershire*

Early English

Many fine towers of this period have stone broach spires
(Plates 41, 42 and 43).

Buckinghamshire	**Haddenham**: The belfry storey has five lancets on each side, three blank and two pierced.
Huntingdonshire	**Bury**: A remarkable tower with two tall lancets as belfry windows above a single one in the stage below.
Norfolk	**West Walton**: This is the finest Early English tower. It is detached and is of stone. The buttresses are large octagonal turrets. Much dog-tooth ornament. The belfry windows are splendid examples of plate-tracery. Later parapet and pinnacles.

28   Black and white half-timbered church at Marton, Cheshire

29   The Saxon tower, St Peter's, Barton-on-Humber, Lincolnshire

| Northampton-shire | **Brackley**: Each side has a double lancet between a blank lancet. |

Decorated

Many fine towers of this period have stone parapet spires.

| Rutland | **Whissendine**: A remarkable tower with tall deep belfry windows and unusual parapet. |

Seventeenth and eighteenth centuries

Towers of this period are of the Classical style with large round-headed windows, often with projecting key-stones, a classical balustrade with urns instead of pinnacles, and possibly a cupola. Three typical and fine examples are:

Buckinghamshire	**Gayhurst** (Plate 32): House and church form a splendid group.
Dorset	**Wimborne St Giles**: In a picturesque setting
Hampshire	**Avington**: Built of delightful red brick

Nineteenth century

Six splendid towers which enhance the countryside:

Dorset	**Cattistock**
Hertfordshire	**Northaw**
Lincolnshire	**Blankney** and **Hackthorn**
Northampton-shire	**Orlingbury**
Staffordshire	**Enville** (based on Somerset)

30   Norman Church, Iffley, Oxfordshire

Bell-cotes and Bell-cages

If there is no tower or timber turret, then a bell or two may be
hung in an open bell-cote. There are several in Rutland, which
is very odd as there is so much fine stone available for a
tower. Here are three typical examples, all of the thirteenth
century, for two bells.

Oxfordshire	**Kelmscott**
Rutland	**Essendine** and **Little Casterton**

Bell-cages are more rare, but there are two charming examples
on small churches in the gardens of the manor-house.

Somerset	**Brympton D'Evercy** (Plate 4)
Wiltshire	**Great Chalfield**: With a small crocketed spire

31 *Norman tower, Old Shoreham, Sussex*

32 *Eighteenth-century Renaissance, Gayhurst, Buckinghamshire*

If there is no stone staircase up a tower, it would probably be ascended by a wooden ladder. The original wooden stairway still remains in the Norman tower of **Brabourne**, Kent. It is an amazing sight and is a good example of the interest often tucked away in unknown places. The oak steps, mere quarter-logs, are over 800 years old, and the huge timbers were obviously cut from a tree then very ancient – so just calculate when that tree must have been planted! Another example in Kent is at **Old Romney**. To ascend a tower is usually rewarding, for a lovely view of the countryside is generally obtained.

The Finest Cathedral Towers

The following are very beautiful and they dominate their cities. We give their main features. Sometimes the height and date may be approximate.

Canterbury	The central tower or Bell Harry Tower (Plate 1). Height 250 feet. Date 1503. Superlatively beautiful is not too high praise. The buttresses are octagonal turrets. There are double windows in two stages, the lower ones having ogee hood-moulds. The four main pinnacles are pinnacled turrets.
	The west towers. Height 157 feet. Dates: south-west tower 1434, north-west tower a copy of 1834. Four main pinnacles.
Durham	The central tower (Plate 3). Height 218 feet. The small double belfry windows are of 1490 and the long double windows below are of 1465. Battlements, but no pinnacles.
	The west towers (Plate 3). Height 145 feet. The lower stages are Norman and the upper stages have early thirteenth-century lancets. Battlements and pinnacles later.

33   Saxon round tower, Forncett St Peter, Norfolk

Ely	The central tower. Height 170 feet. Date 1342. This tower is a unique stone octagon with crocketed pinnacles and a rich wooden vault with timbers 63 feet long, making the finest lantern anywhere. This supports a wooden octagon with square-topped pinnacles.
	The west tower. Height 215 feet. Thirteenth century, supporting another effective octagon with flanking octagonal turrets of 1400.
Gloucester	Height 225 feet. Date 1455. There are double windows in two stages and rather much panelling, but outstanding are the four exceptionally elaborate turrets and spirelets for the pinnacles (followed in some Somerset towers).
Hereford	Height 160 feet. The ball-flower ornament proves the date of 1320. There are four windows in each stage, but they are mostly blank panelling. The four pinnacles are later.
Lincoln	The central tower. Height 271 feet (the highest central tower in England). Dates, thirteenth century below and 1311 above. Octagonal buttresses. Double windows for almost the whole length. Parapet and four pinnacles of lead later.
	The west towers. Height 206 feet. Lower stages Norman, and early fifteenth-century stage above, which copies the central tower. These towers rise behind a screen wall so that they seem to be perched on the top of the wall instead of rising from the ground.
Wells	The central tower. Height 165 feet. Date 1322, slightly altered in 1440. Three double-light belfry windows continued

34 *Round tower, apse, and thatched roofs at Fritton, Suffolk*

below as blank panelling (again influencing Somerset towers). Eight figures on the buttresses. Four main richly pinnacled pinnacles and eight median pinnacles.

The west towers. Height 125 feet. Dates, south-west tower 1386, and north-west tower copied from it in 1424. Both imitate the central tower. Two double-light windows continued as blank panelling below. Straight parapet and no pinnacles, but there is an off-standing pinnacle halfway up.

Worcester   Height 196 feet. The date is 1375, but the sandstone has been much renewed. Double

windows in the belfry stage and panelling below. Three figures on each side between the windows. Straight parapet. Four octagonal pinnacles. This tower may have influenced the later tower of Gloucester Cathedral.

York The central tower (Plate 2). Height 198 feet. Date 1423. This vast tower is the largest in England, yet simplicity (as so typical of England) sums it up. There are double windows for almost the whole of its length. There are battlements, but no pinnacles. All very lovely.

The west towers. Height 196 feet. Dates, south-west tower 1450, and north-west tower 1470. The belfry storey has a large single window with panelling above. Eight pinnacles. These towers seem to rise from the parapet of the fourteenth-century west front rather than from the ground.

35   Round tower with octagonal upper storey, thatched roof, Theberton, Suffolk

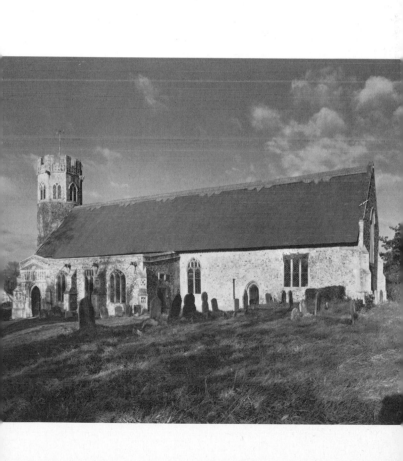

Bells

A tower was built to contain bells, and over 3,000 medieval ones are still hanging and ringing in belfries. Such bells were often dedicated to a saint and they might have a prayer or inscription inscribed in beautiful lettering. Initial letters in the form of crosses, word stops, lettering and foundry marks are of great interest and beauty, and yet are rarely seen as few people climb to the belfry.

There are about 5,200 churches in England with rings of five or more bells. The greatest numbers are in Devon, followed by Somerset, and the richest counties for old bells are those two counties and Norfolk and Suffolk.

Good examples of medieval bells can be studied at:

Cambridgeshire	**Bartlow**, **Cambridge**, St Botolph, **Conington**
Essex	**Margaretting**
Lincolnshire	**Somerby** (Brigg), **South Somercotes**
Norfolk	**Ketteringham**, **North Burlingham**
Nottinghamshire	**Scarrington**
Oxfordshire	**Dorchester** Abbey, **Oxford** Cathedral
Suffolk	**Boxford**

After the Reformation, inscriptions, usually in English, were often rhymes of a somewhat secular nature and incorporated the name of the founder.

Good examples of post-Reformation bells of the late sixteenth and seventeenth centuries can again be found at **Dorchester** Abbey and at **Oxford** (St Mary the Virgin) and **Cambridge** (St Bene't).

The bells ring out with messages of hope, joy and worship. Surely there is no sweeter or more melodious sound, in this age of noise, than that of church bells echoing over the countryside.

Spires

Timber Belfries and Spires

Spires may be of timber or stone according to the locality.

The earliest form of covering of a tower would have been a low hipped roof pyramidal cap, slightly pitched and overlapping the tower in order to throw rainwater clear of the wall, as at **Eastleach Martin**, Gloucestershire. The material would be that of the locality (see section on exterior roofs, page 132). This form was soon heightened, as at **Rudgwick** and **Yapton** of timber shingles, **Telscombe**, **East Dean**, near Eastbourne, and **Tarring Neville** of red tiles, and **Old Shoreham** (Plate 31) of Horsham stone tiles, all in Sussex. The four-sided form was again heightened to become an octagonal spire.

The pyramidal cap could later be constructed within the parapet of the tower (when the use of guttering had been discovered) and this always remained popular in Sussex, as at **Boxgrove** Priory and **Steyning** (both red-tiled).

In the south-east of England, where timber is plentiful, small timber belfries were often placed on the roof of the nave at its west end, and these belfries had either a small cap (as at **Ford** and **Tortington**, Sussex, where belfry and cap are painted white), or a spire, usually covered with wooden shingles or weather-boarded which might be either of moderate height, as at **Tangmere**, Sussex, **Alfold**, Surrey, **Brenzett**, Kent and **Aythorpe Roding** and **Birdbrook** (Plate 36), Essex, or tall and slender as at **Crowhurst**, Surrey, and **Cowden**, Kent. These belfries are supported inside the church on a massive timber framework. A red-tiled belfry and cap is very charming and homely, as at **Friston**, Sussex (Plate 37).

In Essex even the whole of some remarkable early towers which support a timber belfry or spire are themselves of timber, as at **Blackmore**, **Greensted**, **Magdalen Laver**, **Margaretting**, **Navestock**, **Stock** (Plate 38) and **West Hanningfield**. There are also two in Surrey, at **Burstow** (very fine) and **Newdigate**.

The huge timber supports, great beams and struts, are certainly an amazing sight, and might be the original Saxon wooden church.

In Surrey and Sussex a large spire of timber shingles overlapping a tower is very common, and the spire may be massive, as at **Compton** (Plate 39), **Merstham**, and **Shere**, Surrey, **Bury**, Sussex, and **Bapchild**, and **Patrixbourne**, Kent, squat, as at **Old Romney**, Kent, or more slender as at **Horsted Keynes** and **Playden**, Sussex, and **Eynsford** and **Hever**, Kent. The timber spire on the ground at **Brookland**, Romney Marsh, Kent (Plate 40), is known to thousands of visitors.

Timber spires overlapping the tower are usually chamfered,

the diagonal sides of the spire being cut away to the four
corners of the tower.

Timber-framed spires can also rise within the parapet of the
tower, as at **West Tarring**, Sussex, and **Great Burstead**, Essex.

Lead Spires

Sometimes a timber-framed spire was covered with lead,
which has a grey or white appearance. These are the finest
lead spires:

Overlapping the tower:

Cambridgeshire	**Ickleton**
Devon	Close together at **Barnstaple**, **Braunton**, and **Swimbridge**
Hampshire	**East Meon**
Lincolnshire	**Long Sutton** (Plate 41); thirteenth century and the oldest
Suffolk	**Hadleigh**
Surrey	**Godalming**

Some of these spires have a bell on them (originally the
sanctus bell).

Rising within the tower parapet:

Essex	**Great Baddow**
Hertfordshire	**Hemel Hempstead** (tall and slender)
Kent	**Ash-next-Sandwich**

On a timber belfry:

Essex	**Stanford Rivers**

36 Timber belfry and spire on nave roof, Birdbrook, Essex

The best known spire is, of course, the twisted and leaning lead spire at **Chesterfield**, Derbyshire.

Some spires are a delightful green colour, as at **Wingham**, Kent. The covering is then of copper.

A needle spire, usually of lead, is popular in Hertfordshire, and therefore called a Herts spike. Examples are at **Hitchin**, **Flamstead**, **Little Munden** and **Great Munden**, and **Little Hadham**.

A favourite feature of churches built today is the needle spire which is characteristic of this Space Age. The new **Coventry** Cathedral is an example.

Stone Spires

There is no more noble sight than the spire of an old church soaring above the cottages of a village. It is a pointer to

37   Simplicity, Friston, Sussex

38 *Timber tower, belfry and spire, Stock, Essex*

39 *Typical timber spire, Compton, Surrey*

40 *Quaint and odd, Brookland Church, Romney Marsh, Kent*

something beyond this world – the eternal truth of the
Gospel.

Barnack, Northamptonshire (famous for its quarries) might
be said to be the earliest stone spire in England, but the
earliest group is a type found around **Oxford**. These spires
overlap the tower and have tall massive pinnacles at the
corners and large dormer windows at the base on the four
cardinal sides. They are all of the early thirteenth century and
are found at **Oxford** Cathedral (Plate 42), **Bampton**,
Broadwell, **Shipton-under-Wychwood** and **Witney**. **Adderbury** is
also of this type, but a century later.

Broach spires

In the same century (thirteenth) broach spires were evolved
and this type is found only in England. The square tower
changes to an octagonal spire by means of broaches or
pyramids at the corners of the spire. Broaches vary
considerably in size, from large and steep pitch (in the eastern
area) to low and insignificant (in the western area).

This type almost always overlaps the tower; there are no
pinnacles, and instead of dormer windows there are two or
more tiers of spire-lights. In late spires, if employed at all,
spire-lights are few and small.

The broach spire is nearly always of the thirteenth century
or sometimes of the fourteenth century. A rare one of the
Perpendicular period is at **Irchester**, Northamptonshire. In
most cases tower and spire form one admirable unit.

Amongst so many in Northamptonshire, south Lincolnshire
and surrounding districts, it is difficult to choose those of
special note, and, moreover, as with towers, the smaller
examples are often just as attractive as the larger ones. This
list, is, however, reasonably comprehensive.

Bedfordshire	**Pertenhall**
Gloucestershire	**Leckhampton** and **Shurdington**: Both are tall and slender and have small broaches.

41   The oldest lead spire, Long Sutton, Lincolnshire

Huntingdonshire	**Brington**, **Broughton**, **Buckworth** (big broaches), **Easton**, **Ellington**, **Keyston**, **Kimbolton**, **Spaldwick**, and **Warboys**. All are very refined and many are along the Huntingdon to Thrapston road.
Leicestershire	**Market Harborough**
Lincolnshire	**Aunsby**, **Dry Doddington** (stumpy), **Ewerby**, **Frampton**, **Lenton**, **Marston**, **North Rauceby** (Plate 43), **Pickworth**, St Mary's, **Stamford**, and **Threekingham**.
Northampton-shire	**Aldwincle** St Peter, **Church Brampton**, **Denford** and **Etton** (both chamfered, unusual with stone spires), **Loddington**, **Polebrook**, **Raunds** (a fine steeple), **Thorpe Malsor** and **Warmington** (large spire-lights).

| Nottinghamshire | **Holme** (stumpy, but picturesque), and **Newark** |
| Rutland | **Barrowden**, **Ketton**, **Langham**, and **Seaton** (chamfer type) |

Outside the stone spire area, old stone spires are rare or quite unknown. There are none in Kent or Surrey. Devon and Cornwall have a few, all of the simplest design. In the south of Cornwall are two thirteenth-century broach spires which are almost identical and are of the crudest possible type: **Rame**, high up on its headland with the sea on three sides and exposed to rain and every wind that blows; and **Sheviock** in an adjoining parish, but completely sheltered in a beautiful combe. On the north Cornish coast near Padstow, **St Enodoc**, delightfully situated in the middle of the golf links, is also similar.

42   One of the earliest stone spires, Oxford Cathedral

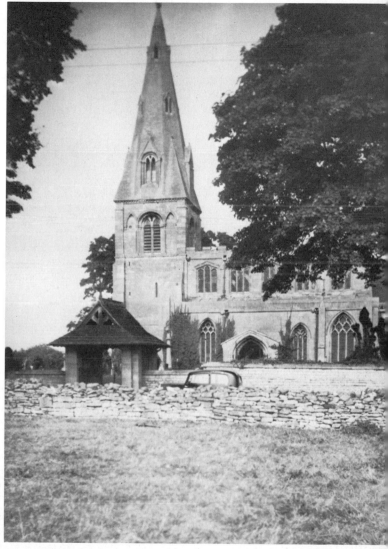

43 *Broach spire, North Rauceby, Lincolnshire*

Parapet spires

These spires do not overlap the tower, but rise from within the parapet owing now to the use of lead guttering. They are usually of the fourteenth or fifteenth centuries. The advantage is that a ladder and scaffolding can be placed on top of the tower if repairs are needed, instead of having to erect them from the ground, as was, of course, necessary with the earlier broach spires. One can also walk round the base of the spire.

Abroad it is often impossible to tell where the spire commences and the tower finishes, but in England there is nearly always a distinct line between the two, and the parapet spire certainly assists in this respect.

This type is more common than the broach type and occurs frequently in the stone areas mentioned, particularly in south Lincolnshire, where it is possible to see at one glance at least a dozen soaring upwards – each one noble.

Spires were particularly favoured in the fourteenth century and they are common in south Lincolnshire as many churches in that area were enlarged or rebuilt at that time. **Heckington** is a marvellous example.

The most superb parish church spire is at **Louth**, Lincolnshire (Plate 44). It is of the early sixteenth century and is 294 feet high. The tower itself is a grand one and from its four crocketed pinnacles (no less than 52 feet high) four most effective flying buttresses jump across to the spire.

The spire has crockets, a feature of late spires. Long lines tend to seem hollow in the middle and so a slight bulge (or entasis) was often given to a spire mid-way. The genius who designed this spire obtained this result by increasing the size of the crockets about one-third of the way up. Tower and spire are of equal height as they should be.

The spire of **Grantham** is also magnificent, and special mention must be made of **Moulton**, also in Lincolnshire, which is a lovely example with most effective flying buttresses.

44   The finest church spire, Louth, Lincolnshire

Other great parapet spires can be seen at:

Cambridgeshire	**Whittlesey**, St Mary (Plate 45)
Northampton-shire	**Higham Ferrers**, **Kettering**, **Oundle**, and **Rushden**
Yorkshire	**Patrington**

Once again, however, it is in innumerable villages that smaller but no less perfect examples are to be found. The following are all lovely, but they will be quite unknown (except perhaps **Norwich** Cathedral):

Bedfordshire	**Dean**: A diminutive spire, but very picturesque. **Harrold**: Effective flying buttresses.
Berkshire	**Shottesbrooke**
Buckinghamshire	**Hanslope**: Effective flying buttresses
Cambridgeshire	**Eltisley**
Huntingdonshire	**Great Gidding**, **Yaxley**: Effective flying buttresses
Leicestershire	**Bottesford**, **Queniborough** (tall), **Waltham-on-the-Wolds**: Tower has tall pinnacles
Lincolnshire	**Asgarby**, **Billingborough**, **Brant Broughton**, **Claypole**, **Donington**, **Gosberton**, **Heckington**, **Helpringham**, **Holbeach**, **Leadenham**, **Quadring** (leaning tower), **Silk Willoughby**, **Spalding**, **Stamford** All Saints, **Surfleet** (leaning tower), **Uffington**.
Norfolk	**Norwich** Cathedral: 315 feet high, on a Norman tower.
Northampton-shire	**Bulwick**, **Easton Maudit**, **Wakerley**, **Weekley**: The diminutive spire makes a fitting end to the picturesque village street.
Oxfordshire	**Church Handborough**
Rutland	**Empingham**, **South Luffenham**
Yorkshire	**Hemingborough** (Plate 46): As mentioned, tower and spire should be of equal height, but here the spire greatly exceeds the height of the tower, with a very satisfying result.

45   Parapet spire, St Mary's, Whittlesey, Cambridgeshire

There is also a small group of stone spires treated rather differently from those mentioned above. They have an arrangement of double pinnacles, one above the other. There are five of them and all are superb works of art.

First and foremost is the world-famous spire of **Salisbury** Cathedral. It is the highest in England and is 404 feet high. The proportions are wonderful so that it never seems to be its great height. How ever did they erect it in the fourteenth century? The tower is of the thirteenth century.

St Mary's, **Oxford** (Plate 47), is also one of the loveliest anywhere, in the same street as one of our most beautiful towers, that of Magdalen College (Plate 21).

King's Sutton, Northamptonshire, certainly earns its title amongst a trio:

> Bloxham for length,
> Adderbury for strength,
> And King's Sutton for beauty.

The remaining two of equal charm are at **Ruardean**, Gloucestershire, and **Laughton-en-le-Morthen**, Yorkshire.

Another small group, but very effective, has a spire rising from an octagonal storey surmounting the tower, as at:

County Durham	**Chester-le-Street**
Northampton-shire	**Nassington** and **Wilby**
Oxfordshire	**Bloxham**
Rutland	**Exton**
Yorkshire	**York**, All Saints' North Street

A small spire poised on elegant flying buttresses rising up from the corners of the tower was a novel idea. **Newcastle** Cathedral has a fifteenth-century example (193 feet high).

46   A prominent parapet spire, Hemingborough, Yorkshire

Wren's Towers and Spires

Sir Christopher Wren, in the late seventeenth century, used this design at St Dunstan's-in-the-East, City of **London**, and in none of his spires did he express greater confidence.

His real genius is shown in his towers (of Portland stone or brick) and spires (of Portland stone or lead) of the City churches. The stone spire of St Mary-le-Bow, Cheapside (Plate 48), is both wonderful and perfect, and every detail is worth careful study. Everyone has heard of the famous Bow Bells. The weather-vane (230 feet up) is a dragon no less than 8 feet 10 inches in length and weighing two hundredweights. A dragon is the supporter of the City Arms.

Other elegant spires of stone are at St Bride, Fleet Street, and St Vedast, Foster Lane.

Three towers are surmounted by elaborate stone structures, somewhat similar and yet differing in detail: St James, Garlickhithe, St Michael, Paternoster Royal and St Stephen, Walbrook.

It is, however, in his black lead turrets and spires that the greatest variety is found. The following are all original and exceptionally pleasing: St Magnus, London Bridge, St Margaret, Lothbury, St Margaret Pattens, St Martin, Ludgate (acting as a foil to the dome of St Paul's which is 364 feet high), St Edmund, Lombard Street, St Mary Abchurch (near Cannon Street), St Peter, Cornhill (the covering is now copper) and St Bene't, Paul's Wharf, Upper Thames Street.

Wren could also build in the Gothic style, as are his towers of St Mary Aldermary, St Michael, Cornhill, and St Alban, Wood Street.

Amongst modern spires, **Truro** Cathedral, Cornwall (Plate 49) has three of the early twentieth century. They are rather French-looking, but are very effective. The central spire is 250 feet high and the western spires are 204 feet high.

47   Beautiful stone spire, St Mary's Church, Oxford

48   Wren's masterpiece, St Mary-le-Bow, Cheapside, City of London

49   *Truro Cathedral, Cornwall*

Weather-Vanes

On top of the tower or spire may be a weather-vane to
indicate the direction of the wind. It is often a cock for
vigilance. There is a very large one at **Knapton**, Norfolk,
combined with a pennon with the crossed keys and sword for
St Peter and St Paul, the Patron Saints.

There is also a very large cock at **Winchcombe**,
Gloucestershire, and at **Priston**, Somerset, it is gold with a red
comb.

A large key for St Peter is above the churches dedicated to
him in Cornhill, City of **London**, and at **Brackley**,
Northamptonshire. Similarly the gridiron emblem of St
Lawrence is above his churches at St Lawrence Jewry, City of
London, **Upminster**, Essex, and **Ramsgate**, Kent.

A dragon is quite a favourite, as at St Mary-le-Bow,
Cheapside (Plate 48), again in the City of **London** (see section
on stone spires, page 97), and at **Sittingbourne**, Kent, a long
dragon is combined with ornamental ironwork.

A fish is popular as it was an early Christian symbol. It may
be seen at **Filey**, and **Flamborough**, Yorkshire, and St John the
Baptist's, **Lewes**, Sussex, and at **Piddinghoe**, further down the
river.

The word nave is derived from the Latin word *navis*,
meaning a ship. A ship is not therefore uncommon. Examples
are at **Southwold**, Suffolk, and **Tollesbury**, Essex.

A flying duck is appropriate on Romney Marsh, Kent; the
one at **Brookland** (Plate 40) can be easily seen by the
numerous visitors.

A violin is not so usual, but it occurs at **Great Ponton**,
Lincolnshire (see section on towers, page 55).

Vanes are often dated and may be heraldic, as at
Etchingham, Sussex.

Even a scene may be depicted, as for instance St Martin and
the Beggar at **Chipping Ongar**, Essex.

50   Early sixteenth-century clock and clock-jacks, Exeter, St Mary Steps, Devon

Clocks and Clock-jacks

The best-known and most notable medieval clock is the astronomical clock in **Wells** Cathedral. Above the dial (itself an ingenious masterpiece) a procession of four carved figures ride round on horseback. A clock-jack is at the side of the clock and there are two more outside. **Exeter** Cathedral and **Ottery St Mary**, Devon, and **Wimborne** Minster, Dorset (coloured quarter-jack), also have medieval clocks.

The hour and its quarters were then often struck on the bell or bells by jacks, ingeniously devised and brightly coloured. The best example is a trio of such figures of the early sixteenth century and still hard at work at **Exeter** St Mary Steps, Devon (Plate 50). Above the painted dial the quarter jacks hold a pike in one hand and in the other a hammer with which they strike the bell under the little platform on which each stands. The central figure is seated and he has a rigid rod in his hands. All he does is to nod his head at each stroke of the hour.

Two jacks with an ornamental framework are known to the many visitors to **Rye**, Sussex, where the pendulum, 18 feet long, swings free in the body of the church.

The fifteenth-century **Southwold** jack is well known and there is another in the neighbouring church of **Blythburgh**, Suffolk.

It would probably be as late as the seventeenth century before the simple clocks of village churches had dials. One of the largest is at **Coningsby**, Lincolnshire.

Projecting clocks became popular in the seventeenth century and Wren often combined them with his towers, as at St Mary-le-Bow, Cheapside (Plate 48) and St Magnus, London Bridge, City of **London**.

Clerestories

When there were aisles and additional light was required in the nave, an upper row of windows above the aisle roofs was often constructed, particularly in East Anglia, where this feature is usually outstandingly beautiful. It is, however, rather rare in some areas, particularly in the south of England, and in the extreme west of England it is almost unknown.

A clerestory can, of course, be of any period, but the great majority are of the Perpendicular period, as are those in the following list of some of the best. The number is the number of windows on one side (and usually a corresponding number on the other side).

Dorset	**Sherborne** Abbey: The nave has five windows of five lights, and the chancel has three windows of six lights.
Essex	**Great Baddow**: Very pleasing, of early Tudor red brick, with corbel-table, stepped battlements and pinnacles,
Gloucestershire	**Bristol**, St Mary Redcliffe: The nave has seven windows, and the choir five windows, all of six lights each.
Leicestershire	**Melton Mowbray**: A wonderful array of clerestory windows of three lights each, round nave, transepts, and chancel – a total of 48.
Lincolnshire	**Gedney**: Perhaps the most beautiful anywhere; there are only 12 windows, but they are of three lights each and they completely cover the whole wall. **Quadring**: Eight windows of three lights.
Norfolk	**Terrington St Clement**: The nave has a magnificent clerestory with 13 windows of three lights and one of two lights. Clerestory windows also continue round the transepts and chancel.

Oxfordshire	**Chipping Norton**: The clerestory is a sheet of glass having four continuous windows of five lights each. The windows are square-headed, as sometimes in the Cotswolds, North Midlands, and the North. **Idbury**: The south wall shows how attractive an exterior view can be due to beautiful Perpendicular clerestory windows.
Somerset	**Bath** Abbey: The nave has five windows and the chancel three windows, all of five lights. More of such windows adorn the transepts.
Suffolk	**Blythburgh** (Plate 51): A most effective group of 18 windows of two lights. **Bury St Edmunds**, St Mary: No less than 20 windows of two lights. **Cavendish**: Only five windows of three lights, but this permits the beautiful flush-work to be displayed. **Coddenham**: Also a good example of flush-work. **Lavenham**: After the great tower, the striking feature of the exterior is the clerestory of 12 windows of three lights. **Long Melford**: The most beautiful feature of the exterior is the clerestory with 18 windows of three lights and an inscription in flush-work. **Southwold**: Also 18 windows, but of two lights. **Stonham Aspall**: The large Perpendicular windows make a splendid exterior.

51   Perpendicular at its best, Blythburgh, Suffolk

Porches

Stone Porches

Great care was usually bestowed upon a porch, as it had certain liturgical uses.

Of Norman date the finest in England is at **Malmesbury** Abbey, Wiltshire. The outer doorway has eight orders of arches filled with figures and scenes. Inside the porch on each side are six Apostles with angels flying above them.

Of the Early English period the finest can be said to be at the Cathedrals of **Lincoln** and **Wells** (the capitals show the martyrdom of St Edmund).

Of the Decorated period, **Heckington**, Lincolnshire, is a masterpiece, with elaborate sculptured gable.

It is, however, in the fifteenth and early sixteenth centuries or Perpendicular date that the porch reaches perfection as in these examples.

Cornwall	**Launceston**, St Mary Magdalene: Amazing carving, considering that the material is granite. Sculptures of St George and the dragon, and St Martin dividing his cloak with the beggar.
Essex	**Ardleigh**: Beautifully proportioned, with flush-work, niches and seated lions; St George and the dragon in the spandrels.
Gloucestershire	**Northleach** (Plate 52): Perhaps the finest of all. Very effective buttressing and pinnacles. Original figures of the Virgin and Child and the Trinity. Inside, the porch has an exquisite stone vault with bosses, and the side walls have pedestals on fascinating sculptures.
Lincolnshire	**Addlethorpe**: A beautiful porch with its original gable cross carved with the Crucifixion and the Virgin and Child. Original roof with bosses.

52   Grand stone porch, Northleach, Gloucestershire

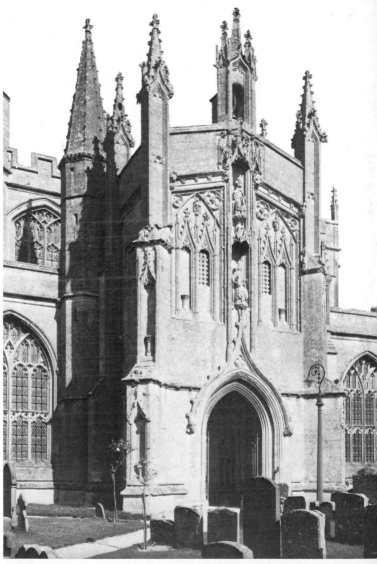

Norfolk	**Cley**: A number of shields, canopied niche between two windows, large sundial and beautiful open-work parapet. Stone vaulted roof with intriguing bosses, one of a boy with trousers down being caned, and another of a woman chasing a fox with her stick. **Pulham, St Mary the Virgin** (Plate 53): Very beautiful, stone-fronted, Annunciation and angels, numbers of niches and shields, grotesques as pinnacles, and pretty open-work parapet.
Suffolk	**Beccles**: Prominent buttresses, pinnacles, shields and niches. Exquisite parapet. 34 feet high. **Framsden**: Attractive with flush-work and niches. **Fressingfield**: Nicely proportioned, with niches and windows. **Kersey**: Small, but, like the village, most attractive. Flush-work is effective. Inside is a beautiful wooden roof with traceried panels. **Woolpit**: Panelling, large niches, and open-work parapet.

One seventeenth-century porch must be mentioned. It is the elaborate porch with spiral columns and notable figures of the Virgin and Child at the University Church of St Mary the Virgin, **Oxford**.

Timber Porches

In the south-east of England, the plentiful supply of timber provides a number of porches of that material dating back to the fourteenth or fifteenth centuries. The gabled portion in front, a barge-board, and the side openings were usually skilfully carved, and the entrance arch was constructed of great tree trunks. The following are some of the finest:

53   The beautiful porch of Pulham St Mary the Virgin, Norfolk

Berkshire	**Long Wittenham, West Challow**: Carving on barge-board
Essex	**Margaretting**
Herefordshire	**Aconbury**
Kent	**High Halden** (Plate 54): One of the most beautiful. **Shoreham**
Suffolk	**Boxford**: A remarkable wooden porch with Decorated two-light windows. There is also a Perpendicular stone-faced porch.
Surrey	**Ewhurst**
Sussex	**West Grinstead**
Warwickshire	**Berkswell**: Picturesque, being of black-and-white half-timbered construction. Room above.
Worcestershire	**Crowle**: Roof with bosses

Brick Porches

These are always of a warm, pleasing colour.

Essex	**Feering**: Stepped battlements and pinnacles, all of brick. The vault has brick ribs. **Sandon**: Stepped battlements on a projecting corbel-table. Harmonizes with the brick tower.
Suffolk	**Great Ashfield**: A charming contrast in colours, for there is brickwork with flint panelling. Also stepped battlements.

54 Wooden porch, High Halden, Kent

Holy Water Stoups

A niche, usually on the right-hand side near the church entrance, to hold holy water. Sometimes it is supported on a shaft. The devout worshipper on entering and leaving the church reverently dips the fingers of his right hand in the water and makes the sign of the cross to indicate self-consecration and a renewal of baptismal vows.

There are two oustanding examples:

Cornwall	**St Endellion**: Three acorns and three shields with coats-of-arms, one shield held by an angel.
Hertfordshire	**Caldecote**: A small church with a huge stoup! Above the panelled shaft is a very tall crocketed canopy.

Doorways

Saxon

Barnack, Northamptonshire, has a typical Saxon doorway – high and narrow, round arch, large square impost stones, and no recessed orders.

Norman

In the Norman period the round arch continues, but there are now usually a number of recessed arches, and under each arch, at the sides, are small shafts.

The arches are often highly ornamented, and all the following are magnificent works of art. The lavish carving, particularly of the Yorkshire group, should be carefully studied.

Cornwall	**St Germans**: Seven orders of arches
Devon	**Bishopsteignton**
Gloucestershire	**Windrush**: Numbers of beak-heads
Herefordshire	**Kilpeck**: The shafts are elaborately decorated, one with two wiry figures and dragons.
Norfolk	**Heckingham**
Oxfordshire	**Barford St Michael**: Numbers of beak-heads. **Iffley** (Plate 30): Two doorways, the west one with numbers of beak-heads, and the south one with carved capitals.
Staffordshire	**Tutbury**: Seven orders of arches
Yorkshire	The Norman doorways of this county are truly wonderful with an amazing amount of detailed carving of medallions, figures, chevron or zig-zag, beak-heads and carved capitals.
	Adel (Plate 55), **Alne**: Medieval beasts.
	Birkin, **Brayton**, **Fishlake**: Particularly

elaborate. **Kirkburn**, **Riccall**, **Stillingfleet**, **Thorpe Salvin**, **Wighill**: Crucifixion and Descent from the Cross on capitals.

Some Norman doorways have an elaborately carved tympanum between the head of the door and the containing arch. All the following are very fine:

Berkshire	**Charney Bassett**: Man with two gryphons.
Buckinghamshire	**Dinton**: Tree of Life and two animals.
	Water Stratford: Christ in Majesty
Cambridgeshire	**Ely** Cathedral: Christ in Majesty
Dorset	**Fordington**: St George and the dragon
Gloucestershire	**Eastleach Turville**: Christ in Majesty.
	Elkstone (Plate 56): Christ in Majesty with the Lamb of God and symbols of the Evangelists. Beak-heads above. **Moreton Valence**: St Michael and the dragon.
	Quenington: Two doorways, the one on the north with the Harrowing of Hell, and the one on the south with the Coronation of the Virgin and symbols of the Evangelists. **Ruardean**: St George and the dragon. **Siddington**: Christ in Majesty.
Herefordshire	**Aston**: Lamb, ox and eagle. **Brinsop**: St George and the dragon. **Fownhope**: Virgin and Child. **Rowlstone**: Christ in Majesty. **Stretton Sugwas**: Samson and the lion.
Kent	**Barfreston**: Christ in Majesty.
	Patrixbourne: Christ in Majesty.
Leicestershire	**Stoney Stanton**: Bishop, ox, and dragons
Oxfordshire	**Church Handborough**: St Peter with a key, Lamb of God and a lion
Shropshire	**Aston Eyre**: Christ's Entry into Jerusalem
Wiltshire	**Malmesbury** Abbey: Christ in Majesty

55   Norman doorway, Adel, Yorkshire

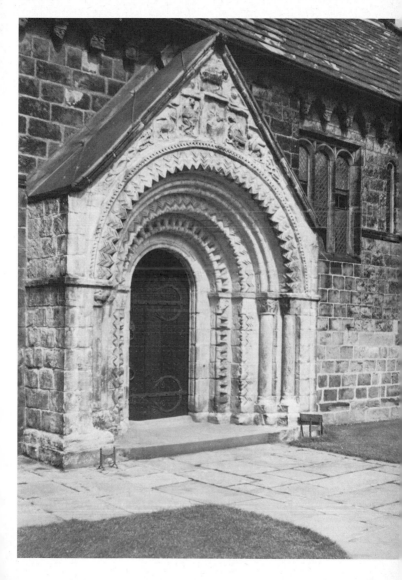

Early English

What a difference to Norman work! Acute pointed arch with mouldings deeply cut, the capitals having the beautiful stiff-leaf foliage, and dog-tooth ornament being popular.

Two excellent and typical examples are at **West Walton**, Norfolk, and **Skelton**, near York.

Decorated

The arch is now broader than previously, mouldings are not so deeply cut, the ball-flower ornament may occur, and the capitals might have the natural foliage of the period. **Cotton**, Suffolk, has a splendid example with much original colour remaining.

Perpendicular

The pointed arch of the doorway is often under a square hood-mould. The spandrels between the two might have tracery, heraldry or sculpture – angels with censers fit in nicely.

Two typical examples are at **Sall** and **Hilborough** (Plate 57), Norfolk.

Renaissance

Doorways of the seventeenth and eighteenth centuries again have round arches, but they are large and they usually have projecting key-stones and big arch-stones or voussoirs (as at St Mary-le-Bow, Cheapside, City of **London** (Plate 48), said to be the finest of the period in England).

56 *Norman tympanum, Elkstone, Gloucestershire*

57 *Fifteenth-century doorway, Hilborough, Norfolk*

Doors

Hadstock, Essex, is remarkable in having its Saxon wooden door of plain oak boards with iron straps.

Before the middle of the fourteenth century the smith decorated the door, and his skill was remarkable. Norman ironwork remains on doors at:

Hertfordshire	**Little Hormead**
Kent	**Hartley** and **Staplehurst**
Shropshire	**Edstaston** (two)
Surrey	**Old Woking**
Yorkshire	**Stillingfleet**

Thirteenth-century iron scrollwork of straps and hinges are on splendid doors at:

Bedfordshire	**Eaton Bray** (Plate 58), **Leighton Buzzard**, and **Turvey**

At St Saviour's, **Darmouth**, Devon, the huge door is covered with fourteenth-century ironwork of large leaf scrolls and two leopards.

Later the craft of the wood-carver prevailed and the ornamentation at the head of the door might follow the window tracery of the period, as at **Wellow**, Somerset (Reticulated), and **Addlethorpe**, Lincolnshire (Plate 59; Perpendicular).

Very elaborate wooden doors adorned with figures can be seen at **Harpley**, Norfolk, and **Stoke-by-Nayland**, Suffolk.

Doors to tower stairways are often original and of great strength (that at **Filby**, Norfolk, has seven locks).

The original door-handle (or sanctuary knocker) often remains. The most famous is the twelfth-century one at **Durham** Cathedral. At **Adel**, Yorkshire (Plate 60), the ring is held in the mouth of a monster swallowing a man, and at **Dormington**, Herefordshire, it is in the mouth of a demon head.

58   Thirteenth-century ironwork, Eaton Bray, Bedfordshire

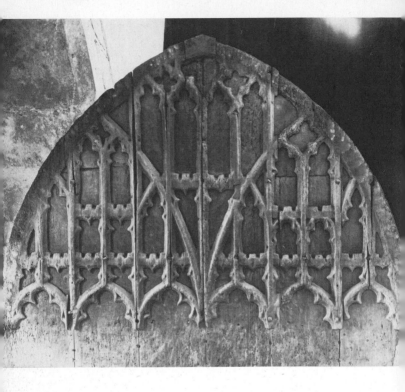

59 *Fifteenth-century door, Addlethorpe, Lincolnshire*

60 *Closing ring on door at Adel, Yorkshire*

Gargoyles

These occur particularly on towers and also often on the upper parts of exterior walls. A gargoyle is a projecting spout to throw the rain-water from the gutter clear of the wall.

The medieval churchman had a sense of humour and he certainly enjoyed his creation of gargoyles, as we can now enjoy studying them. They depict fantastic monsters and figures in every possible attitude and very rarely do they ever have any drawing-room manners. They would certainly not have passed present-day Diocesan Advisory Committees! Almost every church has one or two gargoyles, but anyone interested in this subject will have an immense amount of enjoyment at any of the following churches:

Cambridgeshire	**Over**: Men with open mouths and a woman emptying a pitcher.
Cheshire	**Malpas**: Monkeys hand in hand, grinning twins, and a man with his tongue out.
Gloucestershire	**Winchcombe**: Some 40 huge grotesques, famous for their ugliness. An ugly winged man in a top hat is notable.
Kent	**Wye**: A snake is held in the mouth of a figure.
Lincolnshire	**Grimoldby**: A man with a beard and another in a brimmed hat. **Heekington**: Rich carvings of numerous figure-stops and gargoyles show the Decorated style at its best. **Theddlethorpe**, All Saints: many grotesques.
Northampton-shire	**Denford**: Many gargoyles, and also numerous quaint heads both outside and inside the church. **Welford**: Two figures hold the spout between them.
Nottinghamshire	**East Markham**: Some winged animals, a creature in armour with a battle-axe, and another with its hand in its mouth.
Somerset	**Evercreech**: Figures climb up and down the

parapet and a cat chases another one. **High Ham**: A trumpet player and a piper, and another listening. A chained monkey nurses her baby. **Monksilver**: Two figures together, one with its hand in the mouth of the other.

Yorkshire

Patrington: Musicians, a monk, a saint being stabbed and another drowning. All rich fourteenth-century work.

Other Exterior Figure Sculpture

The Normans were fond of corbel-tables – projecting masonry supported on a row of small corbels, usually just underneath the roof which projected over them in order to throw the rain-water clear of the wall. There is nearly always such a corbel-table at the top of a tower supporting a thirteenth-century stone broach spire, and for the same reason many of the best later towers have a band of ornament in that position below the parapet.

These little corbels were often elaborately carved in the forms of monsters and figures.

Fascinating Norman corbel-tables can be well studied at:

Gloucestershire	**Elkstone**: Signs of the Zodiac, winged horses, hares, stags, greyhounds and centaurs.
Herefordshire	**Kilpeck**: There are some 80 corbels encircling the outside, humorous and fascinating. There are a sad-looking dog and a rabbit together, two wrestlers, a grotesque man playing a fiddle, Lamb and Cross, and numerous birds and beasts, including a muzzled bear. Dragon mouths with curling tongues also jut out from the walls.
Kent	**Barfreston**: Grotesque heads and quaint figures
Warwickshire	**Berkswell**: Grotesque heads
Wiltshire	**Steeple Langford**: The corbel-table proves the wall to be Norman
Yorkshire	**Bossall**: The Norman corbel-table remains round the nave and transepts

Exterior string-courses of figures or foliage continued to be used from time to time, one of the best examples being of the fourteenth century at **Adderbury**, Oxfordshire, where there are about 100 delightful sculptures, including a dragon with a knotted tail, a boy with two dogs, a knight fighting an animal, a mermaid with two tails, and a medieval orchestra with men playing trumpets, cymbals, fiddle, harp and bagpipes.

The most remarkable external carving is the Saxon Crucifix at **Romsey** Abbey, Hampshire (and there is another of the same date inside which is a very valuable piece of Anglo-Saxon sculpture).

The finest exterior figure sculpture is on the west front of **Wells** Cathedral, Somerset. It is of the thirteenth century and there are some 350 figures. The view of this front from the Close is therefore one of the most superb views in England. The beauty of the Close of an English Cathedral is proverbial. **Salisbury** takes pride of place, but **Wells** runs it closely!

Only second to **Wells** Cathedral for external figure sculpture is the west front of **Exeter** Cathedral. Its figures of saints and kings are of the fourteenth century.

Other very lovely cathedral west fronts are those of **York**, **Lincoln** and **Peterborough**.

Figure sculpture on Somerset towers has been mentioned. The following figures on towers are noteworthy:

Devon	**Hartland**: 144 feet high and a landmark for shipping. On the east wall is a large figure of St Nectan.
Gloucestershire	**Fairford**: Quaint men at each corner
Oxfordshire	**Clanfield**: On the stair-turret a big figure of St Stephen with the stones of his martyrdom and a book.
Somerset	**Minehead**: On the south wall is the Holy Trinity, and on the east wall St Michael is weighing a soul in scales upon which St Mary is more successful than the devil.
	Haslingfield, Cambridgeshire, **Tilty**, Essex, and **Skelton**, near York, have original gable crosses.

Mass Dials and Sundials

Scientific sundials on churches generally date from the end of the seventeenth or beginning of the eighteenth century. The brick porch of 1720 at **Ellingham**, Hampshire, has a fine painted sundial.

Rather curiously about 20 Saxon ones remain. The most famous is at **Kirkdale**, Yorkshire. The long inscription proves the date 1060.

There are other Saxon sundials at:

Gloucestershire	**Daglingworth**
Hampshire	**Warnford**
Oxfordshire	**Marsh Baldon** (surrounded by cable ornament)
Yorkshire	**Edstone**

Medieval Mass dials or scratch dials were, however, constructed differently and they vary in form, size, detail and position in the most remarkable manner, and there may be several on the same wall (as at **Barfreston**, Kent).

They are most common around the Cotswolds and in Somerset and Hampshire.

A good example, having figures for the hours, is at **Farmington**, Gloucestershire.

A pillar sundial 'makes' the English country garden. There is a remarkable one of the seventeenth century in the picturesque churchyard of **Elmley Castle**, Worcestershire.

61   The charm of the small church, Winterborne Tomson, Dorset

Plan

The simplest plan is a single cell, as at **Winterborne Tomson**, Dorset (Plates 61 and 92).

In Norman times a tower between nave and chancel was popular, as at **Stewkley**, Buckinghamshire, **Studland**, Dorset, and **Cassington** and **Iffley** (Plate 30), Oxfordshire. Transepts were then often added. Such central towers are usual in the line of the Wiltshire, Berkshire Downs, and North Chilterns, as at **Edington**, Wiltshire, **Uffington**, Berkshire, and **Ivinghoe**, Buckinghamshire, and also in the East Riding of Yorkshire, as at **St Mary's**, **Beverley** (Plate 25), and **Hedon** (Plate 26).

The Celtic Church always had a square east end, but some early Norman churches followed the Roman basilica plan of a round east end called an apse, as again at **Winterborne Tomson** (Plates 61 and 92). There are charming examples at **Hales** and **Heckingham**, Norfolk, and **Fritton**, Suffolk (Plate 34).

Some churches are called round churches, but only the nave is circular. There are four: Temple Church, City of **London**, and at **Cambridge**, **Northampton**, and **Little Maplestead**, Essex.

The smallest complete medieval church in England is at **Culbone**, Somerset (Plate 62). There are other claimants, but they were formerly larger.

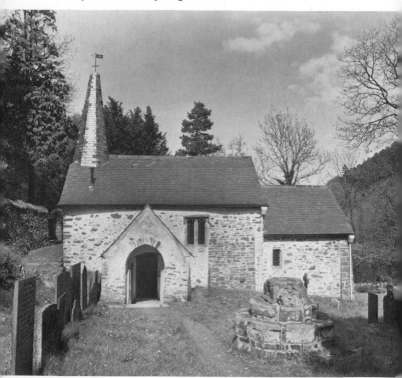

Orientation

Old churches and cathedrals invariably follow approximately a west to east axis with the altar at the east end. There is, however, often a slight deviation at the present time to the north, and much more rarely to the south.

The reason for this eastward position is not definitely known. Light comes from the east with the rising sun (possibly a connection with sun-worship). The Holy Land is, of course, in that direction, and it was also thought that Our Lord's second coming would be from that quarter.

Quite often the chancel is out of alignment with the nave. Guide books like to state that such inclined or weeping chancels represent Christ's head on the cross, but this is quite incorrect, and in any case chancels weep to the south as well as to the north!

Owing to the skill of the medieval builders, it is also hard to believe that this was purely accidental.

Many churches no doubt did face sunrise on their dedication or patronal festivals when they were built, but over the centuries owing to a changing calendar that position could also change slightly, and a new or rebuilt chancel might be set out to face the new sunrise position.

Leatherhead, Surrey, is a splendid example where the three parts of the church, tower, nave and chancel, are all off axis with each other.

62   The smallest complete medieval church, Culbone, Somerset

Crypts

The finest crypt is at **Canterbury** Cathedral. It is of Norman date. Another cathedral also has one of the same period, namely **Worcester**.

Three parish churches also have splendid Norman crypts, namely the well-known one at **Lastingham**, Yorkshire, and at St Peter-in-the-East, **Oxford**, and at **Berkswell**, Warwickshire.

There are, however, some Saxon crypts, for those at **Wing**, Buckinghamshire, and **Repton**, Derbyshire, are of the tenth century, and the crypt at **Hexham** Priory, Northumberland, is even earlier, being *c*. 680,

The bone-hole at **Hythe**, Kent, known to many visitors on account of its skulls and bones, is not a crypt, but was constructed in the thirteenth century as a processional path when the chancel was lengthened and no right of way was possible beyond it (compare **Walpole St Peter**, Norfolk).

Exterior Roofs

The material of the roof covering will, of course, depend upon the locality. Lead may be found anywhere, and also copper. Red tiles (usually mellowed) are found in the south, old grey slates in the south-west, and stone tiles in the Cotswolds. Red pantiles are picturesque, as at **Bawburgh**, Norfolk, and **Holme**, Nottinghamshire, but surely there is no more charming or homely material than the thatch of the Broads district, as at **Edingthorpe**, **Filby**, **Hales** and **Potter Heigham**, Norfolk, and **Bramfield**, **Fritton** (Plate 34) and **Thornham Parva**, Suffolk. Even the tower of the last has a thatched conical cap.

Windows

As one approaches the church, one has often dated the
different parts of the church by looking at the windows, but
this can be quite inaccurate, as the windows may have been
inserted in a wall that had already been in existence for
hundreds of years. All that can be said is that if the window is
original, then the wall must be at least as early as the window
of that particular type.

The following are the characteristics of the various periods;
the change from one to another was, of course, gradual, and
often one window can combine current and earlier designs.
The change was fairly consistent throughout the country.

Saxon

Round-headed, but sometimes triangular-headed (**Barton-on-
Humber**, Lincolnshire – Plate 29). The latter is an infallible
clue to this period. The semi-circular heads are frequently cut
out of a single stone. The sides or jambs may slope slightly
towards one another.

The earliest Saxon windows were cut straight through the
wall, with little, if any, splay. Normally a window is flush with
the outer wall face and splayed or sloped within, thus
enlarging the window opening. There is, however, one
exception, for in the later (but not in the latest) Saxon era,
windows were sometimes splayed within and without (the
glass therefore being set in the middle of the wall); this is
another infallible clue to date (as at **Tichborne**, Hampshire –
Plate 63).

Round-headed openings divided by a baluster-shaped shaft
are a feature of the period, particularly as belfry windows
(**Barton-on-Humber**, Lincolnshire – Plate 29). Saxon windows
were never recessed.

Small circular openings were sometimes favoured and may
be late Saxon or early Norman.

Norman

The semi-circular arch continues and the jambs are now
perfectly upright. Proportions vary, but generally windows are
small owing to the high cost of glass. Larger windows were
sometimes treated outside much like a doorway, with two
orders to the arch and perhaps shafts to the jambs.

Windows were usually high up in the walls and equal
spacing was not often attempted. The east window might be a
single small light, as at **Newhaven** and **Ovingdean**, Sussex,
Elkstone, Gloucestershire, and **Fritton**, Suffolk, but
occasionally three such lights might be grouped together, as at
Darenth, Kent.

Large circular windows may sometimes be found, as at
Barfreston, Kent, and **Castle Hedingham**, Essex, where a
miniature arcade radiates in and from the centre of the
window making a wheel-window. (This was the forerunner of

the rose windows of the Gothic period, which were very popular on the Continent, but were rarely favoured in England, **Boyton**, Wiltshire, having a fine one. Circular windows, however, continued to be used throughout the medieval period in some East Anglian clerestories, often alternating with ordinary windows, as at **Cley**, Norfolk.) The usual arrangement of belfry windows is two round-headed arches divided by a shaft and recessed within a large round-headed containing arch (**Old Shoreham**, Sussex – Plate 31).

Early English

The pointed arch is now used for the first time. The tall, narrow windows of the earlier part of this period (around 1220) are called lancets. They are usually of severe simplicity, but three grouped together at the east end, as so often in Sussex, make a most pleasing and satisfying background to the altar. The centre of the three lights usually rises above the others. Such lancet triplets may be well seen at **Amberley** (Plate 85), **Barnham**, **Boxgrove** Priory (Plate 78), **Burpham**, **Burwash**, **Climping** and **Udimore**, Sussex, **Minster-in-Thanet**, Kent, and **Easthorpe**, Essex. In the North, lancets are tall and slender.

Two lancets together at the east end are much less common – **Tangmere**, Sussex, is an example. Occasionally there are five together, as at **Bosham**, Sussex, but special mention must be made of the beautiful chancel ends of **Blakeney**, Norfolk (Plate 160), and **Ockham**, Surrey (Plate 64), where the number is seven.

Tracery, or stone bars, in the heads of windows was not invented – it gradually evolved itself. A window on its exterior now usually had a hood-mould to protect the window from rain-water. When two lancets, each with a hood-mould, were grouped together, the dip in the middle would collect water which could only escape over the hood-mould and on to the windows. To avoid this the lancets were enclosed by one

63   Saxon double-splay window, Tichborne, Hampshire

hood-mould, and this also enclosed a small piece of wall.
When this blank wall was itself pierced (cut in the solid
stonework) plate-tracery resulted (**Chalton**, Hampshire – Plate
65), and this is therefore the germ of church window tracery.

When such a group forms one window with openings
formed of thin bars of stone, this is then called bar-tracery,
which became universal (**Long Wittenham**, Berkshire – Plate
66).

The tracery is supported on vertical bars of stone called
mullions.

Plate tracery, whether with two lancets or three lancets,
with the blank space or spaces above pierced with a circle or
quatrefoil (four hollows between four cusps), is therefore the
origin of the Geometrical window, our first bar-tracery.

The church could now for the first time have large
windows, which might have seven lights below, giving a large
space above for the tracery. The wall was, of course,
weakened, but buttresses were given greater projection.

Decorated

At the end of the last period and the beginning of this period,
the tracery is appropriately called Geometrical, the earliest
form being the circle, which at first was uncusped, but later
cusps were added within the circles (a cusp is a projecting
point intersecting small arc openings). Windows with tracery
comprising only such circles can usually be dated in the
second half of the thirteenth century (**Long Wittenham**,
Berkshire – Plate 66).

At the end of that century and in the first 15 years of the
fourteenth century other forms exist side by side with the
circle or are substituted for it; the long-lobed pointed trefoil is
very popular, as are trefoils giving the appearance of daggers.
Trefoils might also be round-lobed (**Besthorpe**, Norfolk –
Plate 67). Such tracery might have a centrepiece, but at this
time there is also tracery without a centrepiece. It may be:

64   Seven lancets of East Window at Ockham Church, Surrey

a) *Intersecting tracery*

From each mullion spring two arched mullions of the same
radius as the containing arch and intersecting with one
another. The curves may be uncusped, but more often they
are cusped (**Besthorpe**, Norfolk – Plate 67).

b) *Graduated lancets*

Usually three or five, rising up to the arch. Again they may or
may not have cusps. They are common in the west of
England, as at **Ottery St Mary**, Devon, and **Wimborne**
Minster, Dorset.

The ball-flower ornament (most common from 1307 to 1327) was used extensively on windows in the Hereford area, as at **Leominster** Priory. Each south aisle window of **Gloucester** Cathedral has as many as 1,400.

Geometrical window tracery is therefore of greater variety than that of any other style.

Slightly later in the Decorated period we have Reticulated or net-like window tracery. The tracery is entirely composed of ogee arches (compound curves, concave and convex – so very popular in the fourteenth century), all producing similar forms, each tier upwards diminishing in numbers (**Beeston-next-Mileham**, Norfolk – Plate 68).

Later still, Flowing tracery became the fashion (**Besthorpe**, Norfolk – Plate 67). Simple geometrical curves (such as circles and trefoils) are still sometimes to be found even amongst the flowing curves, as at **Beverley Minster**, but normally they were completely eliminated.

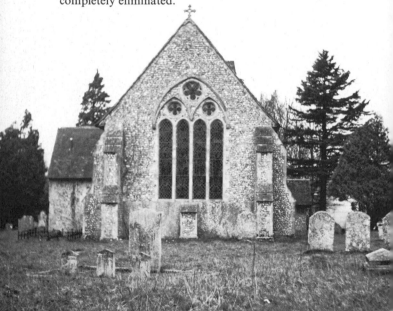

65   Geometrical plate tracery, Chalton, Hampshire

66 *Geometrical bar tracery, Long Wittenham, Berkshire*

Previously the beauty of tracery lay in the form of the openings, but now the eye follows the curves of the bars. There, is, of course, infinite variety in the designs.

South Lincolnshire and the East Riding of Yorkshire have numerous churches of the period of Flowing tracery and therefore abound in good examples, as at **Sleaford** and **Heckington**, Lincolnshire, and **Patrington**, **Hull** and **Cottingham**, East Riding. Among village churches are **Ducklington**, Oxfordshire, **Great Horwood**, Buckinghamshire, **Wymington**, Bedfordshire, **Ringstead**, Northamptonshire, and **Snettisham**, Norfolk.

In Kent and occasionally elsewhere a local and beautiful type of tracery is found. It is indeed called Kentish tracery, and it consists of an elaborately split-cusped indented quatrefoil of starlike form with prominent spikes protruding from it, as at **Chartham**, Kent.

67   Varied window tracery, Besthorpe, Norfolk

68 *Reticulated window tracery, Beeston-next-Mileham, Norfolk*

Perpendicular

In France, Flowing tracery developed into the even more
elaborate style known as the Flamboyant, but in England
there was then a complete change to straight lines. It began at
Gloucester Cathedral, and it was indeed a great revolution, for
it set the fashion for windows for nearly two hundred years
during the great church building period before the
Reformation, when the merchant classes were at the height of
their prosperity.

Such a window gave the maximum amount of light and
every possible scope to the glass-painter, whose art was then
reaching its highest point of development. He could insert his
figures of saints in the rectangular panels, which was quite
impossible with the earlier Flowing tracery.

It is always easy to detect a Perpendicular window. The
design is most satisfying, there is infinite variety, and its
detailed study is rewarding.

This rectilinear tracery can be seen to perfection in the great
East Anglian churches. There are huge east windows, as at
Sall (Plate 69), **Walpole St Peter**, and St Nicholas, **King's
Lynn**, Norfolk, and **Cavendish**, Suffolk, and large aisle
windows and numerous clerestory windows.

Rather curiously a small piece of Flowing tracery is often
retained in the side lights of the Perpendicular tracery in this
area.

That most superb of all buildings, King's College Chapel,
Cambridge, is really just a row of Perpendicular windows,
with buttresses between them to support the wonderful fan
vault – all completely English.

Perhaps, however, the most beautiful stonework of the
windows of the period is to be found in some Somerset
churches, such as **Curry Rivel** and **Crowcombe**, and in many
east Devon churches, such as **Cullompton** and **Kentisbeare.** A
type peculiar to the extreme West is well seen at **St Neot**,
Cornwall (with much of its original glass), and **Ashburton**,
Devon.

The vertical bars continuing upward into the head of the

69   Perpendicular window tracery, Sall, Norfolk

window were much stronger than the earlier bars with their
geometrical or flowing curves. Advantage was taken of this to
increase the size of the window; but mullions now perhaps 50
or 60 feet high had themselves to be stayed to prevent bulge,
and this was effected by the insertion of horizontal bars called
transoms across the lower lights as well as in the tracery –
again to the great satisfaction of the glass-painter.

A Perpendicular window seems to be nothing but mullions;
a bar starting from the apex of an arch is, however, called a
supermullion.

Arches at this time were usually more obtuse, but the
special arch of the period is the four-centred arch, which
admirably suited the tracery.

Square-headed windows now occur, and indeed in the
North they are quite common. Some fifteenth-century
windows, however, in less prosperous areas, were of the
simplest type with perhaps no tracery at all but a few cusps at
the tops of the lights.

The delightful Tudor oriel window so often found in houses
is rare in churches. Charming examples may however be seen
at **Adderbury**, Oxfordshire, on the porch of **Stoke Dry**,
Rutland, and on the tower of **Royston**, Yorkshire.

Post-Reformation

The Gothic style lingered in **Oxford** until the seventeenth
century as shown in several college chapels (Wadham), but
elsewhere the Renaissance style soon predominated. This
produced large plain windows with once again the
semicircular arch, and often with a projecting keystone, as in
Wren's City churches (**Gayhurst**, Buckinghamshire – Plate 32).

Interior Roofs (Wooden)

The most simple form is the high-pitched single-framed trussed rafter roof in which each pair of rafters is a complete truss in itself. Examples are at the interesting churches of **South Burlingham**, Norfolk, and **Dennington**, Suffolk.

The king-post roof is of this type, but with a strong beam at intervals from wall to wall, on the centre of which stands the king-post supporting the rafters above. Many such roofs remain in the small ancient churches of the south-east and may be of thirteenth or fourteenth century date. Examples are at **Lyminster**, Sussex, and **Barking**, Suffolk.

Tie-beam Roofs

Later roofs were usually double-framed with principal tie-beams placed at intervals. Sometimes the tie-beam is supported on arched braces which may have traceried spandrels. Sometimes a roof may be boarded or ceiled between the principal rafters with bosses at the intersections of the rafters.

Somerset and Cheshire have the finest tie-beam roofs, usually ceiled, which adds to their richness.

Somerset   Angels abound; their wings are usually more closed up than those of East Anglia. The following tie-beam roofs are all magnificent: **Bruton**, **Evercreech** (angels, beams, and bosses richly coloured and gilt, and which can be well studied from the galleries), **High Ham**, **Leigh-on-Mendip**, **Long Sutton**, **Martock** (Plate 70 – the most lavish with 736 panels), **Somerton** (very fine), **Wellow**, **Wells** St Cuthbert (very beautifully coloured), and **Weston Zoyland** (very fine). Similar roofs will be found over side aisles at **Brent Knoll** and **Mark**, and

<table>
<tr><td>Cheshire</td><td>over transept and chapel at **Crewkerne**. Cheshire is also noted for its tie-beam roofs, adorned with numerous bosses. The following are all very lovely: **Astbury** (with open-work pendants), **Barthomley**, **Chester**, St Mary-on-the-Hill, **Disley**, **Malpas** (coloured bosses and angels), **Mobberley**, and **Northwich** (or **Witton**), which is particularly fine with colour.</td></tr>
</table>

Wales has rich tie-beam roofs at **Gresford**, **Ruthin**, and **St David's** Cathedral, and mention must be made of those at **Oxford** Cathedral, **Sefton**, Lancashire, **Blythburgh**, Suffolk (much original colour), and particularly **Beverley St Mary**, Yorkshire, with its paintings of 40 English kings up to Henry VI.

Wagon Roofs

West Country roofs are almost invariably rounded and are called wagon or barrel roofs.

The most remarkable example is at **Shepton Mallet**, Somerset, with 350 wooden panels with a design only duplicated once. When the carved panels are coloured and gilded, the result is magnificent, as can be seen at **Cullompton**, Devon (Plate 71). It was, however, more usual to plaster the space between the principal rafters, giving a homely effect, and adding largely to the attractiveness of West Country churches. Two splendid examples are at **Watchet** and **Selworthy** (Plate 72), Somerset. Again right colouring always enhances a church and there are two gorgeous examples with coloured bosses at **Ilfracombe** and **Combe Martin**, Devon, the former having an ornate rood celure.

The wagon roof at **Muchelney**, Somerset, is covered with angels coming out of clouds painted in the seventeenth century.

70   Panelled tie-beam roof, Martock, Somerset

Hammer-beam Roofs

The most ornamental type of roof is, however, the hammer-beam variety and it is almost confined to the eastern counties. A hammer-beam projects into the church and then stops and from the end of it the main arch springs, thereby considerably lessening its width and reducing outward thrust. In a double hammer-beam roof there are two tiers of such beams on each side. There are usually an immense number of angels, often over a hundred, and in this part of the country they usually have outspread wings. Cornices or wall-plates and wall-posts are adorned with angels, and spandrels under the hammer-beams are often elaborately traceried.

Single hammer-beam roofs are more usual in Norfolk and double ones in Suffolk. As these roofs are so beautiful, the list which follows is a fairly complete one.

Norfolk	**Banningham**, **Blakeney** (Plate 160), **Cawston** (very fine), **East Harling** (steep pitch), **Emneth** (partly tie-beam), **Gissing** (double and most attractive), **Knapton** (Plate 73) (double and very fine with 138 angels with some colour), **Ludham**, **Necton** (partly arch-braced and very fine with 16 figures on the wall-posts), **North Burlingham**, **North Creake** (elaborate cornice), **Norwich** St Stephen, **Potter Heigham**, **South Creake** (coloured angels), **Swaffham** (double and very fine), **Tilney All Saints** (double and very fine), **Trunch** (spandrels have lace-like tracery), **Upwell** (partly tie-beam; very fine aisle roofs with hammer-beams; and angels everywhere which can be well studied from the galleries), and **Wymondham** Abbey.
Suffolk	**Bacton** (coloured rood celure), **Badingham** (very fine), **Bury St Edmunds** St Mary (partly arch-braced and very fine), **Coddenham**, **Cotton** (partly arch-braced), **Earl Stonham** (very fine with elaborate cornice), **Framsden**, **Fressingfield**, **Gislingham**, **Grundisburgh** (very fine), **Heveningham**, **Hopton** (near Botesdale, much colour), **Lakenheath** (partly tie-beam), **Little Stonham**, **Mildenhall** (partly tie-beam, and over aisles, very fine), **Rattlesden**, **Shotley**, **Walsham-le-Willows** (partly tie-beam, with colour, very fine), **Wetherden**, **Woolpit** (very fine), and **Worlingworth**. (All are double hammer-beam roofs except numbers 2, 3, 6, 8, 12, 13, 15, and 18.)

71 Wagon roof, Cullompton, Devon

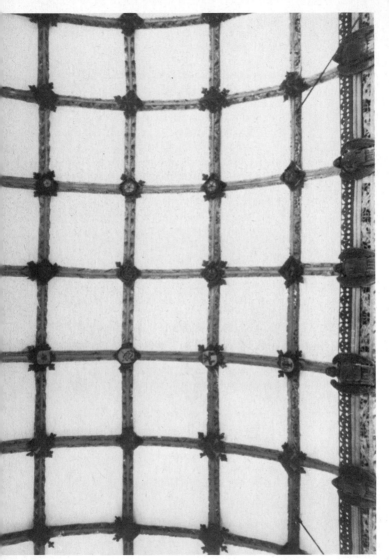

72   *Wagon roof, Selworthy, Somerset*

73   *Hammer-beam roof, Knapton, Norfolk*

| Cambridgeshire | Two notable hammer-beam roofs: **March** (Plate 74), has a double one and is one of the very finest with nearly 200 angels; **Ely** transept has a single one with colour. |
| Essex | Three double hammer-beam roofs: **Castle Hedingham, Gestingthorpe** and **Great Bromley**. |

There are also three beautiful hammer-beam roofs in which the hammer-beams are hidden by vaulting, namely St Peter Mancroft, **Norwich** (very fine), and **Ringland**, Norfolk, and **Framlingham**, Suffolk. Perhaps the most astonishing medieval roof is at **Needham Market**, Suffolk, which is amazing medieval craftsmanship. It is, in effect, a hammer-beam roof.

Another superb roof that appears to be a hammer-beam roof is at **Bere Regis**, Dorset (Plate 75). It has huge coloured bosses and large brightly-painted figures of the Twelve Apostles which are very fascinating.

For a roof of a forest of tremendous timbers, **Grasmere**, Westmorland, must surely be unrivalled.

Bosses of wood on a wooden roof are often carved with a variety of figures and subjects, and if coloured they enhance the church. Nine bosses at **Sall**, Norfolk (Plate 76) depict scenes from the Life of Our Lord. At **Sampford Courtenay**, Devon, the bosses include the favourite subject of a sow and litter, and three rabbits, but only three ears had to be carved!

The wall-posts of a roof (for preventing thrust), whether of the main roof or that of an aisle, nearly always rest on corbels. They are usually of stone and should be carefully studied, for they are full of interest and are often amusing. They might be human heads or angels or grotesque monsters, seen to perfection at **Sharrington**, Norfolk (Plate 77). Again, they should be coloured, as the four fine medieval musicians at **Duston**, Northamptonshire. (On the subject of musicians and colour there is the most charming group of five early sixteenth-century musicians with long hair, brown and blue coats and pink shoes at **Beverley St Mary**, Yorkshire.)

The wall-posts themselves may occasionally house figures, as at **Necton**, Norfolk.

74   Hammer-beam roof, March, Cambridgeshire

75 *Apostles on the roof at Bere Regis, Dorset*

76 *Wooden roof boss of the Entry into Jerusalem, Sall, Norfolk*

77 *Corbel, Sharrington, Norfolk*

Stone Roofs (or Vaults)

The simplest vault known to the Normans was the groined vault, whereby two barrel vaults intersect, as at **Darenth**, Kent. Vaulting ribs were not then known, but they soon became known as they were the arches upon which the roof was erected. The simplest type is quadripartite with four cells, as in the round Norman chancel roof of **Hemel Hempstead**, Herts., and in the pointed thirteenth-century roofs at **Boxgrove** Priory, Sussex (Plate 78), and **Beverley Minster**.

When additional ribs were introduced the cells increased in number and decreased in size.

A tierceron rib rises not to the central boss but to some point on one of the ridge ribs. **Exeter** Cathedral and **Beverley Minster** central tower have fine examples.

In the fourteenth century, ribs became mainly decorative and they did not spring from the wall, as previously, but crossed the spandrels from rib to rib, thereby making elaborate star-like patterns. Such a vault is known as a lierne vault. It is extremely beautiful with innumerable bosses. There are wonderful examples at **Tewkesbury** Abbey, Gloucestershire (Plate 79), St George's Chapel, **Windsor**, and in the Cathedrals of **Gloucester**, **Norwich** (Plate 80) and **Oxford**.

In the fifteenth century the most beautiful and purely English form of vault known as the fan vault was introduced in the Cloisters at **Gloucester**. Quite the finest is in the superb chapel of King's College, **Cambridge**, but Henry VII's Chapel, **Westminster** Abbey, is a close rival. **Sherborne** Abbey, Dorset (Plate 81) then follows very closely.

The East Chapels of **Peterborough** Cathedral have fan vaults.

Equally lovely though smaller fan vaults exist at **Cullompton**, Devon, and **North Leigh**, Oxfordshire (Plate 82). Being lower they can more easily be seen and they show to perfection the beauty of Perpendicular architecture with corresponding windows.

The beautiful fan vaults of the Divinity School, **Oxford**,

78   The beauty of Boxgrove Priory, Sussex

and at **Ottery St Mary**, Devon, have prolonged bosses or pendants, which are very effective.

In the whole of English Gothic architecture, it is doubtful if there is any more amazing work than the sculpture on vault bosses. There may be several hundred in one cathedral (such as **Norwich** and **Exeter**) or church. The majority are so high that details cannot be seen from the ground: yet all the details are there, and this proves that such work was done for the glory of God and not for man – hence its beauty.

Biblical and other subjects are portrayed, and the chief events in Our Lord's Life may be depicted, as on 15 bosses in **Tewkesbury** Abbey, Gloucestershire, all showing the most exquisite details.

Foliage and grotesques are also common, and a sow and litter are favoured in stone as well as in wood.

St Mary Redcliffe, **Bristol**, has a vast number of bosses.

Photography and binoculars are now able to reveal all this beauty to us.

79   *Lierne vault, Tewkesbury Abbey, Gloucestershire*

80 Norwich Cathedral vault

81   Fan vault, Sherborne Abbey, Dorset

82   Fan vault, North Leigh, Oxfordshire

Cathedrals

Main Styles

Norman	**Durham** (the finest Norman work in England), **Ely**, **Gloucester** (and Perpendicular), **Norwich**, **Peterborough** (the oldest timber roof), and **Winchester** (and Perpendicular – the longest medieval cathedral in the world).
Early English	**Canterbury** (and Perpendicular), **Durham** – the Chapel of the Nine Altars, **Lincoln**, **Salisbury** and **Wells** (and Decorated).
Decorated	**Exeter** (the two towers at the ends of the transepts are Norman), **Wells** (and Early English), and **York** (and Perpendicular).
Perpendicular	**Canterbury** (Plate 1) (and Early English), **Gloucester** (and Norman), **Winchester** (and Norman), and **York** (Plate 2) (and Decorated).
Renaissance (late 17th century)	St Paul's Cathedral, **London** (Wren)
Late 19th and early 20th century	**Truro** (Plate 49) (but Perpendicular south aisle)
1962	**Coventry** (and Perpendicular tower and spire of former building)

The finest east windows are at **Carlisle** (Flowing), **Gloucester** (Perpendicular), **Lincoln** (Geometrical), **Ripon** (Geometrical), and **York** (Perpendicular).

The pulpitum is the stone screen west of the stalls. There are sumptous Decorated examples at **Exeter**, **Lincoln** and **Southwell** (each side different), and a Perpendicular one at **Ripon** (now having brightly-coloured figures).

Chapter Houses

The meeting room of the cathedral chapter known as the
Chapter House is often one of the most splendid parts of an
English Cathedral. The vault is usually a triumph of
craftsmanship in stone. The following are the finest:

Norman	**Bristol**
Early English	**Lincoln** and **Westminster** Abbey
Decorated	**Salisbury** (Geometrical style, with carvings of Old Testament scenes), **Southwell** (also Geometrical style with beautiful natural foliage carving), and **Wells** (with the famous branching stairway, which is one of the most graceful flights of steps in the world).

Piers and Arches and Complete Churches in one Style

Saxon

Round arches and only of one order springing from massive impost blocks. Interlaced carving was popular. Exterior corners may have the long-and-short work of the later Saxon period, and exterior walls of herring-bone masonry (forming zig-zags) are usually an indication of Saxon or very early Norman workmanship.

Here are four amazing chancel arches:

Lincolnshire	**Stow**
Northampton-shire	**Wittering** (Plate 83) (interesting to compare it with the Norman arch adjoining)
Sussex	**Bosham** and **Worth**

Cambridge, St Bene'ts, has a most remarkable tower arch of this period.

Equally amazing arcades can be seen at:

Huntingdonshire	**Great Paxton**

Saxon crosses have been noted, but Saxon sculpture will be found at:

Derbyshire	**Wirksworth**: Coffin-lid
Gloucestershire	**Daglingworth**: Panels of the Crucifixion, St Peter and Our Lord enthroned
Leicestershire	**Breedon-on-the-Hill**: Remarkable friezes
Northampton-shire	**Barnack**: Exquisite sculpture of Christ in Majesty. **Castor**: A small sculpture of a man

Complete churches:

Buckinghamshire	**Wing** (with crypt)
County Durham	**Escomb**, **Jarrow** and **Monkwearmouth**
Essex	**Bradwell-on-Sea** (isolated on the coast), and **Greensted** (nave of split oak tree-trunks, the oldest wooden walls in England; just think when such trees were planted).
Gloucestershire	**Deerhurst** (and a Saxon chapel nearby)
Hampshire	**Boarhunt**, **Breamore** (inscription on arch) and **Corhampton**
Northampton shire-	**Brixworth** (probably the oldest complete church still used)

Sussex	**Worth**
Wiltshire	St Lawrence, **Bradford-on-Avon**
Yorkshire	**Kirk Hammerton**

It is interesting to note that our cathedrals do not have such early work.

Norman

The round arch continues, usually with several recessed orders. The columns are nearly always massive and cylindrical, and the capital is always square-edged on top. The most frequent ornament is the chevron or zig-zag, and later in the period the fascinating beak-heads.

Chichester Cathedral, Sussex, has two wonderful sculptured panels of about 1140; Christ coming to the house of Mary of Bethany and the Raising of Lazarus.

The chancel arches are usually wonderful works of art, and the capitals should be studied in detail for they often have marvellous carvings of human figures, weird animals and birds, and grotesques and monsters in all kinds of positions and postures.

The most magnificent chancel arch in England is at **Tickencote**, Rutland (Plate 84).

Other notable chancel arches are at:

Cumberland	**Torpenhow**
Gloucestershire	**Elkstone**
Herefordshire	**Kilpeck** and **Rowlstone**
Northampton-shire	**Wakerley**
Rutland	**Stoke Dry**
Sussex	**Amberley** (Plate 85), **Old Shoreham**, **Selham** and **Tortington**
Warwickshire	**Stoneleigh**
Yorkshire	**Adel** (Plate 86), **Brayton**, **Kirkburn**, **Liverton**, and **North Grimston**

84   Norman chancel arch, Tickencote, Rutland

Fine arcades may be seen at:

Kent	**St Margaret-at-Cliffe**
Norfolk	**Walsoken** (Plate 87)
Northampton-shire	St Peter's **Northampton** (elaborate capitals)
Sussex	**Steyning**

Complete churches:

Berkshire	**Avington**
Buckinghamshire	**Stewkley**
Derbyshire	**Melbourne** and **Steetley**
Dorset	**Studland** and **Worth Matravers**
Herefordshire	**Kilpeck** and **Moccas**
Kent	**Barfreston** and **St Margaret-at-Cliffe**
Oxfordshire	**Iffley** (Plate 30)
Shropshire	**Heath Chapel**
Sussex	**Old Shoreham** (Plate 31)
Yorkshire	**Adel** and **Birkin**

Transitional Norman

Churches of this period show the gradual change from the rather massive Norman work with round arches to the lighter Gothic work with the pointed arch, and often a mixture of both.

Such churches abound in Sussex, as at **Boxgrove** Priory (Plate 78), **Burpham** and **New Shoreham**.

The Chancel arch at **Walsoken**, Norfolk (Plate 87), is a good example – the arch has become pointed, but the ornamentation is zig-zags as on the Norman arcades.

85   Norman chancel arch and Early English chancel, Amberley, Sussex

Early English

The acute pointed arch with deeply undercut rounds and hollows is now usual, and the capitals, now with a rounded upper edge, are either moulded or have exquisite conventional stiff-leaf foliage with long stalks. The ornament of the period is the dog-tooth (a completely hollowed four-leaf pyramid).

Fine arcades with sumptuous foliage on the capitals may be seen at:

Bedfordshire	**Eaton Bray** and **Studham**
Berkshire	**East Hendred** (Plate 88)
Buckinghamshire	**Ivinghoe**
County Durham	**Sedgefield**
Gloucestershire	**Slimbridge**
Hertfordshire	**Kimpton**
Lincolnshire	**Weston**
Norfolk	**West Walton**
Somerset	**Wells** Cathedral: The foliage capitals with exciting figure sculpture are very notable.

Complete churches:

Berkshire	**Uffington**
Lincolnshire	**Bottesford**
Norfolk	**West Walton**
Northampton-shire	**Warmington**
Northumberland	**Haltwhistle**
Sussex	**Climping**
Yorkshire	**Skelton**, near York (even original gable crosses)

Decorated

Arches are not so acutely pointed, and the mouldings are more numerous but are not so deeply cut and there are few hollows.

86   The Baptism of Christ on a Norman capital at Adel, Yorkshire

Capitals again are usually moulded, but if with foliage, it is now quite different from that of the previous century, for it is beautiful life-like foliage which follows nature, as for instance the leaves of the oak, ivy, maple and vine. The ornament of the period is the ball-flower (a globular flower with three incurved petals).

The ogee arch (concave and convex curves like a bracket) and crockets (projecting foliage) and foliage finials are now very popular.

This foliage can be seen to perfection at **Southwell** Minster, Nottinghamshire.

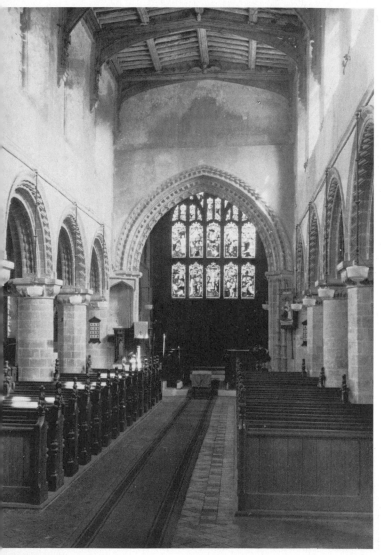

87   Walsoken, Norfolk

88 *Thirteenth-century foliage capital, East Hendred, Berkshire*

Fine arcades with foliage capitals may be seen at:

Leicestershire	**Stoke Golding**
Lincolnshire	**Claypole**
Rutland	**Oakham**
Yorkshire	**Patrington** (Plate 89)

Complete churches:

Berkshire	**Shottesbrooke**
Essex	**Tilty** – chancel with superb windows
Lincolnshire	Many fine churches of this date are in the south of the county. **Ewerby**, **Heckington** (particularly elaborate), **Holbeach** and **Swaton**.
Norfolk	**Snettisham**
Oxfordshire	**Dorchester** Abbey (Plate 151) (the unique sanctuary is especially notable)
Sussex	**Winchelsea**
Yorkshire	**Patrington**

Perpendicular

Arches have become still more obtuse, and the four-centred arch is now common. The mouldings are wide and shallow. As the arch is now blunt, the pier occupies a large proportion of the total height of an arcade.

Foliage on capitals is almost entirely confined to the West Country. Undulating foliage surrounding the capital is popular in Devon, as at **Broad Clyst**, **Molland**, and **Wolborough** (Plate 90), and in Cornwall small leaves often occur on each face of the capital, as at **St Veep**.

Perpendicular arcades are very numerous, as there was so much rebuilding at that time. It is appropriate, therefore, to give particulars of two main types.

89   *Fourteenth-century foliage capitals, Patrington, Yorkshire*

90   *Fifteenth-century foliage capital, Wolborough, Devon*

a) *West Country*

Four semi-circular half-shafts are connected by wave mouldings. Good examples are at **Altarnun** and **St Teath**, Cornwall.

b) *East Anglia*

Semi-circular half-shafts alternate with wide shallow hollows, the former alone having small capitals and bases, the hollows continuing up into the corresponding hollows of the arch. Good examples are at **Sall**, **Shelton**, and **Wighton**, Norfolk, and **Denston**, **Southwold**, and **Stoke-by-Nayland**, Suffolk.

Complete churches:

There are so many that any list would be quite inadequate, but these are a few of our special glories.

Berkshire	St George's Chapel, **Windsor**
Buckinghamshire	**Hillesden** and **Maids Moreton**
Cambridgeshire	**Cambridge**, King's College Chapel
Devon	**Cullompton**
Essex	**Saffron Walden** and **Thaxted**
Gloucestershire	**Chipping Campden**, **Cirencester**, **Fairford** and **Northleach**
Norfolk	**King's Lynn**, St Nicholas, **Sall**, **Terrington St Clement**, and **Walpole St Peter**
Oxfordshire	**Ewelme**
Somerset	**Crewkerne** and **Ilminster**
Suffolk	**Blythburgh** (Plate 51), **Lavenham** (tower and nave), **Long Melford**, **Southwold**, **Stoke-by-Nayland** and **Woodbridge**
Wiltshire	**Edington**: A very early example. **Steeple Ashton**

Renaissance or Seventeenth and Eighteenth Century

After the Reformation, the Gothic style was gradually
superseded by the very different style of the Renaissance
based upon classical traditions. The arch is again round, but
of course windows are much larger than in Norman times.
The piers follow one of the classical orders.

There are two exquisite examples of seventeenth-century
architecture – in the Chapels of the Colleges of Trinity,
Oxford, and Pembroke, **Cambridge**, which is one of Sir
Christopher Wren's earliest designs.

London   Of his famous architecture many of his
                      City of **London** churches still remain, apart
                      from St Paul's Cathedral. He rebuilt 51 in
                      the square mile of the City after the Great
                      Fire of 1666. His towers and spires are
                      included in the section on spires. The
                      following interiors escaped damage or
                      severe damage in the war and are good
                      examples of his work:

                      St Bene't, Paul's Wharf
                      St Clement, Eastcheap
                      St Edmund, Lombard Street
                      St James, Garlickhithe
                      St Magnus, London Bridge
                      St Margaret, Lothbury
                      St Margaret, Pattens
                      St Martin, Ludgate
                      St Mary Abchurch
                      St Mary Aldermary (Gothic style)
                      St Mary-at-Hill (many original fittings)
                      St Michael, Cornhill
                      St Peter, Cornhill

The following interiors are also Wren churches, but have
been beautifully restored and considerably altered after severe
war damage:

> St Andrew-by-the-Wardrobe
> St Andrew, Holborn
> Sts Anne and Agnes, Gresham Street
> St Bride, Fleet Street (pews face one
> another)
> St Lawrence Jewry (the City Corporation
> church)
> St Mary-le-Bow
> St Michael, Paternoster Royal
> St Nicholas, Cole Abbey
> St Stephen, Walbrook
> St Vedast, Foster Lane (pews face one
> another)

There are also notable late seventeenth-century churches at:

Buckinghamshire	**Willen** (red brick)
Huntingdonshire	**Little Gidding**: Built, isolated in fields, in the time of Charles I by Nicholas Ferrar in connection with his revival of semi-monastic life. The pews are arranged facing one another.
Staffordshire	**Ingestre**: A beautiful example
Suffolk	**Euston** (partly medieval) (Plate 91): In the grounds of the Hall
Surrey	**Petersham** (partly medieval)
Westmorland	**Brougham (Ninekirk)**, 1660

Notable eighteenth-century churches are at:

Buckinghamshire	**Gayhurst** (Plate 32): Adjoins the fine Elizabethan house
Dorset	**Blandford** and **Wimborne St Giles**
Hampshire	**Avington** (red brick)
Leicestershire	**King's Norton** (an early example of Gothic Revival)
Oxfordshire	**Chiselhampton** (very charming)

91   A Renaissance church, Euston, Suffolk

Rutland	**Teigh**: A remarkable interior. Pews face one another
Shropshire	**Shrewsbury**, St Chad
Westmorland	**Ravenstonedale**
Worcestershire	**Great Witley**: A magnificent interior, beautifully decorated.

Sometimes a medieval church is encased in eighteenth-century work to make it look like a Georgian church. Such are:

Essex	**Lambourne**
Hampshire	**Farley Chamberlayne** and **Wolverton** (red brick)
Oxfordshire	**Wheatfield**

Interiors

Eighteenth-century Furnishings

At this time 'three-deckers' became the fashion. They are prayer-desk, lectern and pulpit combined in one, but at different levels. The pulpit then dominated the church (not the altar), and plaster ceilings were the fashion so that the voice of the preacher could be heard. High box-pews (to keep out draughts) were the usual form of seating, and the squire would have a particularly cosy and select family pew, possibly with a fire-place, as he liked to keep himself to himself (and probably the villagers were pleased that he did so!). Galleries became usual (facing the pulpit, of course) for the increased congregations, due largely to the influence of Charles Wesley.

Even the numerous pegs for hats or wigs often remain in such churches.

There is no doubt that most of our churches would have been furnished in some such way by the beginning of the nineteenth century. All this was, of course, in aid of a Protestant form of worship. The Oxford Movement of the beginning of the century, however, stressed that the Church of England possessed the Apostolic Succession and was therefore a part of the Catholic Church, and that the altar should again be the centre of worship. That is why so many chancels, then ruinous, had to be re-built by the Victorians, and we must give them credit for saving what might otherwise have disappeared. At the same time, however, they swept away all the Protestant woodwork in the body of the church. This is now often regretted and churches become of great interest where such woodwork has been allowed to remain. One reason for the latter is that the Victorians built a new church altogether elsewhere in the parish, leaving the old church untouched (for example, **Parracombe**, Devon).

Churches completely of the late seventeenth century or Georgian period as above mentioned, would, of course, have had all such fittings as part of the structure and are more likely therefore to have retained them. The following list,

which we hope will be useful, is of those medieval churches
which still retain such fittings without any Victorian
restoration removing them.

Cheshire	**Baddiley**
Devon	**Molland**, **Offwell**, **Parracombe** and **West Ogwell**
Dorset	**Chalbury** (particularly charming), **Winterborne Tomson** (Plates 61 and 92): In a farmyard and also particularly charming. The rood-loft front is now the west gallery. Restored in memory of Thomas Hardy.
Hampshire	**Minstead**: In the New Forest and well known
Hertfordshire	**Stanstead Abbots**
Kent	**Fairfield**: Isolated in fields. **Stelling**: The gallery and all the box-pews still face the pulpit.
Nottinghamshire	**Teversal**
Wiltshire	**Old Dilton**: Lovely view through the east window to the hill beyond.
Yorkshire	**Whitby**: Quite the best and most complete of all.

Charming Interiors

The last list leads on to interiors whose charm is not
necessarily due to eighteenth-century fittings, but to medieval
furnishings of all dates and which are unrestored, the whole
structure being charming, lovable and quaint.

A visit to any one of these is always very rewarding.

Buckinghamshire	**Dorney**
Cornwall	**Launcells**
Essex	**Bradwell-juxta-Coggeshall**
Hampshire	**Stoke Charity**
Herefordshire	**Pixley**
Kent	**Graveney** and **Old Romney**

92   Eighteenth-century fittings in Norman church, Winterborne Tomson, Dorset

Lincolnshire	**Cotes-by-Stow** and **Saltfleetby All Saints** (leaning tower)
Rutland	**Stoke Dry**
Somerset	**Cameley, Hinton Blewett**, and **Puxton** (leaning tower)

Interiors with Complete Medieval Furnishings

The last list then leads on to interiors which have nearly all their medieval fittings complete and a visit to them is therefore most rewarding.

Buckinghamshire	**Edlesborough**: On a hill. The only medieval wooden pulpit canopy.
Cheshire	**Astbury**
Devon	**Swimbridge** and **Tawstock** (particularly monuments)
Essex	**Wendens Ambo**
Hertfordshire	**Flamstead**
Lincolnshire	**Croft**
Norfolk	**South Burlingham**
Northampton-shire	**Stanford**
Somerset	**Banwell, Trull** and **Wellow**
Worcestershire	**Strensham**

Interiors – Devotion and Colour

This list comprises churches which have been most tastefully restored and are full of beauty with colour and the atmosphere of devotion.

Cornwall	**Blisland**: Very lovely. **Lanreath, Mullion**: The Cove is lovely and so is the church.
Devon	**Harberton** and **Torbryan**
Essex	**Thaxted**
Gloucestershire	**North Cerney**
Norfolk	**South Creake**

Nottinghamshire	**East Markham**, **Egmanton**, and **Holme**
Oxfordshire	**Horley**
Suffolk	**Lound** (work by Sir Ninian Comper)

Some very excellent restoration work is often carried out today on cathedrals and churches.

There is no fairer scene than a small country church, often remote, beautified and cleaned by loving and sympathetic treatment of its white walls and all its fittings with a touch of colour hopefully in the right place.

The atmosphere of devotion then immediately becomes apparent, and the church fulfils the function of every church – to make one fall down on one's knees.

Quite at random here are three examples:

Berkshire	**Shellingford**
Buckinghamshire	**Chearsley**
Sussex	**Coates**

Two modern churches with interiors of great beauty must also be mentioned – St Cyprian's, Clarence Gate, Baker Street, **London**, and St Mary's, **Wellingborough**, Northamptonshire, both by Sir Ninian Comper.

Fonts

We are admitted into the Church by baptism. The font is therefore nearly always at the west end of the church.

Saxon

Devon	**Dolton**: From a Saxon cross with dragons and interlaced serpents.
Dorset	**Melbury Bubb**: Also formerly a Saxon Cross – turned upside down with hounds chasing deer.
Gloucestershire	**Deerhurst**: Spiral ornament
Northampton-shire	**Little Billing**: Inscription
Warwickshire	**Curdworth**: Triumph of goodness over evil.

Norman

Innumerable Norman fonts remain. They are massive and are often amazingly carved with wonderful monsters and figures. They are usually square or circular.

East Yorkshire group	All have a marvellous gallery of figures: **Cowlam** (Plate 93): The Wise Men are splendid. **Langtoft**: Adam and Eve and serpent with apple in mouth. The Martyrdoms of St Lawrence, St Andrew and St Margaret are realistic. **North Grimston**: The Last Supper and Descent from the Cross are captivating. **Kirkburn**: The principal scenes are the Baptism of Our Lord, the charge to St Peter, and the Ascension. **Reighton**: Richly carved designs.
North-west Norfolk group	An outstanding group: **Shernborne**: On four columns. Grotesque heads and

93   Norman font, Cowlam, Yorkshire

interlacing work. **Toftrees**: Very similar to Shernborne. **South Wootton**: On nine pillars with some monster faces. **Sculthorpe**: Lions and rams, and the Visit of the Wise Men. **Breccles**: Arcading and row of robed figures. **Castle Rising**: Demon faces and foliage. **Fincham**: Nativity, Wise Men, Baptism of Christ, and Adam and Eve. **Burnham Deepdale** (Plate 94): Scenes of the Occupations of the Twelve Months.

Aylesbury group
Chalice-shaped with circular bowl on inverted square capital, all richly carved. Typical are: **Aylesbury**, **Bledlow**, **Great Kimble**, **Weston Turville**.

Cornish groups
a) A cup-bowl elaborately carved and supported on a massive central stem: four angle shafts rise outside the bowl and support heads projecting from the corners. Examples: **Bodmin**, **Roche** and **St Austell**. b) A font following the form of a Norman capital and having roundels on the bowl and large heads at the corners. Examples: **Altarnun**, **St Thomas-by-Launceston**, and **Laneast**.

Magnificent Norman fonts may also be found at:

Berkshire
Avington: Eleven arches with figures, including a bishop and a devil.

Buckinghamshire
Stone: Spiral ornament framing reptiles, and men fighting beasts.

Cumberland
Bridekirk (Plate 95): Ornate with mythical monsters, the Baptism of Christ, and a remarkable inscription.

94   Norman font, Burnham Deepdale, Norfolk. September – threshing, October – grinding corn, November – killing a pig, and December – four persons seated at Christmas dinner

Devon	**Luppitt**: Fantastic creatures with centaur and men fighting. **South Milton**: Thick rope ornament and crude figures. **Alphington**: Intersecting round arches and roundels with St Michael and other figures. **Hartland**: Highly decorated. Also with intersecting round arches.
Dorset	**Toller Fratrum**: A medley of heads.
Gloucestershire	**Southrop** (Plate 96): Figures of virtues trample on vices, the names of the vices being inscribed backwards. **Bisley**: Leaves and rosettes and fish.

95   *Norman font, Bridekirk, Cumberland. Baptism of Christ*

96 *Norman font of virtues and vices, Southrop, Gloucestershire*

Herefordshire	**Castle Frome** (Plate 97): Perhaps the most remarkable font anywhere. It squashes evil monsters. The Baptism of Christ is most realistic (note fish in the water); also the symbols of the Four Evangelists. **Eardisley**: Similar carving. The Harrowing of Hell by Christ, two men fighting, and a large lion. **Orleton**: Nine apostles in arcading.
Kent	**Darenth**: Eight figures under arcading, including Sagittarius and King David.
Northampton-shire	**Harpole**: A remarkable tangle of leaf trails and dragons. **Wansford**: Figures under an arcade. **West Haddon**: Remarkable scenes of the Nativity, Baptism of Christ, Entry into Jerusalem and Christ in Glory.
Nottinghamshire	**Lenton**: Angels, Baptism of Christ, Crucifixion and possibly the Raising of Lazarus.
Oxfordshire	**Hook Norton** (Plate 98): Adam and Eve, Sagittarius and Aquarius.
Shropshire	**Holdgate**: Serpents and a medley of carving. **Stottesdon**: Animals, birds and faces.
Somerset	**Locking**: Four figures stretch out their long arms to join hands. Beaded plaits turn out to be snakes. **Lullington**: Human faces, animal heads, rosettes and arcading.
Staffordshire	**Ilam**: Barbaric figures and beasts. **Stafford**, St Mary. Figures on the bowl, and below are four massive lions and other animals. Inscription.
Sussex	**Brighton**: Last Supper, Baptism of Christ, and life of St Nicholas.
Warwickshire	**Coleshill**: Crucifixion and figures of saints under arcading. **Stoneleigh**: The Twelve Apostles under arcading, and rows of faces.

97   Baptism of Christ on Norman font, Castle Frome, Herefordshire

Wiltshire	**Avebury**: Intersecting round arches and a bishop with two serpents. **Stanton Fitzwarren**: Similar to Southrop.
Worcestershire	**Chaddesley Corbett**: Dragons biting one another's tails.
Yorkshire	**Bessingby**: Zig-zag carving, very rare on fonts, and two animals. **Thorpe Salvin**: Two scenes show a baptism, and four scenes show Spring, Summer, Autumn and Winter.

Lead Fonts

There are about 40 fonts made completely of lead, the majority being late Norman. Examples:

Derbyshire	**Ashover** (Plate 99): Twenty figures of men under arches
Gloucestershire	**Frampton-on-Severn**, **Sandhurst** and **Tidenham**: All with scroll-work alternating with figures under arches.
Kent	**Brookland** (Plate 100): A remarkable gallery of 40 scenes of the Signs of the Zodiac and the months of the year.
Lincolnshire	**Barnetby**: Scroll-work and leaf patterns.
Oxfordshire	**Dorchester** Abbey: Well-preserved. Apostles under arches

Tournai Marble Fonts

There are several richly ornamented Norman fonts of this material.

Hampshire	**Winchester** Cathedral: Two scenes from the life of St Nicholas, and birds. **East Meon**: Adam and Eve, and birds and foliage.

Early English

Bedfordshire	**Studham**: Dragons devour foliage. **Eaton Bray**: Stiff-leaf capitals
Northampton-shire	**East Haddon**: Foliage trails and a man holding two dragons

98   Norman font, Hook Norton, Oxfordshire. Sagittarius as an archer, and Aquarius as a water-bearer

Decorated

Cornwall	**Lostwithiel**: Interesting sculpture. A Rood group, huntsman, two snakes coiled over a grotesque head, a bishop with foliage from mouth and ears, a dog and wolf, and lions.
Hertfordshire	**Hitchin**: Figures of saints under ogee canopies. **Ware** (Plate 101): Annunciation, St Margaret, St Christopher, St George, St Catherine, St James, and St John the Baptist.
Oxfordshire	**Shilton**: Scenes from the Passion and figures of the Four Evangelists.
Warwickshire	**Brailes**: Eight tracery patterns and ball-flowers. **Tysoe**: St Mary, St Catherine, St Peter, St Paul, St Michael and St Mary Magdalene.
Yorkshire	**Fishlake**: Saints under ogee canopies.

99   *Norman lead font, Ashover, Derbyshire*

Perpendicular

It is in this century, and in East Anglia, that the font reaches
its highest development.

   It is frequently raised on steps to give it greater dignity.
There are two main types:

a) The stem is surrounded by lions and sometimes also by
wild, hairy men with big clubs. The panels of the bowl have
the symbols of the Four Evangelists alternating with angels
holding musical instruments or shields. Sometimes lions take
the place of the Evangelists. This type is very common in
Norfolk and Suffolk. Examples:

Norfolk	**Acle**, **Happisburgh** (Plate 102), **Surlingham** and **Upton**
Suffolk	**Chediston** and **Saxmundham**

100   *Norman lead font, Brookland, Kent. The months and the signs of the Zodiac*

101   Font showing St Christopher and St George, Ware, Hertfordshire

102 *Typical East Anglian font, Happisburgh, Norfolk*

b) Quite the most beautiful as well as the most interesting are those which show the Seven Sacraments of the Church on seven of the panels of the bowl (and usually the Baptism of Our Lord or the Crucifixion on the remaining panel). The Sacraments are Baptism, Confirmation, Mass, Eucharist or Communion, Penance or Confession, Holy Orders, Holy Matrimony and Unction or anointing of the body. There are 22 such fonts in Norfolk and 11 in Suffolk (and only two elsewhere at **Farningham**, Kent and **Nettlecombe**, Somerset). At **Little Walsingham**, Norfolk, and **Laxfield**, Suffolk (Plate 103), the steps are works of art. Other fine ones are at **Walsoken**, Norfolk, and **Badingham**, **Cratfield** and **Weston**, Suffolk.

The best preserved panels (for studying costume and vestments) are at **Gresham**, and **Sloley** (Plate 104), Norfolk, and **Badingham**, Suffolk.

Colour remains at **Great Witchingham**, Norfolk, and **Westhall**, Suffolk.

Other notable Perpendicular fonts exist at:

Norfolk	**Hemblington**: Saints on the stem and bowl, with the Trinity and Crucifixion. **Stalham**: Saints on the stem, and on the bowl the Trinity, Baptism of Christ, and the Twelve Apostles.
Suffolk	**Snape**: Symbols of the Evangelists and saints on the stem, and the Trinity and figures with scrolls on the bowl.
Kent	**Shorne**: Chalice with a rayed Host, Baptism of Christ, St Michael, Lamb with banner, St Peter, and the Resurrection. **Southfleet**: Similar to Shorne.
Lincolnshire	**Huttoft**: The Virgin and Child and the Trinity with the Twelve Apostles in pairs on the bowl, saints on the stem, and symbols of the Evangelists at the base. **South Ormsby**: Angels with shields on the bowl

Middlesex	**West Drayton**: Angels, a pièta, and Crucifixion on the bowl, hooded men below, and four monsters at the base.
Somerset	**Taunton** St James: A Rood group and 21 figures in groups of three.

Old light red brick is always a pleasing colour. It is very rare for fonts, but there are examples at **Potter Heigham**, Norfolk, and **Chignal Smealy**, Essex.

103   Seven Sacrament font, Laxfield, Suffolk

104 *Holy Matrimony on Seven Sacrament Font, Sloley, Norfolk*

Font Covers

The holy water was only blessed at certain seasons (Holy Saturday being the chief one) and it therefore had to remain in the font and a wooden cover was necessary to keep it clean.

An eight-sided cone is very common, and the boarding may be straight, as at **Monksilver**, Somerset, or of ogee form, as at **Colebrooke**, Devon, which has two angels as a finial. Both these covers are medieval.

Jacobean examples of the former type will be found at **Lanreath**, Cornwall, and **Banwell**, **Congresbury** and **Rodney Stoke**, Somerset. **Mendlesham**, Suffolk, also has a splendid Jacobean cover.

In the medieval period in East Anglia the cover became the most splendid soaring mass of wonderful tabernacle work and it usually reached almost to the roof. The finest example is at **Ufford**, Suffolk (Plate 105), and it is indeed the finest font cover in the world. It is crowned by a pelican. Amazing as it is, it would have been even more gorgeous with all its colour and gilt and figures.

Other similar marvellous medieval covers can be seen at **Castle Acre** (colour), **Elsing** (some colour renewed), **Sall**, and **Worstead**, Norfolk, and **Hepworth** (turrets with tiny men), St Gregory's, **Sudbury** (colour), and **Worlingworth** (closed type), Suffolk.

There are also some examples in the north-east of England, as at **Thirsk** and **Well**, Yorkshire.

The cover would be raised by means of a counterpoise. The tallest covers were telescopic with the counterpoise inside the upper part of the cover, so that the lower portion of the cover telescopes over the upper portion (and all made in the fifteenth century).

In other cases the counterpoise is outside the cover, as with the lovely fifteenth-century cover at **Ewelme**, Oxfordshire (St Michael being the finial). The whole cover then, of course, moves.

Yet again, but only very occasionally, the counterpoise is

105   Font cover, Ufford, Suffolk

hidden by canopied panelling, as in two very fine examples of the sixteenth century, at **Pilton**, Devon (the cover being yet of another shape – concave), and of the seventeenth century at **Astbury**, Cheshire.

Occasionally the whole font was completely encased within its cover with doors giving access. The best example is at **Swimbridge**, Devon (Plate 106), which has canopied panelling as well, all showing the early Renaissance carving typical of the West Country.

An amazing piece of medieval woodwork is the independent canopy standing on six posts elaborately decorated and vaulted at **Trunch**, Norfolk, and an excellent one of 1663 is in **Durham** Cathedral. There is also one of stone at **Luton**, Bedfordshire, of the fourteenth century with eight crocketed gables and vaulted.

There is a remarkable coloured animal's head at **Whaddon**, Buckinghamshire. It is the bracket for the suspension of the font cover (which was more usually suspended from a beam in the roof).

106   Jacobean font cover, Swimbridge, Devon

Chests

The valuables of the church were kept in the chest and they must have been quite safe considering the number of locks and bolts.

The earliest chests, twelfth-century, were 'dug-outs': a great log was roughly squared, a slice sawn off the top to act as a lid, whilst the lower portion was hollowed out. There are many in Warwickshire, as at **Curdworth**.

Thirteenth-century chests often consisted of a great slab of wood flanked by two front uprights or stiles prolonged below the chest itself to raise it from the damp; roundels of geometrical designs occur in the central portion and stiles, as at **Earl Stonham**, Suffolk and **Stoke D'Abernon**, Surrey.

In the fourteenth century, heavy slabs of oak were clamped and bound with ironwork, either for strength in a number of bands (as at **Selworthy**, Somerset, and **Warbleton**, Sussex), or for ornament in elaborate scrollwork, as at **Church Brampton**, Northamptonshire, and **Icklingham** All Saints, Suffolk.

The most elaborate carving, however, is on those fourteenth-century chests where the central portion and the stiles are treated differently; the stiles are divided into horizontal panels filled with carvings, dragons and grotesque figures, and the central portion has tracery (as at **Saltwood**, Kent, **Fillingham**, and **Glentham**, Lincolnshire, and **Wath**, Yorkshire), or even a tilting scene at **Harty**, Kent. The chest at **Dersingham**, Norfolk, is carved with the symbols of the Four Evangelists, with their names on labels. Splendid chests panelled throughout with tracery may be seen at **Crediton**, Devon, **Faversham** and **Rainham**, Kent, and **Huttoft**, Lincolnshire. The one in Magdalen College Chapel, **Oxford**, is beautifully coloured.

The thirteenth-century chest at **Newport**, Essex, is remarkable. The inside of the cover has paintings of the Crucifixion and saints which are the earliest English oil paintings on wood. These formed a reredos and the chest is therefore a portable altar. There are five locks and a false bottom with a secret sliding panel for the altar stone.

Wall-paintings

The walls of old churches were Bible picture books and glowed with gorgeous colour, which is difficult to realize today. The great truths of the Gospel blazed forth in bright colours so that one must have felt in the midst of the saints.

Many incidents in Christ's life were shown, but the emphasis was on the nativity and the events of the Passion, thereby rightly stressing Our Lord's redemptive work (and the same applies to old glass).

Doom or Last Judgment. This subject is usually over the chancel arch or on a wooden board filling up the arch. Such a scene usually formed a background to the great rood and attendant figures. The usual arrangement was the figure of Christ Triumphant, showing His wounds, seated on a rainbow in judgment, with heaven on one side and hell on the other, and sometimes St Michael with scales. The dead rise from their graves. The heavenly mansions look uncomfortable, but the artist really enjoyed himself much more on the other side – hell. Here are usually the jaws of a large dragon with huge teeth and all enveloped in bright red flames. Horrible-looking demons with red-hot chains and pitchforks secure as many customers as possible. Three splendid examples on boards, now moved down for inspection, can be seen at **Wenhaston**, Suffolk (Plate 107), **Dauntsey**, Wiltshire, and **Penn**, Buckinghamshire. Above the chancel arch, there are fine examples at St Thomas, **Salisbury** (restored), the Guild Chapel, **Stratford-on-Avon**, **Combe**, **North Leigh** and **South Leigh**, Oxfordshire, **Great Shelford**, Cambridgeshire, and **Patcham**, Sussex.

St Michael usually appears weighing souls in scales, which demons try to pull down, but are never successful. The Virgin sometimes intercedes. He can be seen at **Swalcliffe** and **South Leigh**, Oxfordshire, and, **Bartlow**, Cambridgeshire.

St Christopher. Easily the most popular single subject on walls. He is almost invariably opposite the principal entrance

107   *The Jaws of Hell, part of the Doom Painting, Wenhaston, Suffolk*

108 St Christopher Wall-painting, Baunton, Gloucestershire

as it was thought that whoever looked upon such a figure would be free from sudden death (and would thus have the opportunity to repent). The huge saint has a long flowering staff and carries the infant Christ on his shoulder across the river, in which may be fish, ships, and even mermaids. The Child holds an orb (representing the world) surmounted by a cross. A hermit with a lantern and his chapel are often included. The subject was popular throughout the medieval period, but more particularly in the fifteenth century and in East Anglia.

This list is fairly complete of the best remaining examples:

Buckinghamshire	**Little Missenden**
Cambridgeshire	**Bartlow** and **Impington**
Cornwall	**Breage**, **Poughill** (two, brightly restored)
Derbyshire	**Haddon Hall** Chapel
Essex	**Lambourne**, **Layer Marney**, and **Little Baddow**
Gloucestershire	**Baunton** (Plate 108) (bright colouring: the boy fishing has a very long line)
Hampshire, Isle of Wight	**Shorwell** (also scenes from the life of St Christopher)
Hertfordshire	**Ridge**
Huntingdonshire	**Molesworth**
Kent	**Brook**
Middlesex	**Hayes**
Norfolk	**Edingthorpe**, **Hardley**, **Paston**, and **Hemblington** (also scenes from the life of St Christopher)
Northampton-shire	**Slapton**
Oxfordshire	**Horley** and **Wood Eaton**
Somerset	**Ditcheat** and **Wedmore**
Suffolk	**Grundisburgh** and **Stowlangtoft**
Surrey	**Warlingham** and **West Horsley**
Wiltshire	**Oaksey** (a splendid mermaid, and a fish bites St Christopher's foot)
Yorkshire	**Pickering**

109   Wall-painting of St George, Pickering, Yorkshire

St George and the dragon is next in popularity. **Hardham**, Sussex, has the earliest (twelfth century). A notable painting is at **Dartford**, Kent, with the king and queen on top of their castle wondering what will happen to their daughter the princess below. Another large painting is at St Gregory, **Norwich**, and there are others at **Bradfield Combust**, Suffolk, **Pickering**, Yorkshire (Plate 109), and **Little Kimble** and **Broughton**, Buckinghamshire (the latter also having a most interesting Dismemberment of Christ by blasphemers).

The Three Living and the Three Dead is a morality picture on the vanity of life – three kings in rich robes hunting and three skeleton kings reminding them of their end. **Raunds**, Northamptonshire, has an excellent example, as also of *The Seven Deadly Sins*, which have always been popular! Pride is the root of all the other sins. (**Little Horwood**, Buckinghamshire, has another example). By contrast, the *Seven Works of Mercy* can be seen at **Trotton**, Sussex (where the sins have nearly disappeared), and **Linkinhorne**, Cornwall.

Christ blessing Trades, shown by various implements, agricultural and mining, is particularly popular in Cornwall, as at **Breage**, and also at **Oaksey**, Wiltshire.

   The following churches (some already referred to above) have notable wall-paintings still remaining:

Cambridgeshire	**Hauxton**: 1250. St Thomas of Canterbury
Dorset	**Tarrant Crawford**: Fourteenth century. Annunciation. Life of St Margaret.
Essex	**Copford**: Twelfth century (but much restored). Christ in Majesty and Apostles. Signs of the Zodiac. **Fairstead**: Thirteenth century. On chancel arch – Passion. **Great Canfield**: Thirteenth century. Very lovely. In east window – the Virgin and Child.
Gloucestershire	**Kempley**: Twelfth century. Extensive. Christ in Majesty and Apostles. **Stowell**: Twelfth century. Last Judgment.

Hampshire	**Idsworth**: Fourteenth century. Lives of St John the Baptist and St Hubert (hunting scenes).
Hertfordshire	**St Albans** Cathedral: Thirteenth-century Crucifixion groups on Norman piers forming reredoses. Decorative motifs.
Kent	**Brook**: Thirteenth century. Extensive. Life of Christ. St Christopher. **Capel**: Thirteenth century. Passion.
Northampton-shire	**Croughton**: Fourteenth and fifteenth centuries. Extensive. Life of Christ and Life of the Virgin. **Peakirk**: Fourteenth century. Passion. **Slapton**: Fourteenth and fifteenth centuries. Some unusual paintings – stigmata of St Francis, Mass of St Gregory and Martyrdom of St Edmund. Also St Christopher.
Oxfordshire	**Black Bourton**: Late thirteenth century. Coronation of the Virgin. Wise Men. Jesse Tree. **Chalgrove**: Fourteenth century. Extensive. Life of Christ. Life of the Virgin. Last Judgment. **South Newington**: Fourteenth and fifteenth centuries. Very beautiful and extensive. Virgin and Child. Passion. St Margaret. Martyrdom of St Thomas of Canterbury.
Shropshire	**Claverley**: Thirteenth century. Knights on horseback in battle between virtues and vices.
Somerset	**Sutton Bingham**: Fourteenth century. Death and Coronation of the Virgin.
Suffolk	**Wissington**: Thirteenth century. Extensive. Early Life of Christ. St Francis and birds.
Surrey	**Chaldon** (Plate 110): A remarkable painting of the Ladder of Salvation of about 1200 covering the whole of the west wall of this small church. The painting is divided horizontally by a band of cloud which is the dividing line between the

salvation of souls and the torments of hell. A ladder forming a cross with the clouds ascends to Christ in the clouds. Souls are struggling or falling on the lower part of the ladder, but above, their ascent is certain.

In the top compartment St Michael is weighing souls in scales which a demon is trying to pull down, Christ tramples on Satan and releases souls, and angels are assisting souls up the ladder. In the lower compartment is the Tree of Knowledge with the serpent hiding amongst the branches. Two large demons hold a beam studded with spikes over which dishonest persons have to walk, and underneath the beam two demons pitchfork a soul into the flames.

Above leaping flames is a large cauldron into which souls are being thrown and stirred up by two great devils. Another huge demon pitchforks a soul over his shoulder.

Underneath the painting is a Consecration cross.

Sussex **Chichester**: Chapel of Bishop's Palace. Thirteenth century. Virgin and Child. Beautiful. **Clayton**: Twelfth century. Extensive. Christ in Majesty and angels. Last Judgment. **Hardham**: Twelfth century. Extensive. Life of Christ. Adam and Eve. St George. **West Chiltington**: Twelfth century – Christ in Majesty and angels. Thirteenth century – Nativity and Passion.

Yorkshire **Easby**: Thirteenth century. Life of Christ. Adam and Eve. **Pickering** (Plate 109): The most complete series in England, but restored. Fifteenth century. Passion.

110 The Ladder of Salvation wall-painting, about 1200, at Chaldon, Surrey

Harrowing of Hell. Seven Acts of Mercy.
Life of St Catherine and Martyrdoms of St
Edmund and St Thomas of Canterbury. St
Christopher and St George.

Benches

Dunsfold, Surrey, has thirteenth-century wooden benches, but most medieval benches are fifteenth century or early sixteenth century and are in East Anglia and the West Country.

East Anglia

The tops of the ends of the benches nearly always take the most fascinating form known as a poppy-head. Below the poppy-head may be delightful carvings of human figures, beasts or birds which sometimes surmount small buttresses at the sides of the standards or ends, which themselves may be panelled or have figures. The backs are often pierced with delicate tracery.

Norfolk

Feltwell St Mary: Charming backs and figures. **Great Walsingham**: A complete set of poppy-head benches with traceried backs, and therefore a wonderful sight. **Harpley**: Open backs and quaint figures on the top of foliage poppy-heads. **Sheringham** (Plate 111): Carvings include a baby in swaddling clothes, a mermaid with a comb, a cat with a kitten in its mouth, and other animals. **Wiggenhall St Mary the Virgin**: These benches are the finest in England. Beneath each poppy-head are two seated figures, and there is a large figure on a pedestal under a canopy on each face. The backs are elaborately pierced. **Wiggenhall St Germans**: Only a mile away from the last, and very similar, but perhaps more interesting as they show the Deadly Sins! The saints are Apostles. **Wilton**: A fine array with carved groups, including a

111   Cat and kitten on a poppy-head bench-end, Sheringham, Norfolk

shepherd with his sheep. **Wimbotsham**: A figure with a rosary, and quite a zoo of animals.

Suffolk

Athelington: A beautiful set with interesting figures, including some Apostles with emblems. **Barningham**: A complete set, with birds, animals and monsters. **Blythburgh**: Figures instead of poppy-heads depicting the Seasons and the Seven Deadly Sins – no difficulty in making out Sloth in bed! **Dennington**: A large number with intricate tracery. An angel, mermaid and sciapus should be noted. The last has huge feet acting as a sunshade over him. **Denston**: Very charming with animals and grotesques. **Fressingfield**: A marvellous sight as this can be said to be the best filled church in the country. The variety of carving includes a number of saints, and a back is carved with the Instruments of the Passion. **Ixworth Thorpe**: Quite a zoo of animals, a mermaid, a harvester with a rake, and a lady with her dog. **Lakenheath**: An interesting set with acrobats and the legend of the tiger and looking-glass. The backs have lace-work patterns. **Stowlangtoft** (Plate 112): Among the finest anywhere. Numerous fine animals and a mermaid. **Tannington**: Some figures of the Sacraments and Deady Sins. **Ufford** (Plate 105): Richly carved. **Wilby**: Carvings of the Sacraments and Works of Mercy. **Withersfield**: Unusual but spirited treatment of the poppy-heads with St George and the dragon, St Michael weighing souls, an angel, and two puppies and two birds. **Woolpit**: Numbers remain, with animals. **Wordwell**: A fine set. The

112   Squirrel on a bench-end at Stowlangtoft, Suffolk

backs are not pierced, but are carved with
quaint animals, grotesques, and a jester.

Huntingdonshire   **Eynesbury**: A large collection with a
wonderful array of animals forming the
tops of the poppy-heads.

Lincolnshire   **Osbournby**: A varied collection with figure
subjects of St George and the dragon,
Adam and Eve, and a fox preaching to
geese.

The West Country

The West of England is also profusely supplied with old
benches, but here the ends are nearly always square-headed;
figure carving (often secular and of an early Renaissance type)
and foliage are common. The fronts and backs of blocks of
benches often have the same rich carving.

    In Devon (old benches are more profuse in the north of the
county than in the south – unlike screens) and Cornwall the
old bench-ends often have heraldic devices. The edges of the
ends have huge scrolls of foliage, usually long pointed leaves
with indented edges.

Cornwall   There is a wealth of old seating in this
county. Carved Instruments of the Passion
are particularly popular. **Altarnun**: A large
and interesting collection, including
sheep, piper, sword-dancer, jester and
a fiddler. **Cardinham**: Another large
collection with tracery, faces and
grotesques. **Kilkhampton**: A great number
of bench-ends and panels, particularly
heraldic and Passion emblems. **Lansallos**:
Heads in profile. **Lanteglos-by-Fowey**:
Quaint heads and birds. **Launcells**:
Unusual representations of the Passion,
Resurrection and Ascension. **Mullion**: The
benches help to make this delightful

church. Instruments of the Passion and profiles. **Poughill**: A wealth of benches similar to Launcells. **St Winnow**: A ship in a storm will be noted. **Talland**: Angels, coats-of-arms, and grotesques.

Devon **Abbotsham**: The Crucifixion and Christ carrying the Cross are unusual on benches. Also a juggler and Renaissance medallions. **Braunton** (Plate 113): A large number. Instruments of the Passion predominate. Fronts and backs also carved. **Combe-in-Teignhead**: Very fascinating with animals, and St Catherine, St Mary Magdalene, Sts Peter and Paul, two wild men, St George, St Agnes, St Genest (as jester), and St Hubert. **Down St Mary**: Profiles, a figure waving a scourge, and a mermaid with a comb and looking-glass. **East Budleigh**: Numerous and varied. Heraldic designs, a ship, shears, and profiles. **High Bickington**: A large collection. Instruments of the Passion, saints, and Renaissance profiles. **Lapford**: Renaissance ornament, profiles, and a figure waving a scourge.

Somerset Many churches around the Quantock Hills have splendid bench-ends with much foliage and traceried panelling. **Barwick**: A man holds up the date 1533, another man shoots a bird, a fox trots off with a goose, and dogs hunt a rabbit. **Bishop's Hull**. Christ rises from the tomb whilst three soldiers are asleep; below is a pelican. Another bench-end shows a night-watchman with his lantern. **Bishop's Lydeard**: A complete set of backs, fronts, and ends of great variety, including a three-masted ship and a windmill with the miller and birds. **Brent Knoll** (Plate 114): Three celebrated ends show the legend of

Reynard the Fox.

a) The fox is disguised as a mitred abbot. Looking up to him are three pigs in cowls, geese and birds. At the foot two monkeys roast a pig on a spit, and above is a chained ape with a money-bag.

b) The fox is stripped and put into stocks, his mitre hanging before him.

c) The fox is hung by triumphant geese all pulling the rope, and two watch-dogs are barking with joy (Plate 114).

Broomfield: A number with tracery, foliage and plants. **Crowcombe**. A wonderful collection, including two men attacking a double-headed dragon, and a man with foliage coming out of his mouth and a merman with a big club and flowers coming out of each ear. **Hatch Beauchamp**: Resurrection with a pelican below, St George and the dragon, and a cock-fight. **Milverton**: A large number of *c.* 1540 with portrait busts, foliage, and two spies with a huge bunch of grapes. **Monksilver**: Some charming foliage and panelling. **North Cadbury**: Dated 1538. Profiles, windmill, two dragons hatching from eggs, and a cat and mouse. **Spaxton**: Plants, Renaissance heads in medallions, and a fuller at work on a piece of cloth with his tools around him. **Stogumber**: Many, with tracery. **Stogursey**: Large plants with many birds, fish and a pelican. **Trull**: Five ends show figures in a religious procession – a crucifer, a candle-bearer, a man with a reliquary, and two choristers with books.

113   Instruments of the Passion (pincers and nails) on a bench-end at Braunton, Devon

In the Midlands medieval bench-ends were normally square-headed and quite plain, but sometimes with small buttresses (**Minster Lovel**, Oxfordshire).

Linen-fold panelling was often used in Tudor times, and bench-ends of that date sometimes have it; it is as if a piece of linen is laid in vertical folds.

114   The fox being hung by birds, bench-end, Brent Knoll, Somerset

Lecterns

Medieval wooden lecterns of desk form:

Huntingdonshire **Bury**: A single desk with exquisite leaves and scrolls of early fourteenth century date.
Kent **Detling**: Four-sided of about 1320 with different geometrical designs on each desk.
Norfolk **Shipdham**: A fifteenth-century double desk carved with circular designs supported on an ornamented shaft resting on three lions.

Beautiful medieval brass lecterns of desk form can be seen at **Yeovil**, Somerset, and in the Chapels of **Eton** College, Merton College, **Oxford**, and King's College, **Cambridge**.

Old brass eagle lecterns are lovely works of art. Three animals at the base are usual. Just over forty remain. Splendid and typical examples will be found at:

Cambridgeshire **Isleham**
Devon **Bovey Tracey** (Plate 115) and **Wolborough**
Northampton- **Oundle**
shire
Nottinghamshire **Southwell Minster**
Suffolk **Clare**

Of old wooden eagles, about twenty still exist. Excellent and characteristic examples are at:

Cheshire **Astbury**
Devon **Ottery St Mary** (with colour)

115 Fifteenth-century brass eagle lectern, Bovey Tracey, Devon

Pulpits

One can nearly always recognize pre-Reformation work by its perfect proportions. This certainly applies to pulpits. At that time they were tall and narrow, and were usually supported on a long slender stem. Many of the Victorian period were quite the reverse.

Pre-Reformation Wooden Pulpits

About 100 remain and they are most numerous in Devon and Norfolk. The oldest is at **Mellor**, Derbyshire, of the fourteenth century, and hewn out of a solid block of oak. The following are of fifteenth or early sixteenth century date:

Devon	Rich and massive foliage and niches are common and when colouring remains the sight is gorgeous. All are in the southern half of the county. **Bigbury**: Shields under arches. **Chivelstone**: Hollowed out of a single block of oak. Shields and much original colour. **Coldridge**: Most intricate canopy-work. **Dartington**: Rich carving **East Allington**: Rich work with badges. **Halberton**: Two tiers of ornament, the upper with nodding canopies. **Holne**: Shields under canopies. **Ipplepen**: Canopied niches, foliage, and colour. **Kenton**: Very rich carving with modern paintings of West Country saints. **North Molton** (North Devon): Canopied niches.
Norfolk	**Burnham Norton** (Plate 116): On the unspoilt Norfolk coast. Painted red and green panels of the Four Latin Doctors (like screen panels). John Goldale and his wife gave the pulpit in about 1475 and they

appear as kneeling figures. **Castle Acre**: Paintings of the Four Latin Doctors. **Horsham St Faith**: Painted panels – Our Lady and Child. St Faith, St Thomas of Canterbury, St Christopher, St Andrew, St John the Evangelist and the Baptist, and St Stephen. On the doors are two abbots, St Benedict and probably St Wandregesilus. **South Burlingham**: Red and green backgrounds powdered with gold flowers and stars. A small church, but full of interest.

Somerset   **Long Sutton**: A beautifully coloured pulpit of 16 sides. The figures of the Twelve Apostles are modern. The stem is of stone. **Monksilver**: Panels are filled with exceptional tracery. **Trull** (Plate 117): Most remarkable. Original figures of the Four Latin Doctors and St John the Evangelist. Angels hold the canopies above. There are also two small saints between each of the larger figures.

Post-Reformation Wooden Pulpits

A large number of wooden pulpits were made just after the Reformation. They are exceedingly pleasing in design. Round-arched arcading is prominent on all the woodwork of the period. Very often above the pulpit is a large sounding-board or tester supported on a standard or back-piece. They are usually termed Jacobean, but might be Elizabethan or Carolean. Here are some examples, all very lovely.

Buckinghamshire   **Cheddington, Ivinghoe**

Cambridgeshire   **Over**: The pulpit has an ogee canopy. This is a beautiful fourteenth and fifteenth-century church, showing what a difference a handsome chancel makes to a church.

117   Medieval wooden pulpit with the Four Latin Doctors, Trull, Somerset

Dorset	**Abbotsbury, Cerne Abbas**
Durham	**Brancepeth**
Hampshire, Isle of Wight	**Newport** (the most elaborate)
Hertfordshire	St Michael's, **St Albans**
Kent	**Lenham**
Lincolnshire	**Alford, Burgh-le-Marsh, Croft**
Oxfordshire	**Merton**
Somerset	**Bishop's Lydeard, Croscombe, Rodney Stoke, Stoke St Gregory** (Plate 118): (with figures of the Virgin and Child, Faith-spear, Hope-anchor, Charity-dove, and Old Father Time – scythe, skull and hour-glass).
Surrey	**Stoke D'Abernon** (elaborate: tester upheld by Sussex iron-work: inscription 'Fides ex auditu' – faith comes from hearing).
Wiltshire	**Brinkworth, Stratford-sub-Castle**

In the late seventeenth and early eighteenth centuries wooden 'three-decker' pulpits became the fashion (see section on eighteenth-century fittings, page 181).

Pre-Reformation Stone Pulpits

About 60 remain and they are most numerous in Devon, Somerset and Gloucestershire.

Devon	**Bovey Tracey**: One of the most beautiful anywhere. Richly coloured and gilt, with original figures of the Four Evangelists, St Peter, St Edward the Confessor, St George, St Margaret, St Andrew and St James the Great. **Chittlehampton**: Little figures under nodding canopies. **Dartmouth**, St Saviour. Very lavish with enormous leaves and colour. Seventeenth-century wooden devices under the canopies – royal lion, portcullis, rose, thistle, harp and fleur-de-

lys. **Dittisham** (Plate 119): On the River
Dart. Very charming and graceful with its
colour and original figures. **Harberton** (Plate
120): Very fine with beautiful colouring.
Seventeenth-century figures. **Pilton**:
Ornamented with canopied niches and
quatrefoils (see section on hour-glasses,
page 240). **South Molton**: Beautifully carved
with Apostles. **Swimbridge**: Rich carving
with figures. **Witheridge**: Richly crocketed
canopies over Rood group and saints.

Gloucestershire   Four similar pulpits with graceful canopied
niches exist at **Cirencester** (coloured and
with perforated panels), **Chedworth**, **North
Cerncy**, and **Northleach**.

Somerset   Around Weston-super-Mare are some 15
medieval stone pulpits, most of similar
design, namely double-light fifteenth-
century tracery and bands of foliage. Very
good examples are at **Banwell** (Plate 121),
Bleadon, **Hutton**, and **Wick St Lawrence**.

Staffordshire   **Wolverhampton** has the most notable stone
pulpit with its original staircase guarded by
a large lion.

118   Figure of Father Time on seventeenth-century pulpit, Stoke St Gregory, Somerset

119 Medieval stone pulpit at Dittisham, Devon

120   *Medieval stone pulpit, Harberton, Devon*

121 Fifteenth-century stone pulpit, Banwell, Somerset

Hour-glasses

These were introduced in the later sixteenth century for regulating the length of the sermon. About 120 stands and some glasses remain.

The usual method was to attach an iron bracket to the pulpit or to the adjacent wall. Most brackets were simple, but sometimes there was considerable skill in ironwork. There are two outstanding examples:

Berkshire	**Binfield** (Plate 122): Painted and enriched with numerous small branches of oak leaves and acorns supporting shields and animals. **Hurst**: This is somewhat similar, but has the date 1636 and a lion and unicorn.
Wiltshire	**Compton Bassett**: A typical example. A fleur-de-lys forms a handle at each end.
Devon	In two neighbouring churches, **Pilton** and **Tawstock**, the bracket is of sheet-iron in the form of an arm holding the glass in the hand.

Rood-screens

So called because above them was the great rood or crucifix.

Devon is noted for its magnificent fifteenth-century wooden screens and most are coloured and gilt. Many fortunately remain as indicated by the following list, and all are lovely.

The panels at the base usually have numerous painted figures (as mentioned later), the tracery at the head is bold and follows the local Perpendicular window tracery, the vaulting is a massive fan-vault, and the cornice on top has several bands of wonderful carving. These screens usually stretch from one side of the church to the other in one unbroken line.

Here are some of the finest:

Berry Pomeroy, **Bovey Tracey**, **Bradninch**, **Burrington** (bright with colour), **Chawleigh**, **Chulmleigh**, **Coldridge**, **Colebrooke** (flamboyant panels), **Cullompton**, **Dartmouth**, St Saviour (notable), **Dunchideock** (note pier-casing), **Harberton**, **Hartland** (massive), **Kentisbeare** (of singular beauty), **Kenton**, **King's Nympton**, **Lapford** (Plate 124 – fine with Renaissance detail), **Payhembury**, **Pinhoe**, **Plymtree** (Plate 123 – very typical), **Swimbridge**, **Talaton**, **Uffculme** (longest in the county), and **Wolborough** (with parclose screens to side chapels and all in lovely red, green and gold).

For a square-headed screen (not vaulted), visit **Willand**. The screens of Somerset are mostly in the west of the county and follow the Devon vaulted type.

Banwell (Plate 125), **Bishop's Lydeard**, **Carhampton** (with colour), **Dunster** (noteworthy), **Halse**, **High Ham**, **Minehead**, **Queen Camel** and **Timberscombe**. All these screens are up to Devon standard, which is, indeed, high praise.

The fifteenth-century wooden screens of East Anglia are quite different, being higher and lighter than the Devon screens. The distinguishing feature is a bold crocketed hood-mould, usually of ogee form, applied to delicate tracery. Many screens were square-headed without a vault, and if

123   A typical Devon interior, Plymtree

there is a vault it is not so massive as in Devon, but it may be
of a rich pendant type giving complete bays. The tracery also
is not so conspicuous, and sometimes, particularly if there is a
vault, there is no tracery at all, but merely plain openings
relieved by a few cusps. These screens, with the gorgeous
colours of medieval times, are priceless works of art of sheer
beauty unrivalled anywhere.

Norfolk   *Vaulted:* **Attleborough**, **Cawston**, **Ranworth**,
                 and **Worstead**. *Square-headed:* **Barnham
                 Broom**, **Bedingham**, **Happisburgh** and
                 Scarning (Plate 126 – with colour). Fine
                 fourteenth-century screens with fourteenth-
                 century tracery can be found at **Merton**
                 and **Thompson**.

Suffolk   *Vaulted:* **Bramfield** (Plate 127) and **Eye**.
                       Both very fine. *Square-headed:* **Barningham**
                       and **Somerleyton**.

The Midland screens are much plainer and are not of such a
distinctive type, but the following are very fine:

Cambridgeshire	**Balsham**
Cheshire	**Astbury** and **Mobberley**
Herefordshire	**Aymestrey**
Huntingdonshire	**Tilbrook**
Kent	**Shoreham** and **Lullingstone**
Lancashire	**Sefton**
Northampton-shire	**Ashby St Ledgers** and **Bugbrooke**
Oxfordshire	**Charlton-on-Otmoor** (linen-fold panels and Brittany influence in its shafts with honeycomb patterns), and **Church Handborough**.
Shropshire	**Hughley**
Warwickshire	**Knowle**

Jacobean screens as chancel screens are rare as every church
had its medieval screen, but excellent examples can be found
at **Croscombe** and **Rodney Stoke**, Somerset. **Carlisle** Cathedral
also has a beautiful early Renaissance screen.

Medieval screens of stone are rare. Devon has one of the
finest at **Totnes** and there is another at **Awliscombe**. Wiltshire
has several, the finest being at **Compton Bassett**, and others
are at **Hillmarton** and **Yatton Keynell**. There are two unique
fourteenth-century stone screens with rood combined in the
neighbouring Essex villages of **Stebbing** and **Great Bardfield**.

Painted Screen Panels

In East Anglia and Devon the panels at the base of the screen
are usually brightly coloured with figures of saints. In Devon
the figures are more stumpy than in East Anglia (but this of
124   Rood-screen, Lapford, Devon

course permits a greater number of them) and of less artistic merit, but nevertheless they are most fascinating and are of the greatest possible interest. The very pretty village of **Ashton** (Plate 131) has the best screen panels with remarkable paintings of prophets on the backs of the panels.

In East Anglia the panels often have a variety of designs in the spandrels – flowers, beasts, birds and grotesques (these are noted in the list, **Suffield**, Norfolk, being one of the best). The backgrounds are alternately red and green (costumes of figures also usually counter-changing). Nothing is more delightful than the figure paintings. The Twelve Apostles are the favourite subject in East Anglia, but angels and archangels, prophets, martyrs, kings, archbishops, bishops,

deacons and the Four Latin Doctors may be found in
different churches and their identification is a fascinating task
(St Catherine with her wheel, and St Lawrence with his
gridiron, for example). Truth and legend are equally well
represented. Many of the saints are obscure, but they
probably had a dramatic death or were useful patron saints,
such as St Apollonia, the patron saint of sufferers from
toothache and usually shown holding a huge tooth in pincers.

At **Southwold** and on some other Suffolk screens the
background is rich gesso work (gold).

The happiest hunting-ground for this subject is the Broads
district of Norfolk – **Barton Turf**, **Belaugh**, **Filby**, **Irstead**,
Ludham, **Potter Heigham**, **Ranworth** and **Upton**. **Ranworth** has
the unusual addition of little parclose screens (side screens) to
enclose the nave altars, the wooden reredoses to which are
also part of the screen, the whole being adorned with figures
considered to be the finest in the whole country.

The following lists of those two great areas of East Anglia
and Devon are fairly complete in respect of unrestored panels.

Norfolk	(Those marked with an asterisk have fine carved spandrels.) **Attleborough**: St John the Baptist, the Virgin and Child, and St John the Evangelist: St Thomas of Canterbury, the Holy Trinity, and St Bartholomew form reredoses to the two nave altars. ***Aylsham**: Fifteen figures, with some Apostles and prophets and St John the Baptist. **Barton Turf**: Superb paintings of the Nine Orders of Angels together with St Apollonia, St Sitha and St Barbara: also four kings – Henry VI, Edmund, Edward the Confessor, and Olaf or Holofius (therefore holding a whole loaf). ***Beeston Regis**: Twelve Apostles. In wonderful preservation. **Belaugh**: Twelve Apostles. **Carleton Rode** (Plate 129): Twelve Apostles. Almost perfect. ***Castle Acre**:

Twelve Apostles. **Cawston**: Thirteen Apostles (note St Matthew wearing spectacles), with St Agnes, St Helen, and Sir John Schorne (with devil in a boot), and the Four Latin Doctors on the doors. Almost perfect. **East Ruston**: The Four Evangelists and the Four Latin Doctors. **Edingthorpe**: Six Apostles. **Filby**: Saints Cecilia, George, Catherine, Peter, Paul, Margaret, Michael, and Barbara. ***Fritton**: The Donor and his family are shown together with the Four Latin Doctors and St Simon and St Jude. **Gateley**: An unusual series. St Etheldreda, St Elizabeth and St Mary (Visitation), Puella Redibowne, St Gregory, Henry VI, St Augustine and Sir John Schorne. **Gooderstone**: Twelve Apostles with Creed scrolls, and the Four Latin Doctors. Very well preserved. **Houghton St Giles**: The Four Latin Doctors, two Popes (St Clement and St Silvester), and four family groups with children – St Mary the Virgin, Mary Salome, Mary Cleophas and Elizabeth. **Hunstanton**: Twelve Apostles in rich robes and very well preserved. **Irstead**: Twelve Apostles. **Loddon**: Scenes of the Crucifixion of St William of Norwich, Annunciation, Nativity, Circumcision, the Wise Men, Presentation, figure with a dagger, and the Ascension. **Ludham**: Saints Mary Magdalene, Stephen, Edmund, King Henry VI, Four Latin Doctors, Edward the Confessor, Walstan, Lawrence, and Apollonia. Very well preserved. ***Mattishall**: Twelve Apostles with Creed Scrolls. ***Morston**: The Four Evangelists and the Four Latin Doctors. **North**

126   Typical East Anglian rood-screen, Scarning, Norfolk

Burlingham: Unusual figures – Saints
Withburga, Benedict, Edward the
Confessor, Thomas of Canterbury, John
the Baptist, Cecilia, Walstan, Catherine,
and Etheldreda. ***North Elmham**: Some
Apostles with Saints Benedict, Barbara,
Cecilia, Dorothy, Sitha, Juliana,
Petronella, Agnes, and Christina. **Potter
Heigham**: The Four Latin Doctors, three
Evangelists, and St Eloy. **Ranworth**: Saints
Etheldreda, Agnes, John the Baptist,
Barbara, Felix, George, Stephen, Twelve
Apostles, Thomas of Canterbury,
Lawrence, Michael, three family groups
with children – Mary Salome, Mary the
Virgin, and Mary Cleophas, and St

Margaret. These panels are renowned as the finest in the country; for delicacy and richness of detail the paintings are unsurpassed. The figures of St Michael and St George are specially notable. ***Suffield**: Four Latin Doctors, two Evangelists, Sir John Schorne, and St Jeron. **Swafield**: Eight Apostles. **Thornham**: Twelve prophets with scrolls, St Barbara, St Paul, Lazarus (most unusual), and St Mary Magdalene. ***Trimingham**: Saints Edmund, Clare, Clement, John the Baptist, Petronella, Dorothy, Cecilia and Jeron. **Trunch**: Twelve Apostles. **Tunstead**: Twelve Apostles and the Four Latin Doctors. **Upton**: Four Latin Doctors, St Helen, St Etheldreda, St Elizabeth of Hungary, and St Agatha. **Walpole St Peter**. St Catherine, The Virgin and Child, St Margaret, Six Apostles, St Mary Magdalene, St Dorothy, and St Barbara. **Wellingham**: St Sebastian, and St Oswald with King Penda, and then three most remarkable scenes wonderfully preserved – St George, St Michael, and the Resurrection. In the first the King and the Princess and others watch the fight with the dragon, in the second St Michael is weighing souls in scales which fascinating devils are trying to pull down, but fortunately St Mary and an angel are too much for them, and in the third all the Instruments of the Passion are most realistically shown. **Weston Longville**: Twelve Apostles with Creed scrolls. **Wigenhall St Mary the Virgin**. Saints Mary Magdalene, Dorothy, Margaret, Scholastica, Catherine, Barbara, the Virgin and Child, and John the Baptist.

127   Beautiful East Anglian vaulted screen. Panels of the Evangelists and St Mary Magdalene, Bramfield, Suffolk

Suffolk

Bramfield (Plate 128): Four superb paintings of the Four Evangelists and St Mary Magdalene. Rich gesso work. **Eye**: This lovely screen has equally lovely and interesting figure paintings – Saints Helen, Edmund, Ursula, King Henry VI, Dorothy, Barbara, Agnes, Edward the Confessor, John the Evangelist, Catherine, William of Norwich, Lucy, Blaise or Thomas of Canterbury and Cecilia. Very well preserved. **Somerleyton** (Plate 130): A most fascinating and very well preserved series of figures. The saints pair with one another from side to side. Saints Michael, Edmund, Apollonia, Lawrence, Faith, Thomas of Canterbury, Anne teaching the Virgin to read, Andrew, John the Evangelist, Mary Magdalene, a bishop, Petronella, Stephen, Dorothy, Edward the Confessor and George. **Southwold**: Twelve angels on the north aisle screen, Twelve Apostles with rich gesso work on the chancel screen, and Eleven prophets on the south aisle screen. **Westhall**: A remote, but very rewarding church. The screen panels show St James the Great, St Leonard, St George, St Clement, Moses, Our Lord, Elias (forming a Transfiguration group and a unique subject on a screen), and St Anthony with his pig, St Etheldreda, St Sitha, St Agnes, St Bridget, St Catherine, St Dorothy, St Margaret and St Apollonia holding a tooth. **Yaxley**: Amid rich gesso work are Saints Ursula, Catherine, Mary Magdalene, Barbara, Dorothy, and Cecilia.

South Devon

As mentioned, the figures on each screen are numerous, so that only a brief summary of the panels is usually given.

128   St Mark and St Matthew on the screen at Bramfield, Suffolk

Alphington: Sir John Schorne, St Helen, St
Christina, St Dunstan and the devil, St
Francis' stigmata, St Denis (with his head
in his hands), and some Apostles. **Ashton**
(Plate 131): As these are the finest in the
West Country, the following is a complete
list – Four Latin Doctors, Saints Sitha,
Michael, Dorothy, Clement, Four
Evangelists, Leonard, female with a
scimitar, Stephen, Sidwell, Blaise,
Catherine, Thomas of Canterbury,
Margaret, John the Baptist, Virgin and
Child, George, Mary Magdalene,
Anthony, Ursula, Leger, Apollonia, a
bishop, Lawrence, Sebastian and Winifred.
On the backs are remarkable paintings of
prophets with scrolls and the Annunciation
and Visitation. **Bradninch** (Plate 132): St
Christopher, St Adrian, St Giles, St
Francis' stigmata, St Michael, St George,
St Sebastian, the Annunciation and
Visitation, and scenes in the Garden of
Eden, as well as Apostles, prophets and
sibyls. **Buckland-in-the-Moor**: The Wise
Men, the Annunciation and some Apostles.
Also some figures on the backs of the
screen. **Chivelstone**: Some Apostles and
Evangelists. **Chudleigh**: Alternate Apostles
and prophets with scrolls. **East
Portlemouth**: The donor of the screen is
seen kneeling next to panels of the
Coronation of the Virgin. Some unusual
saints, including St Cornelius, St Peter
Martyr and St Lawrence. **Hennock**: The
Annunciation and various saints, including
St Erasmus, St Roch, St Sitha, St Peter
Martyr and St Margaret. **Holne**: Forty
painted panels of the Coronation of the

129   Rood-screen panels of Apostles, Carleton Rode, Norfolk

Virgin, Twelve Apostles, Four Evangelists,
Four Latin Doctors and some other saints.
Ipplepen: Alternate Apostles and prophets.
Kenn: Round a pier are the Holy Trinity
and the Annunciation. With Apostles,
Evangelists, and Latin Doctors are St
Sebastian, St Roch, St Francis' stigmata, St
Hubert, St Apollonia, St Anne and the
Virgin, St Mary of Egypt, St Bridget, St
Genevieve, St Juliana, St Catherine, and
other saints of interest, all well preserved.
Kenton: Forty panels of the Twelve
Apostles, alternating with prophets, St
Cecilia, St Lawrence, St Stephen, and other
saints. **Manaton**: Twelve Apostles, Four
Latin Doctors, and other saints. **Plymtree**

(Plate 123). One of the most complete series, with the Annunciation, Salutation, Wise Men, and some unusual saints, including St Anthony, St Sitha, St Sidwell, St Agnes, and St Edward the Confessor. **Torbryan**: Forty panels, including the Coronation of the Virgin, Twelve Apostles, Four Evangelists, and some unusual saints, including St Vincent, St Victor, St Alexis, St Apollonia, St Ursula, and St Armil. **Ugborough**: The Annunciation, Wise Men, Assumption, Martyrdom of St Sebastian, and a number of sibyls. **Widecombe**: The numerous visitors will be able to appreciate the panels of the Apostles, Latin Doctors, and a number of saints. **Wolborough**: No less than 66 painted panels. With the Annunciation and the Apostles are many unusual saints such as St William of York, St Ursula, St Victor, Saints Cosmas and Damian, and Sir John Schorne (noted in East Anglia). **Bridford** is exceptional in having small carved figures of Apostles and prophets.

Buckinghamshire **North Crawley**: Painted figure panels are rare in the Midlands, but this screen has four saints (including St Blaise), and twelve prophets with scrolls.

Worcestershire **Strensham**: Twenty-three figures of Our Lord, the Twelve Apostles and saints, including St Blaise. These panels were the rood-loft parapet and then became the West Gallery front after the Reformation.

130 Saints Michael, Edmund, and Apollonia on the rood-screen at Somerleyton, Suffolk

131   Screen panels at Ashton, Devon. St John the Baptist, the Virgin and Child,
St George, and St Mary Magdalene

132   A female figure, St Christopher, and St Adrian on the rood-screen at
Bradninch, Devon

Rood-lofts

On the tops of the rood-screens were the rood-lofts. These were used by the choir, instrumentalists and organ (if any). They were protected front and back by panelling. Only about a dozen remain in England, but many remain in Wales, often with delicate filigree patterns. The following are the finest in that country – **Bettws Newydd**, **Derwen**, **Llananno**, **Llanegryn**, **Llaneilian**, **Llanengan**, **Llanfilo**, **Llangwm**, **Llangwm Uchaf**, **Llanrwst**, **Llanwnog**, **Montgomery** and **Patricio**.

In England the finest are at **Flamborough** (Plate 133) and **Attleborough**, but all are fine and are of great interest.

Bedfordshire	**Oakley**: Open double-light traceried panels
Berkshire	**Warfield**: Panelled with traceried heads
Devon	**Atherington**: Gorgeous nichework of canopies
Herefordshire	**St Margarets**: Panelled with continuous cornice
Lincolnshire	**Cotes-by-Stow**: A delightful interior. Panelled with traceried heads. The pulpit-like projection is unusual.
Norfolk	**Attleborough**: Very striking. The loft is supported on a marvellous vault. After the Reformation the 24 panels were painted with the arms of the old Dioceses of England and Wales (Canterbury and York arms must have been elsewhere).
Suffolk	**Dennington**: The two screens and lofts, with double-light tracery, surround the east ends of the aisles.
Wiltshire	**Avebury**: Twenty-two open panels with crocketed gables. A continuous cornice. Much colouring remains – red, blue and gold.
Worcestershire	**Besford**: A simple but effective row of quatrefoils enclosing a rose.

133   Rood-loft front, Flamborough, Yorkshire

Yorkshire   **Flamborough** (Plate 133): Very splendid.
                          There is a double cornice, and the canopies
                          above the panels are of exceptionally
                          elaborate tabernacle work. Even the
                          muntins between the main panels have
                          niches. If one can imagine this loft front in
                          all its glory, with figures, gilt and
                          colouring, one can visualize a little the
                          magnificence of a church just before the
                          Reformation. **Hubberholme**. A rare late
                          example dated 1558 (reign of Queen Mary).
                          Completely traceried panels (after Welsh
                          fashion). Colour is pink and gold.

On top of the rood-loft front or on a separate beam above it
was the great rood or crucifix. On either side of the cross
would have been figures of St Mary the Virgin and St John
the Evangelist.

Behind this group of figures was usually the Doom or Last
Judgment painting (see section on wall-paintings, page 209),
and often these paintings show the unpainted spaces against
which were placed the great cross and the figures.

It was most appropriate that such a group should be at the
entrance to the chancel. The great crucifix was then the most
prominent object in, and dominated the nave in the later
medieval period. Walls were heightened, clerestories added, or
additional windows inserted in order to set off and give
prominence to this representation of the greatest fact in
history, showing that mankind had not been left to struggle
alone, but had been redeemed by Christ on the Cross. The
Passion of Our Lord and the shadow of the Cross were very
properly the predominant thoughts of a medieval Christian.

Every old church would have had some such screen and loft
– many no doubt very simple.

The screen was not meant to be a barrier, but a window
and a guide. Screen, loft, rood and Doom were one
composition, the saints who have triumphed painted in the
panels below leading through the Crucifixion to Christ
Triumphant above.

Rood Celures

Above the rood was often a canopy of honour called a *rood celure*, usually formed by panelling or enriching and colouring the eastern bay of the nave roof.

Here are some examples, all beautifully coloured.

Devon	**Hennock, Ideford** and **King's Nympton**: All have panels with diagonal ribs and fine bosses and gilt stars.
Hampshire	**Dummer**: Unusual, but most effective. The roof is formed into a concave arch.
Hertfordshire	**Braughing**: Particularly beautiful with numerous bosses and gilt stars.
Somerset	**West Camel**: Bosses and gilt stars.
Suffolk	**Stowlangtoft**: Painted with the sacred monogram, IHC.

Stalls

The chancels of most churches had wooden stalls which would be placed against the north and south walls and are often returned or set against the back of the screen, that is, three or four on each side of the entrance facing eastwards.

The stall-ends nearly always have poppy-heads and are similar to bench-ends, but they are usually more elaborate. The fronts of the desks often have traceried heads, and the elbows might be adorned with angels whose wings neatly follow the curve.

The greatest triumphs of the medieval wood-carvers were in the magnificent tabernacled canopies of the stalls of some of the cathedrals and greater churches of the north of England. This is a complete list in chronological order from the late fourteenth century to the early sixteenth century and all are very lovely:

Lancashire	**Lancaster**: The most luxuriant canopies in the country. The gables have thick foliage and the tracery is Flamboyant.
Lincolnshire	**Lincoln** Cathedral: In three tiers. Kings and angels on the front desks. Fascinating arm-rests and poppy-heads.
Cheshire	**Chester** Cathedral (Plate 134): Particularly fine canopies with spirelets. The Dean's stall-end is carved with the Tree of Jesse. Interesting arm-rests. **Nantwich**: Exceptionally rich canopies.
Cumberland	**Carlisle** Cathedral: High canopies with crocketed spirelets.
Berkshire	St George's Chapel, **Windsor**: In three tiers. The topmost tier is occupied by the Knights of the Garter, whose colourful banners are above. The carvings on the poppy-heads and desk-fronts should be noted. The Garter stall plates are an amazing heraldic record.

134   Stalls, Chester Cathedral

Yorkshire	**Ripon** Cathedral: The stall-ends are particularly fine, one with an elephant and castle.
Lancashire	**Manchester** Cathedral: The stalls are probably the finest anywhere. Animals and grotesques curve up to the poppy-heads.
London	Henry VII's Chapel, **Westminster** Abbey: The heads of the canopies are dome-shaped. Little lierne vaults. Above are the banners of the Knights of the Bath.
Yorkshire	**Beverley Minster**: A glorious array. Intricate vaulted canopies. The poppy-head ends deserve careful study.
County Durham	**Durham** Cathedral: Purely Gothic in style, but erected in 1665 by Bishop Cosin.

The stalls in the following cathedrals all have canopies, but the canopies are not tabernacled as in the previous list. The order is again chronological from the early fourteenth century to the early sixteenth century.

Hampshire	**Winchester** Cathedral: These stalls are the earliest in England, the date being about 1300. The Geometrical designs in the back panels and in the crocketed gables are typical of that date.
Sussex	**Chichester** Cathedral: Slightly later, but still fourteenth century as confirmed by the ogee arches on detached shafts.
Cambridgeshire	**Ely** Cathedral: Tall niches with cusped arches and crocketed gables. Modern Belgian reliefs.
Gloucestershire	**Gloucester** Cathedral: The canopies are formed by nodding ogee arches, quite three dimensional.
Herefordshire	**Hereford** Cathedral: Nodding ogee canopies on detached shafts, with panelling on the canopies.
Norfolk	**Norwich** Cathedral: The straight top-

cresting is beautiful blank panelling of
Perpendicular window tracery with cusped
arches superimposed. Interesting arm-rests.

Gloucestershire   **Bristol** Cathedral: Flamboyant traceried
panels surmounted by a horizontal coved
cornice. Early sixteenth century.

Cambridgeshire   **Cambridge**, King's College Chapel: The
118 stalls of about 1535 are the purest early
Renaissance work in England. The
balusters, cornice, and coats-of-arms on the
backs were added a hundred years later.

London   St Paul's Cathedral, **City**: The stalls of 1697
are famous for the exquisite carving of
Grinling Gibbons.

Parish church stalls at the most had traceried backs and
cornice and never more than one row of seats. Such seats
would then have been occupied by the parish priest, parish
clerk, any chaplains or chantry priests, and by the patron,
squire and leading churchfolk (the choir was then on the
rood-loft, then in the west gallery and only in the nineteenth
century did they come into the chancel).

The following list is of some of the finest stalls in parish
churches:

Cambridgeshire   **Balsham**: The feature is the arm-rests. Both
the upper and the lower rows (for standing
or sitting), are carved with human figures
or animals.

Herefordshire   All Saints', **Hereford**: An excellent set.
Very similar to those in the cathedral. The
backs and canopies have richly cusped
arches.

Kent   **Minster-in-Thanet**: Early fifteenth century
and particularly beautiful fronts, ends and
arm-rests.

Lancashire   **Cartmel** Priory: The stalls are fifteenth
century, but the backs are of the early

seventeenth century and are very lovely.
There are most elaborate openwork tracery
panels, and the columns are covered with a
vine trail, amidst which are Instruments of
the Passion.

Lincolnshire	**Winthorpe**: Fine stall-ends with intricate tracery, but on one is the legend of St Hubert and the stag. A variety of poppy-heads, one with boys beating down acorns. Beasts adorn the arm-rests.
Norfolk	**Sall**: Good carving on the panelled fronts, and poppy-heads, and arm-rests with faces and monsters.
Northampton-shire	**Higham Ferrers**: Many of the collegiate stalls still remain here.
Shropshire	**Tong** (Plate 135): Tall backs with tracery. Panelled fronts. Arm-rests and poppy-heads with figures.
Suffolk	**Southwold**: Finely carved arm-rests with animals, figures and heads, and the fronts are completely covered with rich tracery. **Stowlangtoft**: Traceried fronts, panelled backs, and coved cornice, but very delightful are the small standing figures instead of poppy-heads, one being of a preacher in the pulpit. **Wingfield**: The stalls are effectively backed on to the vaulted parclose screens. Arm-rests with animals and human faces.

135   Stalls and misericords, Tong, Shropshire

Bishops' Thrones

Devon	**Exeter** Cathedral: The earliest (*c.*1317) and finest. It is indeed said to be the most exquisite piece of woodwork of its date in England. The mass of woodwork consists of crocketed gables, nodding ogee arches, and receding upper stages surmounted by a fantastic pinnacle. Human and animal heads are beautifully carved.
Herefordshire	**Hereford** Cathedral: This throne is later than that at Exeter, but it is three-seated, that is to say the chaplains seats on either side have their own compartments with crocketed canopies, but much smaller than the main throne.
Wales	**St David's**: The throne is similar to the throne at Hereford, but it is of the end of the fifteenth century.

Misericords

Tip-up seats in stalls are called misericords and underneath them are projections which when turned up afford some support when one is standing, and one's elbows can rest on the arms of the stalls (Plate 135).

On either side of the main projection or centre-piece are nearly always subsidiary carvings known as supporters, which are generally different in design and subject from the centre-piece – often human heads, birds, beasts or foliage.

The carvings can be appreciated by anyone, but their meaning will only be understood by very few who have learnt their 'language'. We can thoroughly recommend a detailed study of the subjects and their meaning which will be most rewarding.

Symbolism by type and anti-type was most popular. For instance, Samson carrying off the gates of Gaza is associated with the Resurrection. The pelican in her piety is very common; the bird pecks its breast and gives its blood to its young ones, as Christ redeemed us by His blood and He still gives it to us in the Communion Service.

The principal subjects covered are mythology, medieval romances, fables, homely domestic life, sport, jesters, heraldry and satires – particularly on monks, doctors and musicians. Humour and wise saws can also be found. Sacred subjects are comparatively rare.

Vast numbers of misericords remain, especially in the greater churches, the average number in one building being around 60.

They range in date from c.1270 at **Exeter** Cathedral to c.1534–35 in King's College Chapel, **Cambridge**.

The following list is reasonably complete in respect of the finest sets.

Those marked º are unsurpassed for their carving. Those marked + have particularly interesting subjects.

In Cathedrals
(In order of numbers reading down)

Lincoln[+]	**Chester**[o]
Winchester	**Carlisle**[o]
Wells[o]	**Chichester**
Norwich[o]	**Worcester**[+]
Gloucester	**Manchester**[o]
Hereford	**Ripon**[o]
Exeter[o]	**Bristol**
Ely[+]	

In Chapels

King's College, **Cambridge**
St George's Chapel, **Windsor**
Henry VII's Chapel, **Westminster** Abbey
New College, **Oxford**[+]
All Souls' College, **Oxford**

In Parish Churches

Cheshire	**Nantwich**
Dorset	**Sherborne** Abbey
Hampshire	**Christchurch** Priory
Kent	**Minster-in-Thanet**
Lancashire	**Cartmel** Priory and **Whalley**
Lincolnshire	**Boston**[+]
Northampton-shire	**Higham Ferrers**
Shropshire	**Ludlow**
Warwickshire	**Stratford-on-Avon**
Worcestershire	**Great Malvern** Priory. **Ripple** [+] (realistic representations of the occupations of the twelve months – Plate 136).
Yorkshire	**Beverley**: Both the **Minster**[+] and **St Mary's Church**[+] have fine sets.

136 Misericord of sowing in March; note horse and harrow. Ripple, Worcestershire

It has not been possible to give even a brief summary of the subjects against each church as the subjects are so varied and numerous.

How could one sum up, say, the 68 in **Beverley Minster**?

The tourist will, however, find an excellent summary of all the above mentioned misericords in Sir Nikolaus Pevsner's *Buildings of England* Series (Penguin Books).

Hatchments

A coat-of-arms on a lozenge-shaped frame is a hatchment. It is usually late seventeenth or eighteenth century in date and was hung for some months in front of the house of a deceased person and then brought into the church.

The word 'Resurgam' often occurs. It is not a motto of the family, but a hopeful statement of belief 'I will rise again'.

The background is either completely black or half-black and half-white according to the married state of the person commemorated. Here are the rules:

Black background
Bachelor. Arms are single (just his family)

274

Widower. Arms are divided into two (that is the husband's and the wife's arms)
Spinster. Arms are single and lozenge-shaped
Widow. Arms are divided into two and are lozenge-shaped

Half-black and half-white backgrounds
Married man dies before wife – left side (as you look at it) black and right side white.
Married woman dies before husband – left side white and right side black.

Many churches possess quite a number. They are colourful and they usually adorn a church wall. They also stress the human element with which the church has been connected.

There are 17 in the church of **Stanford**, Northamptonshire. **Theydon Garnon**, Essex, has a remarkable display, all beautifully restored and very colourful.

Plate 137 is an example from **Hoveton St Peter**, Norfolk.

137 A hatchment at Hoveton St Peter, Norfolk

Royal Arms

From earliest times Royal Arms have been useful clues to dates.

The Royal Arms in churches are usually painted on a square board or on canvas, but sometimes they are carved in plaster, stone, or wood. Such Royal Arms are not earlier than the reign of Henry VIII. There is a large and magnificent one of that date with its supporters of a greyhound and dragon and with Tudor rose and portcullis on the chancel arch at **Rushbrooke**, Suffolk.

They became general under Elizabeth I. There are two very notable examples, both in Norfolk. At **Tivetshall St Margaret** the arms are again in the chancel arch and are painted on oak boards which may formerly have had the usual Doom painting. With the arms and its supporters of a lion and a dragon are the Ten Commandments and badges of the other four Tudor sovereigns and Anne Boleyn. Above is the Divine emblem, the sun in splendour, radiating its influence over all.

The other fine example is at **Kenninghall**.

After the Restoration of Charles II Royal Arms became compulsory in churches. A splendid example of 1663 with Creed, Lord's Prayer, and the Ten Commandments is in the chancel arch of **Baddiley**, Cheshire. There is a similar arrangement at **Ellingham**, Hampshire.

With the hatchments at **Theydon Garnon**, Essex, is an equally beautiful restored Royal Arms of the earlier years of George III, the elaborate Hanoverian arms now appearing in one of the quarters.

This is a complete summary (quarters being numbered 1 2
             3 4):

Before 1340	Three gold lions on red.
1340 to 1405	1 and 4 France, many gold fleurs-de-lys on blue, 2 and 3 England, three gold lions on red.

| 1405 to 1603 | As before, but the fleurs-de-lys are now only three in number. |
| 1603 to 1707 | 1 and 4 England and France quarterly as in the previous period, 2 Scotland, red lion and border on gold, 3 Ireland, gold harp on blue. |

(From 1689 to 1702 William and Mary added a gold lion on blue in the centre.)

| 1707 to 1714 | 1 and 4 England impaling Scotland, 2 three fleurs-de-lys of France, and 3 harp of Ireland. |
| 1714 to 1801 | As previously, but with the arms of Hanover in the fourth quarter. |

| 1801 to 1837 | 1 and 4 England, 2 Scotland, 3 Ireland, and the arms of Hanover in the centre (as illustrated in Plate 138 from **Norton Subcourse**, Norfolk). |
| 1837 to the present time | As in the previous period, but without the centrepiece. |

James I substituted the unicorn as a supporter with the lion in place of the Welsh dragon, which had been adopted by the Tudor sovereigns. The lion had been introduced by Edward VI in place of a greyhound.

Monuments

These show the personal elements in the parish and the various fashions throughout the ages. Even if a church appears to be rebuilt and uninteresting, it may well have monuments of great interest from its medieval predecessor.

They are of all dates and vast numbers remain. The lists following are therefore merely some typical and noteworthy examples of each period.

The material was alabaster (which was our English marble from Chellaston, Derbyshire), or stone (including much Purbeck marble in the earlier medieval period), or very occasionally wood. The most costly material was bronze of which there are only ten old effigies in three places.

Bronze Effigies

London	**Westminster** Abbey: Queen Eleanor, wife of Edward I, 1290. Henry III, 1292. Edward III, 1377. Delightful weepers. Richard II and his Queen, 1395. Lady Margaret Beaufort, Countess of Derby, 1511. Henry VII and his Queen, 1518. Magnificent tomb with weepers.
Kent	**Canterbury** Cathedral: Prince Edward, the Black Prince, 1376. Painting of the Trinity on the wooden canopy.
Warwickshire	**Warwick**, St Mary's: Richard Beauchamp, Earl of Warwick, 1453. Weepers: This could be said to be the most sumptuous monument anywhere.

Wooden Effigies

This material is rather a contrast to bronze, but it must be remembered that wooden figures were lavishly coloured and gilt, as still at **Goudhurst,** Kent.

Only about 80 old wooden effigies exist, most being in Essex.

Buckinghamshire	**Clifton Reynes**: Two knights and their wives, early fourteenth century.
Cambridgeshire	**Hildersham**: Cross-legged knight and lady. Early fourteenth century.
Essex	**Danbury**: Three cross-legged knights, but each one is different. Late thirteenth century or early fourteenth century. **Little Baddow**: Civilian and lady, 1320.
Herefordshire	**Much Marcle**: A yeoman, 1350. Coloured. Other monuments here should be noted.
Kent	**Goudhurst**: In an oriel window. Sir Alexander Culpeper and wife, 1537. Brightly coloured.
Norfolk	**Fersfield**: Sir Robert de Bois, 1311. Coloured.
Shropshire	**Pitchford**: Sir John Pitchford, 1285
Somerset	**Chew Magna**: A fourteenth-century knight. Most unusual. Semi-reclining, with feet on a standing lion. Colour.
Suffolk	**Boxted**: William Poley and wife, 1587. **Wingfield**: Michael de la Pole, Earl of Suffolk, and wife, 1415.
Sussex	**Slindon**: Sir Anthony St Leger, 1539
Yorkshire	**Thornhill**: Sir John Savile and two wives, 1529. There are many other monuments to this family in the church. **Worsborough**: Roger Rockley, 1534. In two tiers, with cadaver below.

Pre-Reformation Effigies and Monuments of Stone or Alabaster

Around the sides of a medieval tomb are sometimes delightful little figures called weepers. They might be members of the family, angels or saints. Angels are either feathered or in albs and they often hold shields.

Throughout the medieval period and later one can date an effigy or a brass by the armour of a knight, the dress and hair of a civilian, or a lady's dress and head-dress. Medieval carved figures, with only one or two exceptions, are in humble recumbent attitudes, with hands clasped in prayer.

Cheshire	**Over Peover**: Sir John Mainwaring and wife, *c*.1420. Sir Randle Mainwaring and wife, 1456.
Derbyshire	**Ashbourne**: John and Edmund Cockayne, 1404. Sir John Cockayne and wife, 1447. **Norbury**: Sir Henry Fitzherbert, fourteenth century. Cross-legged. Sir Nicholas Fitzherbert and wives and children, 1473. Sir Ralph Fitzherbert and wife, 1483. Weepers and a monk with a rosary. **Youlgreave**: Thomas Cockayne, 1488. A diminutive monument. Cock's head crest. Angels with shields.
Devon	**Feniton**: A good example of a medieval cadaver. **Haccombe**: A diminutive fifteenth-century monument to a boy, Edward Courtenay.
Hampshire	**Winchester** Cathedral: Bishop William of Wykeham, 1404.
Kent	**Canterbury** Cathedral: Archbishop Chichele, 1443. Very sumptuous.
London	**Westminster** Abbey: Three together, all with canopies and weepers, and somewhat similar – Edmund Crouchback, Earl of Lancaster, 1296. Aveline, Countess of Lancaster, 1290, and Aymer de Valence, 1326.
Norfolk	**Ashwellthorpe**: Sir Edmund de Thorpe and wife, 1417.
Northampton-shire	**Lowick**: Sir Ralph Greene and wife, hand in hand, 1419. Canopies at the heads, and angels round the sides.
Northumberland	**Chillingham**: Sir Ralph Gray and wife,

1443. Very fine, with saints and angels
around the sides.

Nottinghamshire   **Strelley** (Plate 139): Sir Sampson de
Strelley and wife, hand in hand, *c.*1400.
Angels with shields. **Whatton**: Sir Richard
de Whatton, 1322. Legs crossed, and
wearing chain mail.

Oxfordshire   **Dorchester** Abbey: Very fine cross-legged
knight of *c.*1280, drawing his sword.
Ewelme: Alice, Duchess of Suffolk, 1475.
She wears a coronet and the Order of the
Garter. The weepers are exquisite angels

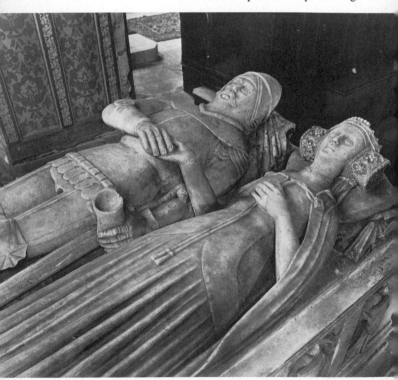

with shields. Through an opening below can be seen a cadaver (above which is a painting). The effigy and tomb are of alabaster, but the elaborate canopy above, with more figures, is of stone, and above all are wooden angels. This is certainly one of the finest monuments in England. **Stanton Harcourt**: Lady Maud Harcourt, *c.* 1400. Colour. Sir Robert Harcourt and wife, 1471. Both wear the Order of the Garter. Sir Robert Harcourt and wife, 1490. Angels and bedesmen.

Shropshire **Tong**: Sir Fulke de Pembruge and wife, *c.* 1420. Sir Richard Vernon and wife, 1451. Angels and saints

Somerset **Chew Magna**: Sir John St Loe and wife, 1450. He is an exceptionally long figure. **Long Ashton**: Sir Richard Choke, Lord Chief Justice, and wife, 1486. Elaborate canopy.

Staffordshire **Elford**: A knight of *c.* 1370. Sir Thomas Arderne and wife, hand in hand, 1391. Weepers. John Stanley, a boy, 1460. Holds a tennis ball. Very attractive.

Suffolk **Dennington**: Lord Bardolph and wife, 1441. Eagle and griffin at feet. **Hawstead**: Cross-legged knight, 1270. **Wingfield**: Sir John Wingfield, 1361. John de la Pole, Duke of Suffolk, Knight of the Garter, and wife, 1491.

Sussex **Arundel**: Thomas Fitzalan, Earl of Arundel, and wife, 1416. Weepers, metal hearse. John Fitzalan, Earl of Arundel, 1435. Cadaver below. William Fitzalan, Earl of Arundel, and wife, 1487. **Winchelsea**: Five notable monuments of

139   Sir Sampson de Strelley and wife, c. 1400, Strelley, Nottinghamshire

	the early fourteenth century with elaborate canopies and profuse carving.
Warwickshire	**Studley**: An excellent example of a thirteenth-century stone grave-cover decorated with a foliated cross. It is a monument to a Prior. **Warwick**, St Mary's: Thomas Beauchamp, Earl of Warwick, and wife, hand in hand, 1369. Weepers.
Yorkshire	**Beverley Minster**: The Percy Monument. Mid-fourteenth century. The spandrels and cusps of the canopy are so elaborately carved that it claims to be the most splendid Decorated monument in England. No effigy. (See section on brasses, page 306). **Methley**: Sir Robert Waterton and wife, 1424. Representation of the Trinity. Lord Wellers and wife, 1461.

Sometimes a medieval monument was surrounded by an iron railing or hearse, as at **Farleigh Hungerford**, Somerset (Sir Thomas Hungerford and wife, 1412), such occasionally having little prickets or spikes for candle-stocks, as at **West Tanfield**, Yorkshire (Sir John Marmion and wife, 1387). (See **Arundel** above.)

In the fifteenth and sixteenth centuries, the figures of the deceased and the family were sometimes incised in the stone or alabaster. This is common in the North Midlands. An excellent example is at **Pitchford**, Shropshire, where four incised alabaster slabs from 1529 to 1587 show eight parents and 50 children, and, of course, the history of costume. Another example is at **Over Peover**, Cheshire (two slabs to the Mainwaring family, 1573 and 1586). Engravings on slate are frequent in Cornwall (**Lelant**).

Tudor Monuments

Great families and rich merchants increased in numbers in Tudor times and often wished to be commemorated by

sumptuous monuments. After the Reformation, with the
changes of religious ideas, the attitude of the figures on
monuments changed as well, and a variety of undevotional
attitudes were adopted, the favourite being that of lolling on
the elbow. The recumbent attitude, of course, continued as
well in the sixteenth and seventeenth centuries, and many
figures are shown kneeling. Needless to say all positions can
sometimes be found on one monument.

Cheshire	**Malpas**: Sir Randle Brereton and wife, 1522. A dog bites her dress. Statuettes.
Derbyshire	**Ashbourne**: Sir Humphrey Bradbourne and wife, 1581. Children. **Ashover**: Thomas Babington and wife, with fascinating weepers, 1518.
Essex	**Layer Marney**: Henry Lord Marney, 1523. Black marble and terracotta.
Kent	**Canterbury**, St Stephen's, Hackington: Sir Roger Manwood, 1592. Waist-length bust. In his robes of Chief Baron of the Exchequer. Below him is a 'life-like' accurate skeleton.
Leicestershire	**Bottesford**: A remarkable group of eight monuments from 1543 to 1679 to eight Earls of Rutland from the first to the eighth Earl. The first six are of alabaster and the last two of marble. All are very fine.
Northampton-shire	**Great Brington**: A fine array of monuments. Sir John Spencer and wife, 1522. Two tiny puppies. Angel. Sir John Spencer and wife, 1586. Robert Baron Spencer and wife, 1599. Sir John Spencer and wife, 1599. William Lord Spencer and wife, 1638. **Fawsley**: Sir Richard Knightley and wife, 1534. Graceful children.
Rutland	**Exton**: John Harington and wife, 1524. Bedesman. Two tiny pet dogs. Robert Kelway and children, 1580. Very fine. Sir

James Harington and wife, 1591. Kneeling at a prayer-desk.

Shropshire   **Condover**: Thomas Scriven and wife, 1587. Children. **Moreton Corbet**: Two delightful coloured monuments to the Corbets, 1513 with eighteen weepers, and 1567 with coats-of-arms on the armour, owl, elephant and castle, and a baby in swaddling clothes. **Tong**: Sir Henry Vernon, and wife, 1515. Arthur Vernon, 1517. Demi-figure on a bracket. Richard Vernon and wife, 1517. Bedesmen.

Somerset   **Chew Magna**: Edward Baker (in a red gown), and wife, 1578. Representations of Labour and Leisure. **Wraxall**: Sir Edmund Gorges and wife, 1512. Angels with coats-of-arms.

Staffordshire   **Brewood**: Sir John Giffard and two wives, 1556. One son, four daughters, and 13 babies in swaddling clothes. Sir Thomas Giffard and two wives, 1560. Seventeen children. John Giffard and wife, 1613. Fourteen children. Walter Giffard and wife, 1632 (no children, which rather lets the side down!). There is also an incised alabaster slab to Richard Lane and wife, 1518, with 11 children. **Elford**: Sir William Smythe and two wives, 1525. Weepers.

Suffolk   **Framlingham**: Henry Fitzroy, Duke of Richmond, 1536. No figures. Stories from Genesis. Shields with Instruments of the Passion. Thomas Howard, Duke of Norfolk, and wife, 1554. Apostles. Two wives of the Duke of Norfolk, 1557 and 1564. Pony and dog at the head, and stag and dragon at the feet.

Sussex   **Arundel**: Thomas Fitzalan, Earl of Arundel, 1524. **Battle**. Sir Anthony Browne, Knight of the Garter, and wife,

	1548. Wife only has canopy. Early Renaissance decoration. Colour.
Warwickshire	**Sutton Coldfield**: Bishop Veysey, 1554.
Yorkshire	**Guisborough**: From the Priory, and to a former Prior, c. 1540. Fine carving of knights, saints, figures and shields.

Seventeenth-century Monuments

Those of the first quarter of this century are of the greatest possible interest and beauty. They are usually of immense size, lavishly coloured, and adorned with innumerable shields with coats-of-arms.

The crests at the heads of the figures and the animals at their feet are often works of art in themselves. Armour and costume are striking, and numerous children nicely fill up the sides. A skull held by a child indicates that he or she had previously died. In a day's visiting of churches, one church at least is likely to have a good example.

Berkshire	**Bisham**: On the edge of the River Thames. Sir Philip and Sir Thomas Hoby, 1566. The bird at the feet is a hobby (falcon). Lady Hoby and family, 1609 (Plate 140). The eldest daughter is shown as a Countess and the little son is shown by the soles of his two feet. Very fine. Lady Margaret Hoby, 1605. A red heart on an obelisk and four life-like swans. Very striking.
Buckinghamshire	**Quainton**: Several of note to the Dormer family.
Cambridgeshire	**Orwell**: Dr Jeremiah Radcliffe, 1612. Head and shoulders and a red gown. Two books, as he was one of the translators of the Bible.
Cheshire	**Gawsworth**: In a delightful setting. Sir Francis Fitton, 1608. Effigy above and skeleton below. Sir Edward Fitton and

wife, 1619. Children. Dame Alice Fitton, 1627. Seated, with her head on her hand. Children kneeling in front of and behind her. Sir Edward Fitton and wife, 1643. One little girl. **Malpas**: Sir Hugh Cholmondeley and wife, 1605. Kneeling children and a baby in swaddling clothes.

Devon

Bishop's Tawton: Daughter of Charles Dart, 1652. Small figure of a baby in swaddling clothes. **Musbury**: Drake family, 1611. Three couples kneel behind each other. **Tawstock**: William Bouchier, 3rd Earl of Bath, and wife, 1623. Perhaps the finest monument of its date in England. Crimson colouring. The Saracen's head, goat, and kneeling children with baby are particularly attractive. Many other monuments of interest, including a typical wall monument with figures facing each other.

Gloucestershire

Longborough: Sir William Leigh and wife, 1631. Three delightful infant children, one in a chrysom robe. Black and white marble. **Miserden**: William Kingston, 1614. A goat eats a cabbage. Anthony Partridge and wife, 1625. Sir William Sandys and wife, 1640. Children.

Hampshire

Catherington: Sir Nicholas Hyde and wife, 1631. Ten children. Beautifully coloured.

Hertfordshire

St Michael's, **St Albans**: Sir Francis Bacon, Lord Chancellor, 1626. The very famous life-size marble figure seated very comfortably, resting his head on his hand, and asleep.

Lincolnshire

Snarford: St Thomas St Pol and wife, 1582. Large six-poster. Kneeling children on top. Sir George St Pol and wife, 1613. Effigies on their sides, he a little above her. Robert

140   Lady Hoby and family, 1609, Bisham, Berkshire

Lord Rich, Earl of Warwick, and wife, 1619. Busts in a medallion.

London
City: St Helen's, Bishopsgate. Sir John Spencer and wife, 1609. Coloured. **Westminster** Abbey: Princess Sophia, daughter of James I, 1606. Three days old. Shown in a cradle. All Saints', **Fulham**: Margaret Lady Legh, 1605. Holds a baby, and another at her side.

Middlesex
Harefield: Alice Spencer, Countess of Derby, 1636. Three kneeling daughters. All four figures have long hair. Cock crest. Domed and curtained canopy. Colour. Many other monuments in this most interesting church.

Norfolk
Besthorpe (Plate 141): Sir William Drury, wife, and children, 1639. One child has a skull and two hold hands.

Northampton-shire
Easton Neston: Sir George Fermor and wife, 1612. Fifteen children. Arch formed by a peacock's tail of 16 pennons brightly coloured with coats-of-arms. **Stowe-Nine-Churches**: Lady Carey, 1620, is exquisite sculpture.

Nottinghamshire
Langar: Thomas Lord Scrope and wife, 1609. He wears the Garter robes and hat. Kneeling son at feet reads a book.

Oxfordshire
Rotherfield Greys: Sir Francis Knollys, K.G., and wife, 1596. He wears the mantle of the Order of the Garter. Elephant and swan at feet. Round the sides are seven sons and six daughters, and the Countess of Essex in her robes. A small infant lies to the side of the mother, and on top of the monument are Lord William Knollys, K.G., and his wife, 1632, at a prayer-desk. The whole is very large. Much colour. **Stanton Harcourt**: Sir Philip Harcourt and

141   Children of Sir William Drury, 1639, Besthorpe, Norfolk

wife, 1688. A good example of two busts.
Swinbrook: Splendid examples of the
lolling attitude. Two adjoining monuments
produce six such figures in tiers of three to
members of the Fettiplace family. The
earlier one erected in 1613 shows the
figures stiffly reclining on one elbow, and
the later one, 1686, shows a more relaxed
attitude with one knee bent.

Shropshire
Condover: Dame Jane Norton with
husband, brother and father at prayer-
desks, 1640. Martha Owen, 1641, a bust
with a baby in front. **Norton-in-Hales**.
Sir Rowland Cotton and wife, 1606. She
holds her naked baby in her arms. **Tong**:
Sir Thomas Stanley and wife, 1632, and
son.

Somerset
Brent Knoll: John Somerset and his two
wives, 1663. Busts in niches. The two wives
have very different head-gear. Two reliefs
below – his family, and rising in his shroud
from his tomb. Brightly coloured.
Churchill: John Latch and wife, 1644.
Brightly coloured. The wife is completely in
her shroud and the husband, reclining
behind her and trying to raise the shroud,
looks rather surprised. Children.
Wellington: Sir John Popham, Lord Chief
Justice, and wife, 1607. In addition there is
a company of 26 persons, all very
charming. Colour.

Suffolk
Bramfield: Arthur Coke and wife, 1629. He
kneels above, whilst his wife is recumbent
holding her baby. The exquisite features,
the draperies and lacework, the ornamental
work on the pillow, and the look of repose
on the face of the infant makes one of the
most wonderful achievements of English

142   Sir Thomas and Lady Vincent, 1619, Stoke D'Abernon, Surrey

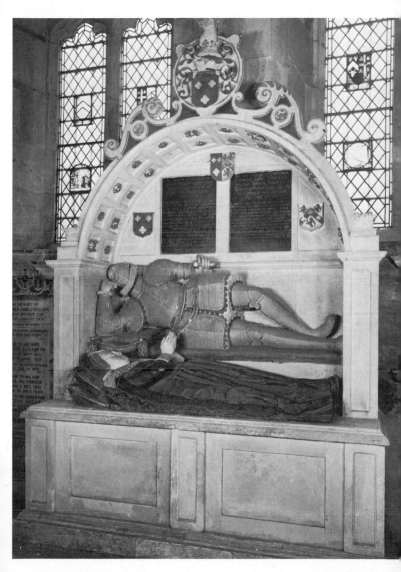

sculpture. A ledger stone nearby records what happens when one decides to run the risk of a second marriage! **Culford**: Lady Jane Bacon, 1654. She is seated, and is surrounded by her family with one child on her lap; her first husband lies on his side and elbow on the ledge below her feet. **Framlingham**: Henry Howard, Earl of Surrey, and wife, 1614. Children. **Helmingham**: A very large monument of 1615 with four kneeling figures of four Lionel Tollemaches from 1550 to 1605. A long inscription.

Surrey

Stoke D'Abernon: Lady Sarah Vincent, 1608. She reclines on an elbow and wears a tightly-waisted dress. Seven children. Sir Thomas Vincent and wife, 1619 (Plate 142). He is above his wife, reclining on an elbow and wearing enormous trunk hose.

Sussex

Ashburnham: John Ash and two wives (one in shroud), 1671. Children. William Ash and wife, 1679. There is a great difference in style between the two monuments – from Jacobean to Baroque. **Withyham**: Thomas Sackville, aged 13, 1677. He holds a skull. His parents kneel life-size on the steps of the monument. Also six brothers and six sisters. This monument begins to show the trend that was fully developed in the next century. It is by Cibber. There are other monuments in the church by sculptors of note – 1802 Nollekens, 1815 Flaxman, and 1825 Chantrey.

Wiltshire

Bishopstone, near Salisbury: A typical monument to a Divine, c.1630. A white-bearded demi-figure in a black gown. **Lydiard Tregoze**: Rich in monuments. Nicholas St John and wife, 1592. Couple

143   Sir William Savage and family, 1631, Elmley Castle, Worcestershire

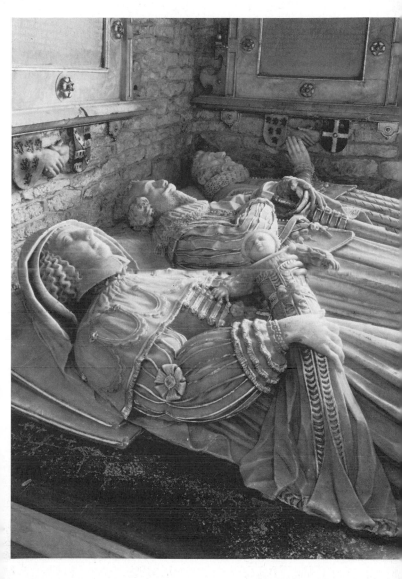

kneel side by side. A number of badges.
A family triptych painted with figures inside
and a family tree outside. The kneeling
couple are Sir John St John and wife, 1594,
and their son who erected it in 1615. Sir
John St John and two wives, 1634. An
eight-poster. One wife holds a child. The
kneeling children are fascinating. Sir Giles
Mompesson and wife, 1633. The two
figures are seated facing one another as if
carrying on a conversation. Her hand is on
a skull. Edward St John, 1645. Standing
gilt figure in armour beneath a canopy held
open by two boys. John, Viscount St John,
1749. Obelisk. Rich with heraldry. **Steeple
Langford**: Another Divine. Joseph Collier,
rector, 1635. Portly three-quarter figure
with a square beard wearing a black gown
and holding a red book.

Worcestershire

Croome D'Abitot: Thomas, 1st Lord
Coventry, 1639. Semi-reclining figures of
Justice and Wisdom. 2nd Lord Coventry
1661 and Lady Coventry, his wife 1634. She
holds a baby. Two small boys. 4th Lord
Coventry, 1687. Semi-reclining in odd
position. Garlands. Figures of Hope and
Mercy. **Elmley Castle** (Plate 143): Sir
William Savage, his son Giles, and the
latter's wife, 1631. She holds a baby with a
ball in its hand. The baby is a masterpiece
and should be compared with that at
Bramfield, Suffolk. Four kneeling sons.
Stag's head pierced by an arrow. 1st Earl of
Coventry, 1699. Semi-reclining effigy with
wig and lace cravat. Two large figures of
Faith and Hope. **Wickhamford**: Double
monument to Sir Samuel Sandys and his
son Sir Edwin Sandys, with their wives,
1629. The son's tomb-chest is slightly lower

than that of his father. Kneeling children,
eleven for Samuel and eight for Edwin.
Samuel's wife is dressed as a widow.
Heraldry.

Eighteenth-century Monuments

Black and white marble superseded alabaster at the end of the
seventeenth century, and colour ceased.

The stupendous monuments of this period will always be
noticed because they often dominate and dwarf the church.

The sculpture is as magnificent as reverence is lacking.
Figures now often stand, and such a position does not
produce humility, but rather self-glorification, which does, of
course, coincide with the low state of the life of the Church.
The attire was often classical costume and wigs.

Epitaphs at this time use the most pompous and verbose
language to describe the innumerable merits of the deceased.
If these were true, it must have been an ideal time in which to
live!

Derbyshire	**Ashbourne**: Penelope Boothby, aged 6, 1791. Very well-known and most attractive.
Devon	**Shute**: William Pole, 1741. Fashionably dressed and holding his staff of office of the Royal Household. No religious intent.
Essex	**Steeple Bumpstead**: Sir Henry Bendyshe, 1717. A reclining figure with a tiny baby at his side. **Wanstead**: Sir Josiah Child, 1699. A showpiece. He stands in Roman attire and a wig. A son reclines on the pedestal below him.
Gloucestershire	**Great Barrington**: Bray children, 1720. A boy and girl in everyday clothes are conducted over clouds by an angel. The girl half looks back! Very fine.
Kent	**Chilham**: Arthur and Edmund Hardy, 1858. Two little boys nestle affectionately

together. A battledore and shuttlecock are shown.

Northampton-shire	**Warkton**: The huge monuments here are not likely to be overlooked. John, Duke of Montagu, 1752. His wife stands watching a cherub and Charity with two children hanging up a medallion with his portrait. Mary, Duchess of Montagu, 1753. Cherubs with garlands and large figures of the three Fates. A naked boy. Mary, Duchess of Montagu, 1775. The architecture of the apse is elegant. A big angel points upwards. Seated Duchess with two children, and a standing female figure. Elizabeth, Duchess of Buccleuch, 1827. A straight-seated figure between a young woman and a youth with an extinguished torch.
Oxfordshire	**Yarnton** (Plate 144): Sir Thomas Spencer, 1709. In classical attire he stands life-size with his wife and son. His four daughters, one with a skull and another with an hourglass, have to find such other positions as they can! Heraldry was still popular.
Staffordshire	**Lichfield** Cathedral: The two little daughters of Prebendary Robinson, 1814. Both are shown asleep. It is very well known, and is one of Chantrey's masterpieces.
Suffolk	**Boxted**: There are two monuments together and somewhat similar. Sir John Poley, end of the seventeenth century, and Dame Abigail Poley, 1725. Both have standing figures in arched niches, but the later one is much plainer and without cherubs. It is said to be the last English monument in alabaster. **Redgrave**: Sir John Holt, Lord Chief Justice, 1710. He is seated in Judge's

144   Eighteenth-century monument, Yarnton, Oxfordshire

robes between figures of Justice and Mercy.
Six cherubs.

Surrey **Bletchingley**: Sir Robert Clayton, Lord
Mayor of London, and wife, 1707. One of
the most splendid and ostentatious
monuments anywhere. He and his wife are
over life-size standing figures full of
character. There is a most attractive little
son below (this same boy can be seen again
by himself at **Ickenham**, Middlesex).
Cherubs.

Worcestershire **Strensham**: Sir Thomas Russell and wife,
1632. The tomb-chest shows a coffin. Sir
Francis Russell and wife, 1705. He is semi-
reclining in a long wig. His wife kneels over
him and points upwards. A cherub in
clouds holds a coronet.

Cartouche Tablets

These are a type of wall monument common in the
seventeenth and eighteenth centuries. They are usually of
marble and are like a sheet of paper with the sides curled up;
the inscription is in the centre and above may be a coat-of-
arms and a crest. There is a good example at **Harefield**,
Middlesex, to John Pricket, Bishop of Gloucester, 1681, and
another at **Petersham**, Surrey.

Ledger Stones

These massive floor slabs of seventeenth or early eighteenth
century date are usually made from a bluish-grey stone. The
armorial carving at the head of the slab and the bold
inscription below are normally great works of art, but they
are often overlooked.

They are particularly common in Norfolk, as at St
Stephen's, **Norwich**.

Brasses

More brasses remain in England than in the whole of Europe.
They are most common in the eastern counties and the Home
Counties.

Brass-rubbing has become very popular. It is a most
fascinating and rewarding hobby. With a roll of detail paper,
black heel-ball, and, of course, permission and payment of a
usually reasonable fee, one obtains a wonderful impression of
the brass on the paper, in fact better than looking at the
original. One can specialize in certain types or make a general
collection of all types and periods. There are now more books
on the subject than on any other branch of church art.

The following are the most notable brasses:

The finest knights of early date

Surrey	**Stoke D'Abernon**: Sir John Daubernoun, 1277
Cambridgeshire	**Trumpington**: Sir Roger de Trumpington, 1289
Suffolk	**Acton**: Sir Robert de Bures, 1302
Kent	**Chartham**: Sir Robert de Setvans, 1306
Cambridgeshire	**Westley Waterless**: Sir John de Creke, 1325
Surrey	**Stoke D'Abernon**: Sir John Daubernoun, 1327

The finest priests in Mass vestments

Northampton-shire	**Higham Ferrers**: Laurence de St Maur, 1337. The finest.
Kent	**Horsmonden**: John de Grovehurst, 1340
Berkshire	**Shottesbrooke**: Unknown, c. 1370
Hampshire	**Crondall**: Nicholas de Caerwent, 1381
Essex	**Great Bromley**: William Bischopton, 1432

The finest priests in copes

An asterisk indicates that figures of saints are engraved on the orphreys of the cope.

Bedfordshire	**Shillington**: Matthew de Asscheton, 1400. Dog at feet.
Cambridgeshire	**Fulbourn**: William de Fulburne, 1391. W.F.s on the orphreys and a coat-of-arms on the morse. **Balsham***: John Sleford, 1401. I.S. on the morse. Canopy. John Blodwell, 1462. The inscription is a dialogue between himself and an angel, the words being in relief or incised. Canopy. **Cambridge**, Trinity Hall*: Walter Hewke, 1517. Half-length figure of Christ on the morse.
Hampshire	St Cross, **Winchester**: John de Campeden, 1382. The marginal inscription is the Burial Service text from Job. **Havant**: Thomas Aileward, 1413. Wheatsheaves, fleurs-de-lys, roses and leopards' masks on the orphreys, and T.A. on the morse. **Ringwood***: John Prophete, 1416, Sacred face on the morse.
Hertfordshire	**Knebworth***: Simon Bache, 1414. Sacred face on the morse.
Leicestershire	**Bottesford***: Henry de Codryngton, 1404. Holy Trinity on the morse. Very fine.
Northampton-shire	**Castle Ashby*** (Plate 145): William Ermyn, 1401. Coat-of-arms on the morse. Very fine.
Oxfordshire	**Oxford**, Merton College*: Henry Sever, 1471. Very fine. Queen's College: Robert Langton, 1518. Cope ornamented with fleurs-de-lys.
Sussex	**Broadwater**: John Mapilton, 1432. M's and maple-leaves on the orphreys, and I.H.S.

145   Brass to William Ermyn, 1401, Castle Ashby, Northamptonshire

on the morse. **Warbleton**: William Prestwick, 1436. Burial Service text from Job on the orphreys, and Credo on the morse.

Bishops

Oxfordshire	**Oxford**, New College: Thomas Cranley, Warden, and Archbishop of Dublin, 1417. The finest.
Cambridgeshire	**Ely** Cathedral: Thomas Goodryke, Bishop of Ely, 1554
Essex	**Chigwell**: Samuel Harsnett, Archbishop of York, 1631

Monastic

Sussex	**Cowfold**: Thomas Nelond, Cluniac Prior of Lewes, 1433. The finest. Very elaborate canopy with figures.
Oxfordshire	**Dorchester** Abbey: Richard Bewfforeste, Augustinian Abbot, 1510.
Bedfordshire	**Elstow**: Elizabeth Herwy, Benedictine Abbess, 1520

Academic costume

Many brasses of this attire can be seen in New College Chapel, **Oxford**.

Norfolk	**Surlingham**: John Alnwik, 1460

Judges

Gloucestershire	**Deerhurst**: Sir John Cassy and wife, 1400. The wife has the only dog with a name, Terri.
Oxfordshire	**Brightwell Baldwin**: John Cottusmore and wife, 1439.

Shroud brasses

Cambridgeshire	**Hildersham**: Skeleton in a shroud, 1530
Hertfordshire	**Digswell**: William Robert and wife, 1484
Norfolk	**Aylsham**: Richard Howard and wife (as skeletons), 1499. Thomas Wymer, 1507.

Floriated cross

Cambridgeshire	**Hildersham**: Robert de Paris and wife, 1408. The Holy Trinity is in the head of the cross.

Flemish brasses

Norfolk	St Margaret's, **King's Lynn**: In foreign work the whole rectangular plate is engraved, and not just the figures as in English brasses. The two finest are in this church – Adam de Walsokne and wife, 1349, and Robert Braunche and two wives, 1364.

There are also two others of note:

Hertfordshire	**St Albans** Cathedral: Abbot Thomas Delamere, *c.*1360
Nottinghamshire	**Newark**: Alan Fleming, *c.*1375

Numerous brasses

Kent	**Cobham**: The most splendid display, not only in this country, but in the whole world. There are no less than nineteen magnificent brasses, many with fine canopies, to members of the great Cobham family and the clergy who staffed the collegiate church. The chancel floor is, of course, covered with them.
Oxfordshire	**Oxford**, New College: Undoubtedly a very good second for the number and beauty of its brasses. As is to be expected, they are of ecclesiastics and fellows.
Gloucestershire	**Northleach**: Being a centre of the medieval woollen trade, the fine collection here is mostly of wool merchants.
Hertfordshire	**Digswell**: The sanctuary floor of the medieval church is covered with brasses, John Peryent and wife, 1415, being outstanding.

That a brass engraving was as respected as a figure carved in any material is proved by the fact that one of the finest monuments, the Percy tomb in **Beverley Minster**, had a brass and not a carved figure. A magnificent brass is therefore a great treasure for any church, as for example Sir Symon de Felbrigge, K.G., and wife, 1416, at **Felbrigg**, Norfolk, and Sir John de la Pole and wife, hand in hand, *c*.1380 at **Chrishall**, Essex. In the splendid church of **East Markham**, Nottinghamshire (Plate 146), is the equally splendid brass to Dame Millicent Meryng, 1419, in typical dress and head-dress of that period. There is a little dog at her feet with bells on its collar.

Dating of brasses to clergy is difficult as vestments have never altered. Hair can give an indication; it was curly in the earlier medieval period and then at a later date hung straight down.

146   Brass to Dame Millicent Meryng, 1419, East Markham, Nottinghamshire

Other brasses can usually be dated to within about twenty or thirty years by the armour, civil dress and hair, and a lady's costume and head-dress.

The following 20 very fine brasses, in order of date, are a complete record of all those features from the thirteenth century to the seventeenth century (and they are all illustrated in the *Observer's Book of Old English Churches*).

Suffolk	**Acton**: Sir Robert de Bures, 1302
Cambridgeshire	**Westley Waterless**: Sir John de Creke, 1325
Oxfordshire	**Chinnor**: Two wives of Reginald de Malyns, 1385
Devon	**Stoke Fleming**: John Corp, 1391
Bedfordshire	**Wymington**: John Curteys, 1391
Gloucestershire	**Chipping Campden**: Wife of William Grevel, 1401
Huntingdonshire	**Sawtry**: Sir William Moyne and wife, 1404
Sussex	**Trotton**: Lord Thomas Camoys, K.G., and wife, hand in hand, 1419
Dorset	**Thorncombe**: Sir Thomas Brook and wife, 1437
Oxfordshire	**Brightwell Baldwin**: Wife of John Cottusmore, 1439
Sussex	**West Grinstead**: Sir Hugh Halsham and wife, 1441
Oxfordshire	**Swinbrook** (Plate 147): John Croston and wives, 1470
Kent	**Ulcombe**: Ralph St Leger and wife, 1470
Buckinghamshire	**Great Linford**: Roger Hunt, 1473
Oxfordshire	**Witney**: Richard Wenman, 1501
Staffordshire	**Kinver**: Sir Edward Grey and wife, 1528
Derbyshire	**Morley**: Sir Henry Sacheverall and wife, 1558
Buckinghamshire	**Upton**: Edward Bulstrode and wife, 1599
Hampshire	**Whitchurch**: Richard Brooke and wife, 1603
Kent	**East Sutton**: Sir Edward Filmer, wife and children, 1629

147   Armour and costume of 1470. Brass at Swinbrook, Oxfordshire

Hic iacet p̄batus iacer Armiger John vodtac̃? Dotroũ vir gratus fuit etiam morigerat?
Morbus devicrus quãdãm tuc fuerat datus Du quem pilatus cuncrer̃ tollc reatus
...rãm̃ q̃ in̄ pauctis tuatus? Noep scindro fuphat omnus ȟomo

Chantry Chapels

It is not generally realized that some of the richest carving and most gorgeous works of art in England are to be found in Chantry chapels. It is Perpendicular work at its best, of the end of the fifteenth century and beginning of the sixteenth century.

Chantry chapels contained the altar at which Mass would frequently be said for the repose of the souls of the founders and their relatives, or of the members of the guilds.

Chantry chapels and guild chapels were either erected within the church surrounded by a screen, or as an addition to the main structure by the extension of an aisle or otherwise.

Some of the best examples of the former are:

Berkshire	St George's Chapel, **Windsor**: There are two here – the Beaufort and Urswick chapels, both with iron grilles and full of colour.
Devon	**Paignton**: The Kirkham Chantry screen is sumptuous with panels depicting the Mass of St Gregory, and the Visitation.
Gloucestershire	**Tewkesbury** Abbey: The Despencer Chantry has a fan vault and a painting of the Trinity, and on top a rare medieval kneeling figure of Edward Despencer. There is also the Beauchamp Chantry which is very beautiful.
Hampshire	**Christchurch** Priory: The Salisbury Chantry, Caen stone. From floor to roof. Gothic and Renaissance. Large windows, tiers of niches and fan vault. **Winchester** Cathedral: There are five enchanting chantries here – Bishop William of Wykeham (very beautiful, with a figure of the Bishop), Bishop Fox (over 50 vaulted niches, all different), Bishop Gardiner (stone figure of a skeleton), Bishop

	Waynflete (elaborate, with a figure of the Bishop), and Cardinal Beaufort (fan vaulted, with a figure of the Cardinal).
Nottinghamshire	**Newark**: Thomas Meryng and Robert Markham both have Chantry chapels here.
Oxfordshire	**Burford**: There are both types at this church. The south aisle was the Guild chapel of the Guild of Merchants, and within the church is a delightful small wooden structure with a wooden canopy.
Somerset	**Wells** Cathedral has two Chantry chapels, Bishop Bubwith, 1424, and Treasurer Sugar, 1489. Identical in plan, but differing in details.
Sussex	**Boxgrove** Priory: The De la Warr Chantry chapel is notable as it shows a mixture of Gothic and Renaissance details.
Worcestershire	**Worcester** Cathedral: Prince Arthur's Chantry, 1504. Numbers of small figures.

Some of the best examples of a separate structure are:

Cambridgeshire	**Ely** Cathedral: There are two Chantry chapels at the east end – that of Bishop Alcock, with rich carving and a fan vault, and that of Bishop West.
Devon	**Cullompton**: The Lane aisle has a beautiful fan vault. **Tiverton**: The Greenway aisle is elaborately decorated.
London	**Westminster** Abbey: Henry VII's Chapel is a Chantry chapel. The fan vault, the figure sculpture of saints around the walls, and the bronze figures of the king and queen, as mentioned, are all superb.
Oxfordshire	**North Leigh** (Plate 82): The Wilcote Chapel. The lovely fan vault and typical large windows show Perpendicular architecture at its best.

Warwickshire   **Warwick**, St Mary's: The Beauchamp
                        Chapel, with its roof, glass, sculpture and
                        bronze figure is the most magnificent of all.
Wiltshire   **Bromham**: The ornate Tocotes and
                        Beauchamp chantry has a painted ceiling.
                        Devizes, St John's: A splendid example of
                        contrasts. The very ornate Perpendicular
                        Beauchamp Chapel adjoins the rich but
                        rather severe Norman chancel.

Stained Glass

Twelfth century

The largest collection in England is in **Canterbury** Cathedral.
The gorgeous colours are ruby and blue. Old and New
Testament subjects remain and also a series of figures from a
Jesse or Genealogy of Christ.

Two other churches must be mentioned:

Kent	**Brabourne**: A small Norman window retains its original glass – semicircles with flowers.
Oxfordshire	**Dorchester** Abbey (Plate 151): At the back of the fourteenth-century sedilia are four medallions of the life of St Birinus.

Thirteenth century

Grisaille glass was introduced. It was white glass with foliage
patterns so arranged that the leadwork also made patterns,
sometimes relieved with lines of colour. The famous example
is the Five Sisters window (five lancets, 55 feet high), in **York**
Minster.

    Canterbury Cathedral also has glass of this period, and
there is also much in **Lincoln** Cathedral.

    In parish churches there are some beautiful roundels in
Madley, Herefordshire, and **Aldermaston**, Berkshire, has two
bright red, blue and yellow roundels of the Annunciation and
Coronation of the Virgin.

Fourteenth century

All colours can now be found, but particularly red, green,
yellow and brown. They are of a very rich deep tone which
has never been excelled.

Gloucestershire	**Deerhurst**: St Catherine with her wheel is very lovely. It is like a rich jewel. **Gloucester** Cathedral: The east window is the largest medieval window in England. The Coronation of the Virgin, with Apostles, saints, bishops, kings and coats-of-arms. **Tewkesbury** Abbey: Well-known for its glass of this century. As the windows are high up, the gorgeous colours can be seen to perfection. There is a fine Last Judgment, and figures of prophets and historical personages.
Herefordshire	**Eaton Bishop**: Above kneeling benefactors are the Crucifixion, St Michael, and a delightful Virgin and Child, the former holding flowers and the latter a bird.
Kent	**Selling**: The east window is complete. Much grisaille glass and five coats-of-arms and figures of saints, including the Virgin and Child and St Margaret.
Lincolnshire	**Heydour**: Six figures of saints
Northampton-shire	**Stanford**: Much fine glass of the period remains in several windows – Apostles, saints and the Crucifixion. The east window is also glorious, but of the time of Henry VII, who is shown with his queen.
Oxfordshire	**Oxford** Cathedral: In the Latin Chapel is some fine glass of the Annunciation, the Virgin and Child, St Margaret, St Friedeswide, and St Catherine. Merton College Chapel: Much original glass remains. Some figures upon grisaille. Kneeling donor makes himself known!
Somerset	**Wells** Cathedral: Jesse Tree in the East window, saints in the clerestory, and some old glass in other windows.
Staffordshire	**Checkley**: Much glass, including the Crucifixion, St Margaret and the Martyrdom of St Thomas of Canterbury.

| Worcestershire | **Kempsey**: Eight figures, including St Margaret, St Catherine, and St Cuthbert. |
| Yorkshire | **York** (see page 318) |

York (see page 318)

Fifteenth century

The rectangular Perpendicular window tracery gave every possible scope to the glass painter, whose art was then reaching its highest point of development.

The colours were now generally lighter with much red, white and blue, and much yellow stain on white glass. Canopies become taller and heraldry becomes more popular.

Buckinghamshire	**Drayton Beauchamp**: The east window is filled with beautiful old glass of ten Apostles with their emblems.
Cambridgeshire	**Leverington**: A fine Jesse Tree of 61 figures, one half being original.
Cornwall	**St Kew**: Almost complete window of the Passion, with donors. The panel of the Washing of the Disciples' feet is particularly attractive. **St Neot**: This church is a 'must' for anyone interested in old glass. Numerous scenes show in detail the Creation and the Lives of Noah, St George and St Neot. There are also the Evangelists and other saints and donors. Tracery lights are also filled with old glass.
Devon	**Doddiscombsleigh** (Plate 148): The glass showing the Seven Sacraments is a great treasure, for it is the only complete one in England. Even so, the figure of Christ is modern (an original figure of Christ can however be seen not far away at **Cadbury**). Blood streams issue from the Wounds of Our Lord and reach to each Sacrament, which are charming little scenes, interesting liturgically as well as for costume. The

	bedroom scene is particularly attractive. In other windows are the Trinity (three figures crowned), and St Christopher, St Michael and St Peter.
Essex	**Margaretting**: The east window is a Jesse Tree formed by 24 vari-coloured figures.
Norfolk	**East Harling** (Plate 149): A well-known east window depicting the early life of Christ and His Passion. **Norwich**, St Peter Mancroft: A famous east window. Very large, with 42 panels. The Nativity, Passion, some saints (St Peter occurs several times), and donors. In the Nativity, the swaddling clothes are being warmed in front of a brazier, as the artist could only visualize Christmas in connection with our cold climate.
Oxfordshire	**Oxford**, All Souls College Chapel: The Twelve Apostles, the Four Latin Doctors, some female saints, and kings and bishops. New College Chapel: Prophets, Apostles, bishops and female saints. In the traceries are the Nine Orders of Angels. **Yarnton**: Various pieces of old glass throughout the church. Two fine feathered angels on red and blue backgrounds respectively. Nine quarries including some birds with scrolls.
Shropshire	**Ludlow**: The large east window has the life of St Lawrence in 27 panels. Elsewhere one can see the story of St Edward the Confessor and the palmers, Annunciation, Apostles and St Christopher.
Somerset	**East Brent**: A complete window of the Passion. **Langport**: The east window has the Annunciation, St Joseph of Arimathea with the Holy Grail, and a number of saints, including St Anthony, St Clement and St Dorothy. **Trull**: In the east window

148   Medieval glass of the Seven Sacraments at Doddiscombsleigh, Devon

is the Crucifixion with St Mary and St John, and in a side window are the three saints connected with a dragon – Michael, Margaret and George. **Winscombe**: An excellent example of donors with the original glass still above them – the Crucifixion with St Mary and St John and St Anthony. There are three figures, slightly later, completely of yellow-stain, and Burne-Jones glass, 1864.

Westmorland
Bowness: In the east window is the Crucifixion with St Mary and St John, with St George, St Barbara and St Catherine and donors.

Worcestershire
Great Malvern Priory: For fifteenth-century glass this church is the most complete in England. It is the Bible in glass. With Bishops of Worcester, saints and angels, we begin with the Creation, and continue with Noah, and Old Testament history, and from the New Testament we have Nativity scenes, Our Lord's Miracles, His Crucifixion, and in the east window scenes from His Passion.

Yorkshire
Almondbury: St Anne teaching the Virgin to read; on either side are St Barbara and St Margaret; also St Elizabeth, St John the Baptist, and St Helen. **Thornhill**: A Jesse Tree; also parts of a Doom, Nativity and Resurrection, and Assumption and Coronation of the Virgin. **York**: Anyone interested in old glass will thoroughly enjoy a visit here. There is so much in the Minster that a short summary is not possible. It must be studied in detail on the spot with the help of a guide book.

The same also applies to the York churches, many of which retain their old

149   Nativity, East Harling, Norfolk, fifteenth-century glass

glass. Special mention must, however, be made about two churches.

All Saints, North Street: There is much old glass in this church. The east window shows St John the Baptist, St Anne teaching the Virgin to read, and St Christopher, with donors below. The Works of Mercy can be seen, and a most remarkable window depicts the last 15 days of the world. The scenes are not far removed from the result of an atomic explosion (but the Church stands for something that will never end).

Holy Trinity, Goodramgate. The east window has St George, St John the Baptist, St John the Evangelist and St Christopher, below which a number of saints depict family life; a curious detail is that in two representations of the Holy Trinity the Son is not shown on the Cross.

Early sixteenth-century glass

The Renaissance influence begins to creep in with more detail and in consequence the main figures are not so clearly defined.

Buckinghamshire	**Hillesden**: This fine Perpendicular church has beautiful richly coloured glass of scenes from the exciting life of St Nicholas.
Cambridgeshire	**Cambridge**, King's College Chapel: This chapel and its glass are rightly world famous. The gorgeous colour of the glass and the white fan vault make a superb interior. As so often, the Crucifixion and Passion occupy the east window. The side windows are parallels between the Old and the New Testament, the Old Testament scenes pointing to the New (for example,

Jonah cast up by the whale is paired with the Resurrection of Christ).

Gloucestershire **Fairford**: As a complete series the glass here is unique. It is the Bible in glass. The whole faith of the Church is presented in vivid colours. All is original, except the top of the west window (damaged in a gale in the eighteenth century).

An interesting detail is that some scenes are typically English, whilst some others are characteristically Flemish.

The Passion occupies the east window, but otherwise we begin with Old Testament scenes, continuing with the early life of the Virgin, the Annunciation, the early life of Christ and the whole Gospel story up to Pentecost.

In the side windows the Twelve Apostles (with scrolls) and the Four Latin Doctors face prophets (also with scrolls) and the Four Evangelists. Similarly in the clerestory saints and martyrs face those who have persecuted the Church (with demons in the traceries). The great west window is a Last Judgment or Doom. Demons of many colours and shapes with red-hot irons drop their victims into cauldrons.

Staffordshire **Lichfield** Cathedral has some beautiful Flemish glass.

Early seventeenth-century glass

Enamels were now mostly used instead of the medieval pot-metals, leaded outlines disappeared, and small leaded rectangular panes took their place.

Oxford provides excellent examples. The most complete is in the Chapel of Lincoln College. In the east window are types and anti-types, scenes from the Old Testament foretelling scenes from the New Testament. In the side windows Apostles face prophets.

Glass of the period can also be well seen in the Chapels of University, Wadham and Queen's Colleges.

Armorial glass of the period can be well studied in **Yarnton** Church (previously mentioned).

Modern glass

Modern glass depicting the church itself and the countryside around it is attractive when seen at close quarters. Examples are:

Devon	**Dean Prior**
Essex	**Colne Engaine**
Middlesex	**Pinner**
Norfolk	**Ringstead**
Somerset	**Nettlecombe**

At **Selborne**, Hampshire, is a window of St Francis with every bird mentioned in Gilbert White's book.

Bright colours rightly often predominate in present-day glass. An example is at **Wellingborough**, Northamptonshire, where the symbols of the Four Evangelists are shown in two windows amidst such brightness.

Reference must also be made to a charming small lancet window in **Great Canfield** Church, Essex, with the flowers and birds at the times of the six festivals of Our Lady.

150   Sanctus bell turret, Castle Eaton, Wiltshire

Low-side Windows

These are sometimes called 'leper windows', but lepers were not, of course, allowed in public, and their hospitals had their own chapels. It would seem that a small bell was rung from them at the Sanctus (Holy, Holy, Holy) and at the Consecration of the Elements, so that the Real Presence might be known outside.

The lower part of these windows was nearly always separated from the upper part for a wooden shutter which could be opened. The shutter still remains at the excellent example at **Melton Constable**, Norfolk, where there is also a stone seat and a stone desk for a book for the server to follow the service and pull the rope of the bell at the appropriate moment.

These windows are most often found at the west end of the chancel, usually on the south side, but sometimes on the north side (particularly if the village is on that side), or even on both sides.

In many churches, however, the Sanctus bell was in its own turret at the east end of the nave, as at **Idbury**, Oxfordshire, which still has its original bell within it. Perhaps most remarkable of all is the turret at **Castle Eaton**, Wiltshire (Plate 150), which is a massive structure with a stone spirelet (and also its original bell).

At **Salhouse** and **Scarning** (Plate 126), Norfolk, the original small bell rung inside the church, the sacring bell, still remains and is attached to the rood-screen.

Piscinas

A piscina is a drain in a niche in the wall, usually surmounted by an arch and ornamented, if at all, in the same manner as doorways and arches of its period.

It is usually on the south side of the chancel near the High Altar. There may be two in the same wall, which, of course, indicates that the chancel has been lengthened (the western one being the earlier of the two). They are also found at the east end of aisles and sometimes in other places, and their presence always proves that there was an altar nearby originally.

In some early piscinas the drain is in a bracket projecting from the wall (as at **Skelton**, near York), or the bracket takes the form of a capital on a small pillar (as at **Finchampstead**, Berkshire).

Sometimes the piscina is a double one having two drains, and this type can broadly be assigned to the reign of Edward I (1272–1307). There was then a separate drain for the lavabo (washing of the priests' fingers before the Consecration) and the ablutions or rinsing of the chalice. Before that period one drain was used for both, and since that date the ablutions have always been consumed by the priest.

In the finest examples the piscina is united with the sedilia in one design.

Here are three beautiful double piscinas:

Cambridgeshire	**Cherry Hinton**: Typical trefoiled arches and dog-tooth ornament
Essex	**Barnston**: Also typical intersecting round arches and stiff-leaf foliage
Norfolk	**Carleton Rode**: Trefoiled arches with quatrefoil above

A local use in East Anglia is an angle piscina, cut out from the side of a window and with a shaft in the middle (as at **Great Snoring**, Norfolk).

Sedilia

These are seats, nearly always of stone and three in number, and either graded towards the east or on the same level. They are invariably found to the south of the altar and were used by the celebrant and his two assistants, the deacon and sub-deacon. They were occupied during the singing of the Creed and Gloria.

Very often the piscina and sedilia were constructed at the same time and are therefore of the same design.

Here are some of the finest sedilia of the different periods:

Norman

Essex	**Castle Hedingham**: Very rich zig-zag ornament on the round arches and richly carved capitals with foliage
Leicestershire	**Leicester**, St Mary de Castro: Very similar to the last. (This church also has a fine group of Early English sedilia.)

Transitional Norman

Derbyshire	**Monyash**: The segmental arches already have thirteenth-century dog-tooth and the capitals crude stiff-leaf foliage

Early English

Cambridgeshire	**Cherry Hinton**: Deeply moulded pointed arches and moulded capitals. (See under piscinas, page 325.)

151 Fourteenth-century Sedilia and Piscina, Dorchester Abbey, Oxfordshire

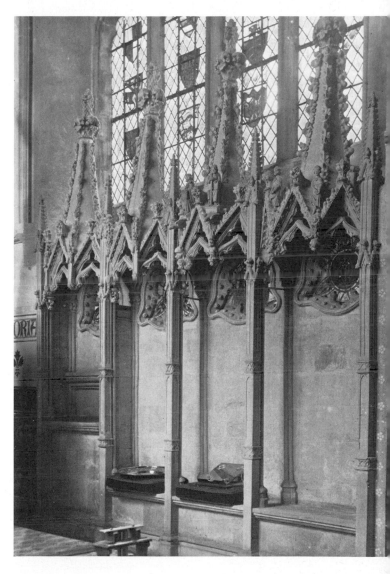

Decorated

Derbyshire	**Sandiacre**: Lofty canopies, richly crocketed
Gloucestershire	**Meysey Hampton**: Beautiful crocketed canopies and pinnacles
Lincolnshire	**Heckington**: The finest of all. Exuberant carving. Little vaults and figures of Christ and some saints.
Norfolk	**Besthorpe**: The crocketed canopies rise up into the window
Nottinghamshire	**Car Colston**: Typical crocketed arches and finials. **Hawton**: Very similar to Heckington which is high praise. A wonderful array of figures.
Oxfordshire	**Dorchester** Abbey (Plate 151): Rich canopies and the unique feature of small windows with twelfth-century glass
Yorkshire	**Beverley Minster**: They are of wood, a most unusual material for sedilia. They are four in number and are similar to the Percy screen and monument – nodding arches, heads as cusps, fruit amongst crockets and little vaults.

Perpendicular

Oxfordshire	**Adderbury**: The lovely fifteenth-century chancel has beautiful though restored sedilia.

152   *Fine fourteenth-century work, Easter Sepulchre, Hawton, Nottinghamshire*

Easter Sepulchres

An Easter Sepulchre is always on the north side of the chancel, usually in the sanctuary. The Blessed Sacrament was placed in an aperture of this structure on Good Friday and remained there until early on Easter Day. Most churches must have used a temporary structure or the top of an altar tomb. A few special structures of stone, mostly of the fourteenth century, do, however, remain.

The three finest examples are:

Lincolnshire	**Heckington**: Very rich Decorated work with figures and foliage. The sleeping soldiers are below, and above are the Risen Christ and the Three Marys.
Nottinghamshire	**Hawton** (Plate 152): Even richer Decorated work. Quite the finest. The sleeping soldiers are in the lower panels, and in the centre are the Resurrection and the Three Marys. Above is the Ascension, represented, as usual, by the two feet of Our Lord showing beneath a cloud, His two footprints being on the finial below. The Apostles gaze upwards.
Yorkshire	**Patrington**: Still of the Decorated period, but not so elaborate, but well preserved. Three soldiers, obviously asleep, below, and in the centre Christ rises from the tomb (rather awkwardly!) between two censing angels.

153   Altar rails, Swinbrook, Oxfordshire (note lolling figure)

Squints

These are apertures, usually oblique, cut through a wall, giving a view of an altar so that one could see the Elevation of the Host. There is an exceptionally long one at **West Chiltington**, Sussex.

Altar Rails

These were gradually introduced after the Reformation to protect the altar when screens were disappearing, and they

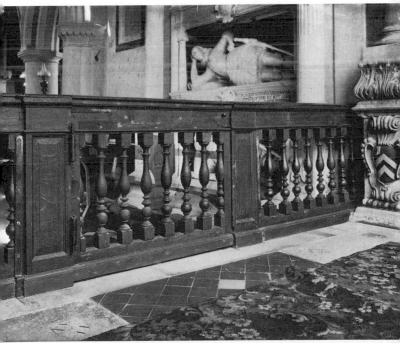

became popular in the time of Archbishop Laud in the seventeenth century to prevent the altar being moved into the body of the church (as desired by the Puritans) and to prevent dogs getting in. They are therefore nearly always of that period and of wood.

The balusters often have a central bulge, as at **Cliffe**, Kent, and **Swinbrook**, Oxfordshire (Plate 153), or they may take the form of columns, as at **Great Walsingham**, Norfolk. The twisted baluster type found at **Great Staughton**, Huntingdonshire, and **Branscombe**, Devon, is probably of the second half of the seventeenth century. The latter enclose the altar on four sides, but more usually they extend from wall to wall.

There are attractive wrought-iron rails at **Lydiard Tragoze**, Wiltshire, of the seventeenth century, and at **Derby** Cathedral, of the eighteenth century.

High Altar and Communion Tables

This is the focal point of the whole church. Here heaven and earth meet in the service commanded by Our Lord, 'Do this in remembrance of Me'. Angels and men join in the worship of the Holy Trinity, pleading before the eternal Father the timeless sacrifice of Christ, once offered on Calvary. The service of the Holy Communion, Eucharist, or Mass, is His perpetual memorial and the chief purpose for which the church was built.

Before the Reformation altars were of stone and the tops or mensa sometimes remain, although not often in their original position. They can always be identified by five crosses indented on them, one at each corner and one in the centre.

After the Reformation, altars were made of wood. Communion tables of Elizabethan and Jacobean date are handsomely carved and have bulbous legs. Here are five very fine examples:

154   Elizabethan Communion table, Carleton Rode, Norfolk

Devon	**Burlescombe**
Norfolk	**Carleton Rode** (Plate 154)
Somerset	**Minehead** and **Weston Zoyland**
Suffolk	**Blyford**

The altar should be long and low and covered with three linen cloths. There is usually an altar frontal of the colour of the day.

Reredoses

The reredos forms a back to the altar. It could be of stone or alabaster or painted wooden panels or just painted on the wall above, as at **St Albans** Cathedral.

There are seven magnificent stone altar screens or retables; in the Cathedrals of **St Albans** and **Winchester** (Plate 155), in the **Oxford** College chapels of All Souls College, Magdalen College and New College, and in **Ottery St Mary**, Devon, and **Christchurch** Priory, Hampshire. A beautiful modern example in gilt and colour is in **Wymondham** Abbey, Norfolk.

Reredoses of stone with figures of Christ and the Apostles in niches remain at **Bampton** and **Somerton**, Oxfordshire, the latter appropriately representing the Last Supper.

From fragments remaining we know that alabaster reredoses must have been gorgeous works of art, particularly if coloured and gilt. For proof, visit **Drayton**, Berkshire, and **Elham**, Kent. **Yarnton**, Oxfordshire (Plate 156), also still retains several panels.

There is a most remarkable fourteenth-century wooden reredos at the charming small thatched church of **Thornham Parva**, Suffolk; it has painted panels of the Crucifixion with St Mary and St John and other saints.

Beautiful painted wooden panels of a reredos can be seen in **Norwich** Cathedral and in **Romsey** Abbey, Hampshire.

The screens of **Attleborough** and **Ranworth**, Norfolk, formed reredoses to the side altars.

A splash of bright colour behind the altar is effective, and it undoubtedly follows medieval tradition. An example, in very modern idiom, is the High Altar of **Chichester** Cathedral.

Sanctuary Chairs

An old chair or chairs, frequently Jacobean, may often be found within the altar rails. A most elaborate one with carvings of the Entry into Jerusalem and the Wise Men is at **Ledbury**, Herefordshire. Somewhat different is the stone sanctuary chair at **Beverley Minster**, which is Saxon.

Church Plate

Pre-Reformation

Inventories show how rich cathedrals and churches were in the number and costliness of their sacred vessels and plate.

Very little survived the Reformation, so that we now have only about 55 chalices and 95 patens (nearly one half of them being in Norfolk) of pre-Reformation date in churches.

Chalices were then usually of silver-gilt, from six to eight inches in height, and consisted of a spreading base, a stem with a swelling or knob for handling easily, and a bowl. These parts differed slightly according to date.

The paten is a small, flat, circular cover for the chalice, but when in use the Sacred Host is placed upon it. There is always a depression in the centre of the paten with a design, both differing according to date.

Seven churches that have their medieval chalice and paten (the Head of Christ being on the paten unless otherwise mentioned) are very good examples:

Herefordshire	**Bacton** and **Leominster** Priory
Middlesex	**West Drayton** (now in the Victoria and Albert Museum for all to see)
Somerset	**Nettlecombe**
Staffordshire	**Hamstall Ridware** (Hand of God on paten)

156 The Three Wise Men, medieval reredos, Yarnton, Oxfordshire

Yorkshire   **Beswick** (Sacred monogram on paten).
                   Hinderwell (Lamb of God on paten)

Three churches have a beautiful medieval chalice, but no
paten:

Dorset   **Coombe Keynes**
Oxfordshire   **Little Faringdon**
Wiltshire   **Wylye** (Plate 157)

One of the earliest pre-Reformation patens is at **Weeke**,
Winchester, of about 1220. The engraving is of The Lamb of
God.

A particularly fine pre-Reformation paten is at **Cliffe**, Kent,
engraved with the Holy Trinity.

Post-Reformation

With the restoration of the communion in both kinds to the
laity a larger cup or chalice became necessary. The paten
changed as well.

The bowl of the Elizabethan chalice is rather like an
inverted bell. Innumerable Elizabethan examples exist in all
parts of the country, but most of all in Somerset.

Sometimes the name of the parish was engraved on the cup,
as at **Dersingham** and **Sall**, Norfolk.

157   Medieval chalice, 1525, Wylye, Wiltshire

Embroidery

There is evidence of the immense wealth of embroidered vestments and hangings possessed by English churches at the time of the Reformation. English needlework was renowned, for it was the finest in the world and was known as Opus Anglicanum.

It is tragic that so little remains. Most are fragments made into altar frontals. A number of copes remain unaltered, because they were not Mass vestments. They are mostly in museums or private ownership.

The materials used were always of the finest, velvet being especially favoured, and great quantities of metal thread, always of pure gold and silver, were employed.

For decoration, angels on wheels, lion masks, double-headed eagles and leopards' heads were popular. Scenes from the life of Our Lord and the saints were shown most realistically.

Copes were often adorned with orphreys with figures of saints under canopies.

The most famous cope remaining is that in the Victoria and Albert Museum, **London**, from Syon Abbey, **Isleworth**, Middlesex. It is of the late thirteenth century and all the splendid figures show the 'S' bend then becoming fashionable.

Some idea of the beauty of this medieval work can still be gained from some cathedrals (**Carlisle** and **Durham**) and churches as follows, where the examples will usually be found in a glass frame on the wall (and covered by a curtain, so always look behind a curtain!):

Devon	**Barnstaple** and **Culmstock**
Gloucestershire	**Baunton**, **Buckland**, **Chipping Campden** (a cope and pair of altar frontals), and **Cirencester**
Kent	**East Langdon** (representation of the Annunciation)

158   Medieval embroidery, Great Bircham, Norfolk (now in St Peter Hungate, Norwich)

Lincolnshire	**Careby**
Norfolk	**Great Bircham** (Plate 158 – now in St Peter, Hungate, **Norwich**) and **Lyng**
Oxfordshire	**Forest Hill**
Shropshire	**Alveley**
Somerset	**Othery**
Wiltshire	**Hullavington** and **Sutton Benger**

A medieval hearse cloth belonging to **Dunstable** Priory, Bedfordshire, is now in the Victoria and Albert Museum.

In Elizabethan times and in the seventeenth century, devotion to the Church continued, as is proved by embroidery still so lovingly worked. The following churches provide good examples. All are altar frontals.

Hampshire	**Mattingley** and **St Mary Bourne**
Herefordshire	**Bacton**
Kent	**Hollingbourne**
Northampton-shire	**Weston Favell** (appropriately showing the Last Supper)

Today ornamental work is sometimes effectively bestowed upon hassocks (kneelers). The small Cotswold church of **Quenington**, Gloucestershire, has a varied and colourful collection. The background for all the hassocks at **Ockham**, Surrey (Plate 64), is the group of seven lancets.

Organs

Before the Reformation most churches had an organ on the rood-loft, hence the meaning of organ-loft. The Puritans strongly objected to beauty and joy, and no pre-Reformation organ case remains in England, but there is one at **Old Radnor** in Wales.

   St Paul's Cathedral and **Bristol Cathedral** have notable seventeenth-century organ cases, and in parish churches they will be found at:

Gloucestershire	**Winchcombe** and **Wotton-under-Edge**
London	The churches of the **City** of London, rebuilt by Sir Christopher Wren, vied with one another over their organs, both in the tone of the instruments and in the beauty of their cases, such as at St Clement's, Eastcheap, and St Magnus, London Bridge.
Northampton-shire	**Stanford**: The organ is in perfect harmony with this attractive interior
Suffolk	**Framlingham**: Originally in Pembroke College Chapel, **Cambridge**
Norfolk	**Great Yarmouth**: A modern case beautifully coloured

West Galleries

After the destruction of rood-lofts at the Reformation, choir, organ and band moved to a gallery erected for the purpose at the west end of the church. The village orchestra in the West gallery was a leading feature of church life until the middle of the nineteenth century when a surpliced choir of men and boys was placed in the chancel.

At **Strensham**, Worcestershire, the panels of the rood-loft have actually been transferred to form the front of the West gallery.

Good examples of early seventeenth-century galleries are at:

Dorset	**Puddletown**: Connected with Thomas Hardy, who often refers to village orchestras
Gloucestershire	**Bishop's Cleeve**
Shropshire	**Moreton Say**
Somerset	**East Brent**

Candelabra or Chandeliers

Rowlstone, Herefordshire, has two thirteenth-century iron brackets ornamented with cocks and with prickets (or spikes) for candle-stocks; in one the tails of the cocks are up and in the other they are down, for variety!

Bristol Cathedral has a magnificent medieval bronze candelabrum. It was the forerunner of those which were so popular in the seventeenth and eighteenth centuries.

They are of brass, having usually two tiers of branched candlesticks on gracefully curved stems springing from a central globe, which generally bears the name of the donor and the date. They are found throughout the country and they always enhance a church. Often the suspension-rod is of fine wrought iron-work.

Here are some excellent examples, taken quite at random:

Devon	**Ashburton** and **Braunton**
Gloucestershire	**Wickwar** (two)
Kent	**Ightham**
Lincolnshire	**Bourne** and **Frampton**
Somerset	**Axbridge**, **Stogumber** and **Wedmore**
Surrey	**Lingfield**
Sussex	**Mayfield**

Family Pews

Such pews followed after Chantry chapels had ceased. They could be open above, as in the splendid Elizabethan example at **Holcombe Rogus**, Devon. More usually they had a canopy making them rather like a four-poster bed, as at **Tawstock**, Devon, **Rycote**, Oxfordshire, and **Stokesay**, Shropshire. Later they were often elevated, as at **Tibenham**, Norfolk, **Warbleton**, Sussex, and **Croft**, Yorkshire, which has a wide balustraded staircase. Later still the pew developed into a cosy furnished apartment with comfortable upholstered armchairs, padded benches, table, carpet, fireplace, and a separate entrance direct from the big house. **Gatton**, Surrey, is a perfect example. **Esher** (the old church) in the same county also retains this interesting feature of former worship.

Libraries and Chained Books

For this subject, **Hereford** must be visited. The Cathedral has the largest library of chained books with about 2,000 volumes, of which about 1,500 are chained. All Saints' Church in the same city also has a notable library of 328 volumes cunningly chained.

Other large libraries with chained books are at **Wimborne** Minster, Dorset, **Cartmel** Priory, Lancashire, and **Grantham**, Lincolnshire.

The seventeenth-century cupboards and fittings of the library at **Langley Marish**, Buckinghamshire, are unaltered and are charming.

Tiles

There were usually two colours only, red and yellow. The fleur-de-lys was very popular and also armorial bearings. Worcestershire and Devon are the best counties for medieval tiles.

The entire floor of the Chapter House at **Westminster** Abbey is composed of decorated encaustic tiles. In parish churches more or less complete floors remain at **West Hendred**, Berkshire, and **Hailes**, Gloucestershire.

Examples can also be well studied at:

Cornwall	**Launcells**
Devon	**Cadeleigh**, **Haccombe** and **Westleigh**
Kent	**Brook**
Somerset	**Old Cleeve** and **Watchet**
Worcestershire	**Bredon**, **Cotheridge**, **Great Malvern** Priory (wall decoration), **Little Malvern** Priory and **Shelsley Walsh**

Consecration Crosses

At the consecration of the church the bishop anointed 12 places inside the church and 12 places on its outside. Those inside were usually marked by 12 crosses painted on the walls.

There are several at **Carleton Rode**, Norfolk, two bright red crosses adorn the east wall of **Bishop's Sutton**, Hampshire, and one still exists below the remarkable wall-painting at **Chaldon**, Surrey (Plate 110).

Exterior ones can be found at **Uffington**, Berkshire, **Ottery St Mary**, Devon, and **Moorlynch**, Somerset.

Votive Crosses and Graffiti

Little scratchings can sometimes be seen on doorways or elsewhere. They may be votive crosses (made as evidence of a vow) or masons' or merchants' marks.

Scratchings of figures and buildings are known as graffiti. They can be well studied inside the churches of **Compton**, Surrey, and **Ashwell**, Hertfordshire, which has a notable one of Old St Paul's.

Two large incised figures of a manticore and a leopard on the outside walls of **North Cerney**, Gloucestershire, are unique.

Aumbries and Banner-stave Lockers

A plain oblong opening originally with a wooden door is an aumbry in which the altar plate would have been kept. The doors still remain at **Great Walsingham**, Norfolk, and **Rothersthorpe**, Northamptonshire.

A tall narrow recess up to 12 feet high would have been for the storage of the long staves of banners. They are most common in east Suffolk and east Norfolk. The one at **Barnby**, Suffolk, still retains its original door.

Dole Cupboards

A dole cupboard, or shelf, was for bread for the poor bequeathed by some kind benefactor. Many are still used for that purpose.

Examples can be seen at **St Albans** Cathedral, Hertfordshire, All Saints', **Hereford**, and **Milton Ernest**, Bedfordshire (brightly coloured).

Anchorite Cells

These were very small apartments which were in effect the walling-up for life of the anchorite. These cells were situated on the cold north side of the sanctuary with one aperture inside to the High Altar and another outside for food.

The form of service of such walling-up is known and there is definite evidence at **Compton** and **Shere**, Surrey. Both these churches are delightful in beautiful settings. At **Compton** there is also a unique Norman upper chancel used probably by pilgrims on the Pilgrims' Way. It has a Norman wooden screen which is the oldest in England and is as hard as iron.

It must, of course, be remembered that the chancel may have been extended further eastwards since the anchorite or anchoress was in residence.

Stations of the Cross

These are modern pictures or carvings of scenes of Our Lord's Passion, and may be seen on the walls of some churches (Plate 105). If bright and colourful they can enhance a church. They are, of course, carrying on the tradition of medieval wall-paintings.

Good examples can be found at **Chesterfield**, Derbyshire, and **Brede**, Sussex.

Alms Boxes

A visit to an old church should be enjoyable, and it will be one's wish, not a burden, to give something for the maintenance of the work of the Church and the upkeep of the fabric, simply out of gratitude for our heritage and that it may continue to function for hundreds of years to come as it has done for hundreds of years past.

Vandalism is not new. If one is interested in ingenuity, one cannot do better than study the intricacies involved in making the contents of a medieval alms box absolutely safe.

There are four pre-Reformation alms boxes in East Anglia, namely at **Cawston**, **Loddon**, and **Ludham**, Norfolk, and **Blythburgh**, Suffolk.

After the dissolution of the monasteries, the relief of the poor became a pressing necessity.

At **Watton**, Norfolk, the box is held by a wooden figure of a beggar dated 1639, and at **Pinhoe**, Devon (Plate 159), a particularly well-dressed gentleman calls himself 'Ye Poor Man of Pinhoe, 1700'.

At **Tunworth**, Hampshire, two sides of the box have a quaintly carved human face with open lips, which serve as the money slots – one figure puts his tongue out, perhaps appropriately at the amount of the donation!

The Instruments of the Passion

They comprise the Five Wounds, the crown of thorns, ladder, three nails, hammer, pincers, scourges, whipping pillar, cords, lantern, three dice, seamless robe, spear, sponge on a reed, thirty pieces of silver or a bag of silver, cock, jug of vinegar, basin, and the fist that buffeted Him.

159   Alms box, Ye Poor Man of Pinhoe, 1700, Devon

Emblems of the Twelve Apostles

St Peter: keys
St Andrew: Cross Saltire (x shaped)
St John the Evangelist: chalice with dragon emerging
St James the Great: scallop shell and pilgrim's staff
St James the Less: fuller's club (a long club with a bend at the lower end)
St Thomas: spear
St Philip: loaves or a basket of loaves
St Bartholomew: flaying knife
St Matthias: axe (or sword or scimitar)
St Simon: fish (or saw or oar)
St Jude: boat
St Matthew: sword or scimitar (or axe)
St Paul: sword

Symbols of the Four Evangelists

St Matthew: angel
St Mark: lion
St Luke: ox
St John: eagle

The Four Latin Doctors

St Augustine: bishop or doctor
St Ambrose: bishop
St Gregory: pope in tiara
St Jerome: cardinal

Emblems of some other 'popular' saints

St John the Baptist: Lamb of God with banner on a book
St Michael, St George and St Margaret: dragon
St Lawrence: gridiron
St Stephen: stones
St Anthony: pig
St Edmund: arrow
St Catherine of Alexandria: wheel
St Mary Magdalene: vase of ointment
St Apollonia: tooth in pincers
St Dorothy: basket of flowers
St Barbara: tower
St Edward the Confessor holds a ring
St Clement: anchor
St Leonard: chains

Sacred Monograms

IHC or IHS: Abbreviated Greek for Jesus
XP or XPC: Abbreviated Greek for Christ
INRI: Latin initials for Jesus of Nazareth, King of the Jews.

A fish was an early Christian symbol because the initial letters of the Greek words for Jesus Christ Son of God Saviour form the Greek word for fish.

A lamb with a halo and a banner represents the Lamb of God, Agnus Dei, that is, Christ.

Conclusion

When all the churches and cathedrals mentioned in this book have been visited, one might like to make a list of the finest. What would be the first half dozen exteriors?

Most lists would probably contain **Canterbury** Cathedral central tower (Plate 1), **Beverley Minster** west towers (Plate 24), Magdalen tower, **Oxford** (Plate 21), and the stone spires of **Salisbury** Cathedral and **Louth**, Lincolnshire (Plate 44). The sixth should be the Somerset tower of your choice, from, say, **Leigh-on-Mendip** (Plate 9), **Evercreech** (Plate 10), or **Chewton Mendip** (Plate 11) (or perhaps another one as all are so beautiful).

The choice of interiors is more difficult. King's College Chapel, **Cambridge**, might head the list, but surely the most beautiful parish church interior is **Walpole St Peter**, Norfolk. **Sall**, Norfolk, and **Blythburgh**, Suffolk, are 'musts', but they rather lack colour, which is so prominent at **Thaxted**, Essex. Colour is certainly the making of the really lovely small Cornish church of **Blisland**, and there we have six.

Perpendicular work at its best will also be found at **Blakeney** (Plate 160), **Cawston** and **Terrington St Clement**, Norfolk, and **Lavenham**, **Long Melford** and **Southwold**, Suffolk, and in the delightful smaller churches of the same period at **Shelton**, Norfolk, and **Denston**, Suffolk.

In contrast to East Anglia, the churches of the West Country are equally charming, as are **Mullion**, Cornwall, and **Plymtree**, Devon (Plate 123), both so typical of that area.

Then again what could be more delightful and worshipful than the tiny churches of Sussex with their beautiful lancet triplets, which form such a perfect background to the altar?

Cathedral interiors usually rather suffer from being of different dates and rather split up by screens and chapels. This is, however, as it should be, as one should be lead gradually and by stages to the High Altar.

It has, however, continually been stressed that it is the simple unassuming churches that are the real gems, probably

160   East Anglia at its best, Blakeney, Norfolk

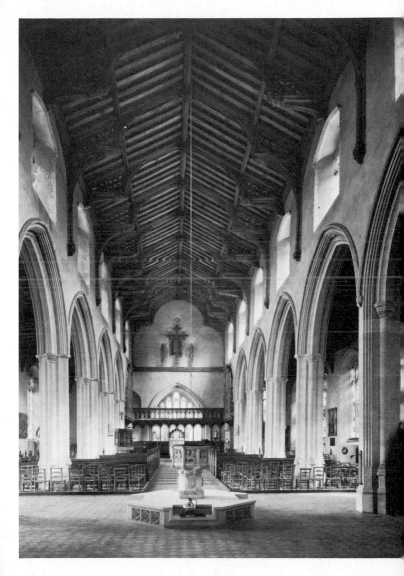

tucked away in some remote spot, unknown (fortunately by restorers) and rarely visited. For instance, **Widford**, Oxfordshire, isolated in the middle of fields by the River Windrush, has a Roman pavement, which, if it were in a house, would be visited by thousands of tourists. If you should be interested in Roman work, then **Ickleton**, Cambridgeshire, has amazing Roman monolith piers.

Small churches packed full of original fittings are always a joy, such as **South Burlingham**, Norfolk, and **Trull**, Somerset (Plate 117). For all periods in one church, from Saxon to the present time, a visit to **North Leigh**, Oxfordshire, is recommended.

We end with a brief summary of a few special glories:

Roofs	**Knapton**, Norfolk (Plate 73), **Hopton**, Suffolk, **Bere Regis**, Dorset (Plate 75), **Cullompton**, Devon (Plate 71) and King's, **Cambridge**
Fonts	**Little Walsingham**, Norfolk
Font Covers	**Ufford**, Suffolk (Plate 105)
Wall-paintings	**Pickering**, Yorkshire (Plate 109)
Benches	**Two Wiggenhalls** – St Mary the Virgin and St Germans, and **Great Walsingham**, Norfolk, and **Fressingfield**, Suffolk
Pulpits	Wood – **Long Sutton**, Somerset. Stone – **Bovey Tracey**, **Dittisham** (Plate 119) and **Harberton** (Plate 120), Devon
Rood-screen panels	**Ranworth** and **Beeston Regis**, Norfolk, and **Ashton** (Plate 131) and **Wolborough**, Devon
Rood-lofts	**Attleborough**, Norfolk, and **Flamborough**, Yorkshire (Plate 133)
Stalls	In some of the greater churches of the north of England, as mentioned
Monuments	**Ewelme**, Oxfordshire, and **Tawstock**, Devon
Glass	**York** Minster and churches, **Great Malvern** Priory, and **Fairford**

Very good work in churches is being done today, particularly by a certain firm of colour specialists.

The extension of our latest cathedral, **Bury St Edmunds**, Suffolk, is in traditional style and is a worthy addition.

Perhaps there could be a final brief note on the beautiful interior of St Mary and All Saints, **Potters Bar**, of 1915 in Gothic style with a west window of 1967 in modern style as fine as any contemporary work anywhere. The church, now in Hertfordshire, is the most northerly parish in the Diocese of **London**, and of which the author has been churchwarden for many years.

The primary object of the medieval builder was to erect a building to the glory of God and His worship, and to express worthily man's belief in the majesty and greatness of God. That is why they are so beautiful – God was put first and not the number of people who might use it.

The piety and love for God of past generations have given each village and old town its crowning glory, its old church.We now have the privilege of being trustees of this priceless heritage and we must not fail in that trust.

Many old churches require thousands of pounds just to keep them wind and watertight. The smallest community (with a huge church) makes heroic efforts, but outside help is vital, and so The Historic Churches Preservation Trust, whose office is at Fulham Palace, **London** S.W.6, has been established for the urgent and important task of raising money to augment local effort, and this is as it should be, for this heritage belongs to all.

The writer stresses the title of the Trust at his lectures for at one meeting he was introduced as representing the Society for the Prevention of Churches! On another occasion he was referred to as the prehistoric churchman!

There is also a society called The Friends of Friendless Churches which helps to preserve churches threatened with collapse and outside the scope of other organizations.

The death-watch beetle is the great enemy today. He, like the congregation, is encouraged by more warmth in old churches.

We must keep the flag flying. It is the red cross of St George on a white background and it should have the arms of its diocese in the first quarter.

Every old church is unique, though all have something in common – the need of man to look beyond himself to something greater, the God of Love and Beauty, as revealed by Our Blessed Lord. In each there is worship, the administration of the Sacraments, and the atmosphere of devotion of hundreds of years. The latter is so often overlooked today, but the unseen can be more important than the seen.

Our glorious churches are not just showpieces. Each is the House of God and the Gate of Heaven in our villages and towns. The village church with its tower or spire dominates the English scene; pointing upwards, it advertises both the fact and the purpose of its existence.

These old churches are still sermons in stone and living witnesses of the Faith for which they were built, and it is our privilege to use them and preserve them for posterity. Let us do so to the greater glory of God, and thereby also fulfil the true purpose of human life – to love, serve and praise God.

Index of Subjects

Alms Boxes, 347
Altar Rails, 331
Anchorite Cells, 347
Arcades, 164
Architectural periods, 19
Aumbries, 346

Banner-stave lockers, 346
Belfries, timber, 81
Bell-cotes, 71
Bells, 80
Benches, 218
   East Anglia, 218
   West Country, 222
Bishops' Thrones, 270
Books, chained, 344
Brasses, 301

Candelabra, 343
Cartouche Tablets, 300
Cathedral styles, 162
Chairs, Sanctuary, 337
Chantry Chapels, 310
Chapter Houses, 163
Chests, 208
Churchyards, 26
Clerestories, 105
Clock-jacks, 104
Clocks, 104
Communion Tables, 332
Complete churches, 164
   Decorated, 170
   Early English, 170
   Norman and Transitional,
     166
   Perpendicular, 174
   Renaissance, 177
   Saxon, 164
Conclusion, 352
Corbel-tables, 126
County boundaries, 13
Crosses
   Churchyard, 26
   Consecration, 345
   Votive, 346
Crypts, 132

Dole cupboards, 346
Doors, 120
Doorways, 115

Easter Sepulchres, 329
Emblems of Apostles, Evangelists
   and Saints, 350
Embroidery, 340

Figure sculpture, 126
Font Covers, 204
Fonts, 186

Galleries, West, 343
Gargoyles, 124
Glass, 313
Graffiti, 346
Gravestones, 26

Hatchments, 274
High Altar, 332
Hour-glasses, 240

Interiors, 181
   Charming, 182
   Devotion and Colour, 184
   Eighteenth century furnishings, 181
   Medieval furnishings, 184
Introduction, 17

Lecterns, 228
Ledger Stones, 300
Libraries, 344
Low-side windows, 323
Lych-gates, 26

Mass dials, 128
Misericords, 271
Monograms, Sacred, 351
Monuments, 279
   Bronze, 279
   Eighteenth century, 297
   Medieval, 280
   Seventeenth century, 287
   Tudor, 284
   Wood, 279

Organs, 342
Orientation, 131

Passion, Instruments of the, 349
Pews, Family, 344
Piscinas, 325
Plan, 129
Plate, 337
Porches, 108
Pulpits, 230
    Stone, 234
    Wood, 230

Reredoses, 334
Rood Celures, 263
Rood-lofts, 260
Rood-screens, 242
    Painted panels, 244
    Devon, 252
    East Anglia, 247
Roofs, Exterior, 132
Roofs, Interior, 145
    Hammer-beam, 148
    Tie-beam, 145
    Wagon, 146
Round churches, 130
Royal Arms, 276

Sedilia, 326
Situation, 20
Spires, 81
    Lead, 83
    Stone-Broach, 88

Stone-Parapet, 92
Timber, 81
Wren, 97
Squints, 331
Stalls, 264
Stations of the Cross, 347
Stoups, Holy Water, 114
Sundials, 128

Tiles, 345
Towers, 31
    Brick, 44
    Cathedrals, 74
    Detached, 48
    Different periods, 63
    Dorset, 36
    East Anglia, 38
    Gabled, 48
    Notable, 52
    Round, 50
    Somerset, 31
    Timber, 81
    West Country, 36
Two churches together, 28

Vaulting, 156
Villages, prettiest, 22

Wall-paintings, 209
Weather-vanes, 102
Windows, 133

Yew Trees, 27

Index of Places

Abbotsbury, 234
Abbotsham, 223
Acle, 51, 197
Aconbury, 112
Acton, 301, 308
Adderbury, 88, 96, 126, 144, 328
Addlethorpe, 108, 120
Adel, 115, 120, 166, 168
Affpuddle, 36
Aldbourne, 25
Aldermaston, 313
Aldham, 51
Aldwincle St. Peter, 89
Alfold, 81
Alford, 234
Almondbury, 318
Alne, 115
Alphington, 109, 254
Altarnun, 176, 188, 222
Alveley, 341
Amberley, 135, 166
Ampney Crucis, 26
Anstey, 26
Appleton-le-Street, 64
Ardleigh, 108
Ardley, 48
Arncliffe, 21
Arundel, 283, 284, 286
Asgarby, 94
Ashbourne, 281, 285, 297
Ashburnham, 294
Ashburton, 38, 142, 344
Ashby St. Ledgers, 244
Ash-next-Sandwich, 83
Ashover, 195, 285
Ashton, 246, 254, 354
Ashwell, 346
Ashwellthorpe, 281
Aslacton, 51
Astbury, 146, 184, 206, 228, 244
Aston, 116
Aston Eyre, 116
Athelington, 220
Atherington, 260
Attleborough, 243, 247, 260, 334, 354
Aunsby, 89

Avebury, 194, 260
Averham, 52
Avington, Berks, 168, 188
Avington, Hants, 70, 178
Awliscombe, 244
Axbridge, 32, 344
Aylesbury, 188
Aylesford, 23
Aylsham, 41, 247, 305
Aymestrey, 244
Aythorpe Roding, 81

Bacton, Herefordshire, 337, 342
Bacton, Norfolk, 41, 43
Bacton, Suffolk, 149
Baddiley, 182, 276
Badingham, 149, 200
Badsey, 52
Bagendon, 48
Bakewell, 20
Balsham, 244, 267, 302
Bamburgh, 21
Bampton, 88, 334
Banningham, 149
Banwell, 32, 184, 204, 235, 242
Bapchild, 82
Bardfield Saling, 50
Barford St. Michael, 115
Barfreston, 116, 126, 128, 134, 168
Barking, Suffolk, 145
Barnack, 88, 115, 164
Barnby, 346
Barnetby, 195
Barnham, 135
Barnham Broom, 243
Barningham, 220, 244
Barnstaple, 83, 340
Barnston, 325
Barrowden, 90
Barthomley, 53, 146
Bartlow, 50, 80, 209, 212
Barton-on-Humber, 64, 133
Barton Turf, 247
Barwick, 223
Batcombe, 32
Bath, 31, 58, 106

Bathampton, 52
Batheaston, 34
Battle, 286
Baunton, 212, 340
Bawburgh, 51, 132
Beaminster, 36
Beccles, 44, 48, 110
Bedingham, 51, 243
Beeford, 62
Beeston-next-Mileham, 138
Beeston Regis, 50, 247, 354
Begbroke, 48
Belaugh, 41, 247
Bere Regis, 152, 354
Berkswell, 112, 126, 132
Berry Pomeroy, 242
Besford, 260
Bessingby, 194
Bessingham, 51
Besthorpe, 136, 137, 138, 290, 328
Beswick, 338
Bettws Newydd, 260
Beverley, 52, 62, 129, 138, 146,
   152, 156, 266, 272, 273, 284, 306,
   328, 337, 352
Bewcastle, 26
Bigbury, 230
Billingborough, 94
Binfield, 240
Birdbrook, 81
Birkin, 115, 168
Bisham, 287
Bishop Burton, 25
Bishop's Cleeve, 343
Bishop's Hull, 223
Bishop's Lydeard, 34, 223, 234, 242
Bishop's Sutton, 345
Bishop's Tawton, 288
Bishopsteignton, 115
Bishopstone, 294
Bisley, 189
Bitton, 53
Black Bourton, 215
Blackmore, 81
Bladon, 26
Blagdon, 34
Blakeney, 41, 135, 149, 352
Blandford, 178
Blankney, 70
Bleadon, 32, 235
Bledlow, 188

Bletchingley, 300
Blisland, 184, 352
Blofield, 41
Bloxham, 96
Blyford, 333
Blythburgh, 104, 106, 146, 176, 220,
   349, 352
Boarhunt, 165
Bobbing, 55
Boconnoc, 20
Bodmin, 188
Bolam, 21, 64
Bosbury, 48
Bosham, 135, 164
Bossall, 126
Boston, 55, 272
Bottesford, Leicestershire, 94, 285, 302
Bottesford, Lincolnshire, 170
Boughton Monchelsea, 26
Boughton-under-Blean, 55
Bourne, 344
Bovey Tracey, 228, 234, 242, 354
Bowness, 318
Boxford, 80, 112
Boxgrove, 81, 135, 156, 168, 311
Boxted, 280, 298
Boyton, 135
Brabourne, 74, 313
Bracebridge, 64
Brackley, 70, 102
Bradenham, 23
Bradfield, 43
Bradfield Combust, 214
Bradford Abbas, 36
Bradford-on-Avon, 166
Bradninch, 38, 242, 254
Bradwell-juxta-Coggeshall, 182
Bradwell-on-Sea, 165
Brailes, 196
Bramfield, 48, 132, 244, 252, 292
Brancepeth, 234
Branscombe, 332
Brant Broughton, 94
Braughing, 23, 263
Braunton, 83, 223, 344
Brayton, 115, 166
Breage, 212, 214
Breamore, 165
Breccles, 188
Brede, 347
Bredon, 345

Breedon-on-the-Hill, 21, 164
Brent Knoll, 32, 145, 223, 292
Brentor, 21
Brenzett, 81
Brewood, 286
Bridekirk, 188
Bridford, 256
Brightlingsea, 41
Brighton, 192
Brightwell Baldwin, 305, 308
Brington, 89
Brinkburn, 21
Brinkworth, 234
Brinsop, 116
Brisley, 41
Brislington, 34
Bristol, 105, 157, 163, 267, 272, 342,
    343
Brixworth, 165
Broad Clyst, 174
Broadwater, 302
Broadwell, 88
Brockenhurst, 28
Bromham, 312
Brook, 212, 215, 345
Brookland, 48, 82, 102, 195
Broomfield, Essex, 50, Somerset, 225
Brougham, 21, 178
Broughton, Buckinghamshire, 214
Broughton, Huntingdonshire, 89
Bruton, 32, 145
Brympton D'Evercy, 20, 71
Buckland, 340
Buckland-in-the-Moor, 254
Buckworth, 89
Bugbrooke, 244
Bulwick, 94
Bungay, 41
Burford, 311
Burgh-le-Marsh, 234
Burgh-next-Aylsham, 40
Burlescombe, 333
Burnham Deepdale, 188
Burnham Norton, 230
Burpham, 135, 168
Burrington, 242
Burstow, 81
Burwash, 135
Bury, Huntingdonshire, 68, 228
Bury, Sussex, 82
Bury St. Edmunds, 106, 149, 355

Bywell St. Andrew, 64

Cadbury, 315
Cadeleigh, 345
Caldecote, 114
Cambridge, 64, 80, 130, 142, 156, 164,
    176, 177, 228, 267, 271, 272, 302,
    320, 342, 352, 354
Cameley, 184
Canterbury, 52, 74, 132, 162, 279,
    281, 285, 313, 352
Capel, 215
Carbrooke, 43
Car Colston, 328
Cardinham, 222
Careby, 341
Carhampton, 242
Carleton Rode, 247, 325, 333, 345
Carlisle, 162, 244, 264, 272, 340
Cartmel, 267, 272, 344
Cartmel Fell, 21
Cassington, 129
Castle Acre, 204, 232, 247
Castle Ashby, 302
Castle Combe, 25
Castle Eaton, 324
Castle Frome, 192
Castle Hedingham, 44, 134, 152, 326
Castle Rising, 188
Castor, 66, 164
Catherington, 288
Cattistock, 70
Cavendish, 24, 26, 106, 142
Caversfield, 48
Cawston, 43, 149, 243, 248, 349, 352
Cerne Abbas, 36, 234
Chaddesley Corbett, 194
Chalbury, 182
Chaldon, 215, 345
Chalgrove, 215
Chalton, 136
Charing, 55
Charlton-on-Otmoor, 244
Charminster, 36
Charney Bassett, 116
Chartham, 140, 301
Chasleton, 20
Chawleigh, 242
Chearsley, 185
Checkley, 314
Cheddar, 32

Cheddington, 232
Chediston, 197
Chedworth, 235
Chedzoy, 34
Chelvey, 52
Cherry Hinton, 325, 326
Chester, 146, 264, 272
Chesterfield, 84, 347
Chester-le-Street, 96
Chew Magna, 34, 280, 283, 286
Chew Stoke, 34
Chewton Mendip, 34, 352
Chichester, 166, 216, 266, 272, 334
Chignal Smealy, 44, 201
Chigwell, 304
Chilham, 23, 297
Chillingham, 281
Chinnor, 308
Chipping Campden, 53, 176, 308, 340
Chipping Norton, 106
Chipping Ongar, 102
Chirton, 52
Chiselhampton, 178
Chittlehampton, 36, 234
Chivelstone, 230, 254
Chrishall, 306
Christchurch, 13, 36, 272, 310, 334
Chudleigh, 254
Chulmleigh, 38, 242
Church Brampton, 89, 208
Church Handborough, 94, 116, 244
Churchill, 292
Cirencester, 176, 235, 340
Clanfield, 127
Clare, 228
Claverley, 215
Claypole, 94, 174
Clayton, 216
Clee, 64
Cley, 110, 135
Cliffe, 332, 338
Clifton Reynes, 280
Climping, 135, 170
Coates, 185
Cobham, 306
Coddenham, 106, 149
Coldridge, 230, 242
Colebrooke, 204, 242
Coleshill, 192
Colne Engaine, 322
Combe, 209

Combe Florey, 38
Combe-in-Teignhead, 223
Combe Martin, 146
Combs, 43
Compton, 82, 346, 347
Compton Bassett, 240, 244
Condover, 286, 292
Congresbury, 204
Coningsby, 104
Conington, Cambridgeshire, 80
Conington, Huntingdonshire, 53
Coombe Keynes, 338
Copford, 214
Corhampton, 28, 165
Cotes-by-Stow, 184, 260
Cotheridge, 345
Cottingham, 140
Cotton, 118, 149
Covehithe, 43
Coventry, 84, 162
Cowden, 81
Cowfold, 304
Cowlam, 186
Coxwold, 62
Cranmore, 32
Cratfield, 200
Crediton, 208
Crewkerne, 34, 146, 176
Croft, Lincolnshire, 184, 234
Croft, Yorkshire, 344
Cromer, 41
Crondall, 301
Croome D'Abitot, 296
Croscombe, 234, 244
Croughton, 215
Crowcombe, 142, 225
Crowhurst, Surrey, 28, 81
Crowhurst, Sussex, 28
Crowle, 112
Culbone, 130
Culford, 294
Cullompton, 38, 142, 146, 156, 176,
    242, 311, 354
Culmstock, 340
Curdworth, 186, 208
Curry Rivel, 142

Daglingworth, 128, 164
Danbury, 280
Darenth, 134, 156, 192
Darley Dale, 28

Dartford, 214
Dartington, 230
Dartmouth, 20, 120, 234, 242
Dauntsey, 209
Dean, 94
Dean Prior, 322
Dedham, 41
Deerhurst, 165, 186, 305, 314
Denford, 89, 124
Dennington, 145, 220, 260,
    283
Denston, 176, 220, 352
Dent, 25
Derby, 53, 332
Dersingham, 208, 338
Derwen, 260
Detling, 228
Devizes, 66, 312
Digswell, 305, 306
Dinton, 116
Disley, 146
Ditcheat, 212
Ditchingham, 41
Dittisham, 235, 354
Doddiscombsleigh, 315
Dolton, 186
Donington, 94
Dorchester, Dorset, 36
Dorchester, Oxfordshire, 80, 174,
    195, 282, 304, 313, 328
Dormington, 120
Dormston, 62
Dorney, 182
Doveridge, 28
Downham, 44
Down St. Mary, 223
Drayton, 334
Drayton Beauchamp, 315
Dry Doddington, 89
Ducklington, 140
Dummer, 263
Dunchideock, 242
Dundry, 22, 34
Dunsfold, 218
Dunstable, 341
Dunster, 242
Duntisbourne Abbots, 48
Duntisbourne Rous, 48
Durham, 22, 74, 120, 162, 206, 266,
    340
Duston, 152

Eardisley, 192
Earls Barton, 64
Earl Stonham, 43, 149, 208
Easby, 216
East Allington, 230
East Bergholt, 48
East Brent, 316, 343
East Budleigh, 223
East Dean, 81
East Dereham, 43
East Haddon, 195
East Harling, 149, 316
East Hendred, 170
Easthorpe, 135
East Langdon, 340
Eastleach Martin, 81
Eastleach Turville, 48, 116
East Markham, 124, 185, 306
East Meon, 65, 83, 195
Easton, 89
Easton Maudit, 94
Easton Neston, 290
East Portlemouth, 254
East Ruston, 248
East Sutton, 308
Eaton Bishop, 314
Eaton Bray, 120, 170, 195
Edingthorpe, 51, 132, 212,
    248
Edington, 129, 176
Edlesborough, 184
Edstaston, 120
Edstone, 128
Egmanton, 185
Elford, 283, 286
Elham, 334
Elkstone, 116, 126, 134, 166
Ellingham, 128, 276
Ellington, 89
Elmley Castle, 128, 296
Elmsted, 28
Elsing, 204
Elstow, 48, 304
Eltisley, 94
Ely, 22, 76, 116, 152, 162, 266, 272,
    304, 311
Emmington, 48
Emneth, 149
Empingham, 94
Enmore, 34
Enville, 70

Epping Upland, 44
Erpingham, 43
Escomb, 165
Esher, 344
Essendine, 71
Etchingham, 102
Eton College, 228
Etton, 89
Euston, 178
Evercreech, 32, 124, 145, 352
Evesham, 58
Ewelme, 176, 204, 282, 354
Ewerby, 89, 174
Ewhurst, 112
Exeter, 104, 127, 156, 157, 162, 270, 271, 272
Exminster, 38
Exton, 96, 285
Eyam, 26
Eye, 42, 244, 252
Eynesbury, 222
Eynsford, 82

Fairfield, 182
Fairford, 127, 176, 321, 354
Fairstead, 214
Fakenham, 41
Falkenham, 43
Farleigh Hungerford, 284
Farley Chamberlayne, 180
Farmington, 128
Farningham, 200
Faversham, 208
Fawsley, 285
Feering, 112
Felbrigg, 306
Feltwell St. Mary, 218
Feniton, 281
Fersfield, 280
Filby, 42, 120, 132, 247, 248
Filey, 102
Fillingham, 208
Fincham, 188
Finchampstead, 325
Finchingfield, 23
Fishlake, 115, 196
Flamborough, 102, 260, 262, 354
Flamstead, 84, 184
Folkingham, 23
Ford, 81
Fordington, 36, 116

Forest Hill, 341
Forncett St. Peter, 51
Fotheringhay, 57
Foulsham, 42
Fownhope, 116
Framingham Earl, 51
Framlingham, 41, 152, 286, 294, 342
Frampton, 89, 344
Frampton-on-Severn, 195
Framsden, 40, 110, 149
Fressingfield, 110, 149, 220, 354
Friston, 81
Fritton, Norfolk, 248
Fritton, Suffolk, 51, 130, 132, 134
Fryerning, 44
Fulbourn, 302

Gamston, 52
Garboldisham, 42
Garthorpe, 52
Gateley, 248
Gatton, 344
Gawsworth, 287
Gayhurst, 70, 144, 178
Geddington, 23
Gedney, 105
Gestingthorpe, 44, 152
Gislingham, 149
Gissing, 51, 149
Glastonbury, 34
Glentham, 208
Glentworth, 64
Gloucester, 76, 138, 142, 156, 162, 266, 272, 314
Godalming, 83
Godshill, 23
Gooderstone, 248
Gosberton, 94
Gosforth, 26
Goudhurst, 279, 280
Grantham, 92, 344
Grasmere, 21, 152
Graveney, 182
Great Ashfield, 112
Great Baddow, 83, 105
Great Bardfield, 244
Great Barrington, 297
Great Barton, 43
Great Bircham, 341
Great Brington, 285
Great Bromley, 152, 301

Great Burstead, 83
Great Canfield, 214, 322
Great Chalfield, 20, 71
Great Driffield, 62
Great Gidding, 94
Great Holland, 44
Great Horwood, 140
Great Kimble, 188
Great Leighs, 50
Great Linford, 308
Great Malvern, 58, 272, 318, 345, 354
Great Massingham, 41
Great Munden, 84
Great Paxton, 164
Great Ponton, 55, 102
Great Rollright, 52
Great Shefford, 51
Great Shelford, 209
Great Snoring, 325
Great Staughton, 53, 332
Great Walsingham, 218, 332, 346, 354
Great Wenham, 43
Great Witchingham, 200
Great Witley, 100
Great Yarmouth, 342
Greensted, 81, 165
Gresford, 52, 53, 146
Gresham, 200
Grimoldby, 124
Grimston, 41
Grinton, 21
Grundisburgh, 149, 212
Guisborough, 287
Gunwalloe, 20, 48
Gwinear, 36

Haccombe, 281, 345
Hackthorn, 70
Haddenham, 68
Haddiscoe, 51
Haddon Hall, 212
Hadleigh, 83
Hadstock, 120
Hailes, 345
Halberton, 230
Hales, 51, 130, 132
Halse, 242
Haltwhistle, 170
Hambledon, 28
Hamerton, 53
Hamstall Ridware, 337

Hanslope, 94
Happisburgh, 41, 43, 197, 243
Harberton, 38, 184, 235, 242, 354
Hardham, 214, 216
Hardley, 212
Harefield, 290, 300
Harpley, 120, 218
Harpole, 192
Harrold, 94
Hartland, 127, 189, 242
Hartley, 120
Harty, 208
Hasketon, 51
Haslingfield, 53, 127
Hatch Beauchamp, 34, 225
Hauxton, 214
Havant, 302
Hawkshead, 21
Hawstead, 283
Hawton, 328, 330
Hayes, 212
Heath Chapel, 168
Heckingham, 115, 130
Heckington, 92, 94, 108, 124, 140,
    174, 328, 330
Hedon, 52, 62, 129
Helmingham, 42, 294
Helpringham, 94
Hemblington, 200, 212
Hemel Hempstead, 83, 156
Hemingborough, 94
Hemley, 44
Hennock, 38, 254, 263
Hepworth, 204
Hereford, 76, 266, 267, 270, 272, 344,
    346
Hernhill, 55
Herringfleet, 51
Hessett, 42
Heveningham, 149
Hever, 82
Hexham, 132
Heydour, 314
Hickling, 43
Higham Ferrers, 94, 268, 272, 301
High Bickington, 223
High Halden, 112
High Ham, 125, 145, 242
Hilborough, 42, 118
Hildersham, 280, 305
Hillesden, 176, 320

Hillmarton, 244
Hinderwell, 338
Hindringham, 43
Hinton Blewett, 184
Hinton St. George, 34
Hitchin, 84, 196
Holbeach, 94, 174
Holcombe Rogus, 344
Holdgate, 192
Hollesley, 43
Hollingbourne, 342
Holme, 90, 132, 185
Holme-upon-Spalding-Moor, 22
Holne, 230, 254
Honing, 43
Hook Norton, 52, 192
Hopton, 149, 354
Horley, 185, 212
Horsham St. Faith, 43, 232
Horsmonden, 301
Horsted Keynes, 82
Houghton St. Giles, 248
Hoveton St Peter, 275
Hubberholme, 262
Hughley, 244
Huish Episcopi, 34
Hull, 140
Hullavington, 341
Hunstanton, 248
Huntingdon, 89
Hurst, 240
Husthwaite, 21
Huttoft, 200, 208
Hutton, 34, 235
Hythe, 132

Ickenham, 300
Ickford, 48
Ickleton, 83, 354
Icklingham All Saints, 208
Idbury, 106, 324
Ideford, 263
Idsworth, 215
Iffley, 66, 115, 129, 168
Ightham, 344
Ilam, 21, 192
Ile Abbots, 34
Ilfracombe, 146
Ilketshall St. Margaret, 51
Ilminster, 32, 176
Impington, 212

Ingatestone, 44
Ingestre, 178
Ingham, 42
Intwood, 51
Ipplepen, 38, 230, 255
Irchester, 88
Irstead, 247, 248
Isel, 20
Isleham, 228
Ivinghoe, 129, 170, 232
Ivychurch, 55
Ixworth Thorpe, 220

Jarrow, 165

Kelmscott, 71
Kempley, 214
Kempsey, 315
Kenn, 255
Kenninghall, 276
Kentisbeare, 142, 242
Kenton, 38, 230, 242, 255
Kersey, 22, 24, 110
Kessingland, 44
Kettering, 94
Ketteringham, 80
Ketton, 90
Keyston, 89
Kilkhampton, 222
Kilmersdon, 34
Kilpeck, 115, 126, 166, 168
Kimbolton, 23, 89
Kimpton, 170
Kingsbury Episcopi, 34
King's Lynn, 142, 176, 305
King's Norton, 178
King's Nympton, 242, 263
King's Sutton, 96
Kingston St. Mary, 34
Kinver, 308
Kirkburn, 116, 166, 186
Kirkdale, 128
Kirk Hammerton, 64, 166
Knapton, 102, 149, 354
Knebworth, 302
Knowle, 244

Lakenheath, 149, 220
Lamarsh, 50
Lambourne, 180, 212
Lancaster, 264
Laneast, 188

Langar, 290
Langham, 90
Langley Marish, 345
Langport, 32, 316
Langtoft, 186
Lanhydrock, 20
Lanreath, 184, 204
Lansallos, 222
Lanteglos-by-Fowey, 222
Lapford, 223, 242
Lastingham, 132
Laughton-en-le-Morthen, 96
Launcells, 182, 222, 345
Launceston, 108, 188
Lavenham, 44, 106, 176, 352
Laxfield, 41, 200
Layer Marney, 44, 212, 285
Leadenham, 94
Leatherhead, 131
Leckhampton, 88
Ledbury, 337
Leicester, 326
Leigh-on-Mendip, 32, 145, 352
Leighton Buzzard, 120
Lelant, 284
Lonham, 221
Lenton, Lincolnshire, 89
Lenton, Nottinghamshire, 192
Leominster, 138, 337
Leverington, 315
Lewes, 50, 102
Lichfield, 298, 321
Lincoln, 22, 64, 76, 108, 127, 162,
    163, 264, 272, 313
Lingfield, 344
Linkinhorne, 36, 214
Liston, 44
Little Baddow, 212, 280
Little Billing, 186
Little Casterton, 71
Little Faringdon, 338
Little Gidding, 178
Little Hadham, 84
Little Hempston, 38
Little Hormead, 120
Little Horwood, 214
Little Kimble, 214
Little Malvern, 345
Little Maplestead, 130
Little Missenden, 212
Little Munden, 84

Little Saxham, 51
Little Stonham, 42, 149
Little Waldingfield, 42
Little Walsingham, 200, 354
Liverton, 166
Llananno, 260
Llanegryn, 260
Llaneilian, 260
Llanengan, 260
Llanfilo, 260
Llangwm, 260
Llangwm Uchaf, 260
Llanrwst, 260
Llanwnog, 260
Locking, 34, 192
Loddington, 89
Loddon, 248, 349
London, 97, 102, 104, 118, 130, 156,
    162, 163, 177, 185, 266, 267, 272,
    279, 281, 290, 311, 340, 342, 345,
    355
Long Ashton, 283
Longborough, 52, 288
Long Melford, 106, 176, 352
Long Sutton, Lincolnshire, 83
Long Sutton, Somerset, 32, 145, 232,
    354
Long Wittenham, 112, 136
Lostwithiel, 196
Lound, 185
Louth, 92, 352
Lower Peover, 62
Lowick, 57, 281
Luccombe, 23
Ludham, 149, 247, 248, 349
Ludlow, 272, 316
Lullingstone, 244
Lullington, 192
Luppitt, 189
Luton, 206
Lyddington, 26
Lydiard Tregoze, 294, 332
Lyminster, 145
Lympsham, 34
Lyng, Norfolk, 341
Lyng, Somerset, 34

Madley, 313
Magdalen Laver, 81
Maids Moreton, 176
Malmesbury, 108, 116

Malpas, 124, 146, 285, 288
Manaton, 255
Manchester, 266, 272
March, 152
Margaretting, 80, 81, 112, 316
Marham, 43
Mark, 32, 145
Market Harborough, 89
Marsh Baldon, 128
Marston, 89
Martock, 34, 145
Marton, Cheshire, 62
Marton, Lincolnshire, 64
Matlask, 51
Mattingley, 342
Mattishall, 248
Mayfield, 344
Melbourne, 168
Melbury Bubb, 186
Mellor, 230
Mells, 32
Melton Constable, 323
Melton Mowbray, 105
Melverley, 62
Mendlesham, 42, 204
Merstham, 82
Merton, Norfolk, 243
Merton, Oxfordshire, 234
Methley, 284
Meysey Hampton, 328
Middlezoy, 34
Mildenhall, 43, 149
Millom, 20
Milton Abbey, 36
Milton Ernest, 346
Milverton, 225
Minehead, 23, 127, 242, 333
Minstead, 182
Minster-in-Thanet, 135, 267, 272
Minster Lovell, 226
Miserden, 288
Mobberley, 146, 244
Moccas, 168
Molesworth, 212
Molland, 174, 182
Monksilver, 125, 204, 225, 232
Monkton, 55
Monkwearmouth, 165
Montacute, 20
Montgomery, 260
Monyash, 326

Moorlynch, 345
Moreton Corbet, 286
Moreton Say, 343
Moreton Valence, 116
Morley, 308
Morston, 248
Morwenstow, 36
Moulton, 92
Muchelney, 34, 146
Much Marcle, 280
Mudford, 34
Mullion, 184, 222, 352
Mundesley, 41
Musbury, 288
Mylor, 20

Nailsea, 34
Nantwich, 264, 272
Narborough, 43
Nassington, 96
Navestock, 81
Nazeing, 44
Necton, 149, 152
Needham Market, 152
Nettlecombe, 200, 322, 337
Nettleton, 58
Newark, 90, 305, 311
Newcastle, 96
Newdigate, 81
Newhaven, 134
Newington-on-the-Street, 55
Newport, Essex, 208
Newport, Isle of Wight, 234
New Shoreham, 168
Ninekirk, 21, 178
Norbury, 281
Northampton, 130, 168
Northaw, 70
North Burlingham, 80, 149, 249
North Cadbury, 20, 225
North Cerney, 184, 235, 346
North Crawley, 256
North Creake, 149
North Curry, 58
North Elmham, 249
North Grimston, 166, 186
North Hill, 36
Northleach, 108, 176, 235, 306
North Leigh, 156, 209, 311, 354
North Molton, 230
North Petherton, 34

North Rauceby, 89
Northrepps, 42
North Weald, 44
Northwich, 146
Norton-in-Hales, 292
Norton Subcourse, 278
Norton-sub-Hamdon, 34
Norwich, 41, 43, 94, 149, 152, 156, 157, 162, 214, 266, 272, 300, 316, 334, 341

Oakham, 174, 342
Oakley, 260
Oaksey, 212, 214
Ockham, 135
Offwell, 182
Old Cleeve, 345
Old Dilton, 182
Old Radnor, 342
Old Romney, 74, 82, 182
Old Shoreham, 66, 81, 135, 166, 168
Old Woking, 120
Orleton, 192
Orlingbury, 70
Orwell, 287
Osbournby, 222
Othery, 34, 341
Ottery St. Mary, 104, 137, 157, 228, 334, 345
Oundle, 94, 228
Over, 124, 232
Over Peover, 281, 284
Ovingdean, 134
Ovingham, 64
Oxford, 31, 52, 57, 64, 80, 88, 96, 110, 132, 144, 146, 156, 177, 208, 228, 272, 302, 304, 306, 314, 316, 321, 334, 352

Padstow, 90
Paignton, 310
Painswick, 28
Parracombe, 181, 182
Paston, 212
Patcham, 209
Patricio, 260
Patrington, 94, 125, 140, 174, 330
Patrixbourne, 82, 116
Payhembury, 242
Peakirk, 215
Pembridge, 48

Penn, 209
Pentlow, 50
Pertenhall, 88
Peterborough, 127, 156, 162
Petersham, 178, 300
Peter Tavy, 38
Pickering, 212, 214, 216, 354
Pickworth, 89
Piddinghoe, 50, 102
Piddlehinton, 36
Piddletrenthide, 36
Pillaton, 36
Pilton, 206, 235, 240
Pinhoe, 242, 349
Pinner, 322
Pirton, 58
Pitchford, 20, 280, 284
Pixley, 182
Playden, 82
Plympton St. Mary, 38
Plymtree, 242, 255, 352
Polebrook, 89
Poringland, 51
Portishead, 34
Potter Heigham, 51, 132, 149, 201, 247, 249
Potters Bar, 355
Poughill, 36, 212, 223
Preston, 62
Priston, 102
Probus, 36
Publow, 34
Puddletown, 343
Pulham St. Mary the Virgin, 41, 110
Puxton, 184

Quadring, 94, 105
Quainton, 287
Queen Camel, 242
Queniborough, 94
Quenington, 116, 342

Rainham, 208
Rame, 90
Ramsgate, 102
Ranworth, 43, 243, 247, 249, 334, 354
Rattlesden, 149
Raunds, 89, 214
Ravenstonedale, 180
Rayne, 44
Redenhall, 42

Redgrave, 298
Reedham, 41
Reepham, 28
Reighton, 186
Repps, 51
Repton, 132
Riccall, 116
Rickinghall Inferior, 51
Ridge, 212
Ringland, 152
Ringstead, Norfolk, 322
Ringstead, Northamptonshire, 140
Ringwood, 302
Ripon, 162, 266, 272
Ripple, 272
Roche, 188
Rochford, 44
Rockingham, 22
Rodmersham, 55
Rodney Stoke, 204, 234, 244
Rolleston, 52
Romaldkirk, 25
Romsey, 127, 334
Rotherfield Greys, 290
Rothersthorpe, 346
Rothwell, 64
Rougham, 42
Roughton, 51
Rowlstone, 116, 166, 343
Royston, 144
Ruardean, 96, 116
Rudgwick, 81
Rudston, 26
Ruishton, 34
Runhall, 51
Rushall, 51
Rushbrooke, 276
Rushden, 94
Ruthin, 146
Rycote, 344
Rye, 104

Saffron Walden, 176
Saham Toney, 41
St. Albans, 65, 215, 234, 288, 305, 334, 346
St. Anthony-in-Meneage, 20
St. Austell, 188
St. Catherines, 20
St. Cleer, 36
St. David's, 146, 270

St. Endellion, 114
St. Enodoc, 20, 90
St. Erme, 36
St. Germans, 115
St. Just-in-Roseland, 20
St. Kew, 315
St. Levan, 38
St. Margaret-at-Cliffe, 168
St. Margarets, 260
St. Mary Bourne, 342
St. Neot, 142, 315
St. Neots, 53
St. Teath, 176
St. Veep, 174
St. Winnow, 20, 223
Salhouse, 324
Salisbury, 96, 127, 162, 163, 209, 352
Sall, 41, 118, 142, 152, 176, 204, 268, 338, 352
Saltfleetby All Saints, 184
Saltwood, 208
Sampford Courtenay, 152
Sancton, 62
Sandhurst, 195
Sandiacre, 328
Sandon, 44, 112
Sandwich, 66
Sawtry, 308
Saxmundham, 197
Scarning, 243, 324
Scarrington, 80
Scartho, 64
Scottow, 43
Sculthorpe, 188
Seal, 55
Seaton, 90
Sedgefield, 170
Sefton, 146, 244
Selborne, 28, 322
Selham, 166
Sellindge, 28
Selling, 314
Selworthy, 22, 146, 208
Sharrington, 44, 152
Shawbury, 52
Sheepstor, 38
Shellingford, 185
Shelsley Walsh, 345
Shelton, 176, 352
Shepton Mallet, 32, 146
Sherborne, 36, 105, 156, 272

Shere, 24, 82, 347
Sheringham, 218
Shernborne, 186
Sheviock, 90
Shillington, 302
Shilton, 196
Shipdham, 228
Shipton-under-Wychwood, 88
Shoreham, Kent, 112, 244
Shoreham, Sussex: see New, Old
Shorne, 200
Shorwell, 212
Shotley, 149
Shottesbrooke, 94, 174, 301
Shrewsbury, 180
Shurdington, 88
Shute, 297
Siddington, 116
Sileby, 55
Silk Willoughby, 94
Silverton, 36
Sittingbourne, 102
Skelton, 118, 127, 170, 325
Slapton, 212, 215
Sleaford, 140
Slimbridge, 170
Slindon, 280
Sloley, 200
Snailwell, 50
Snape, 43, 200
Snarford, 288
Snettisham, 140, 174
Soham, 53
Somerby, 80
Somerleyton, 244, 252
Somersby, 26
Somerton, Oxfordshire, 52, 334
Somerton, Somerset, 145
Sompting, 64
South Burlingham, 145, 184, 232, 354
South Creake, 149, 184
Southease, 50
Southfleet, 200
South Harting, 24
South Hayling, 28
South Leigh, 209
South Luffenham, 94
South Milton, 189
South Molton, 235
South Newington, 215
South Ockendon, 50

South Ormsby, 200
Southrepps, 43
Southrop, 189
South Somercotes, 80
South Walsham, 28
Southwell, 162, 163, 171, 228
Southwold, 44, 102, 104, 106, 176, 247, 252, 268, 352
South Wootton, 188
Spalding, 94
Spaldwick, 89
Sparham, 41
Spaxton, 225
Stafford, 192
Stalham, 200
Stamford, 89, 94
Stanford, 184, 275, 314, 342
Stanford Rivers, 83
Stanstead Abbots, 182
Stanton Fitzwarren, 194
Stanton Harcourt, 52, 283, 290
Staple Fitzpaine, 34
Staplehurst, 120
Stebbing, 244
Steeple Ashton, 25, 176
Steeple Bumpstead, 297
Steeple Langford, 126, 296
Steetley, 168
Stelling, 28, 182
Stewkley, 65, 129, 168
Steyning, 81, 168
Stillingfleet, 116, 120
Stock, 81
Stogumber, 225, 344
Stogursey, 225
Stoke-by-Nayland, 42, 120, 176
Stoke Charity, 182
Stoke Climsland, 36
Stoke D'Abernon, 208, 234, 294, 301
Stoke Dry, 144, 166, 184
Stoke Fleming, 308
Stoke Golding, 174
Stoke Pero, 48
Stoke St. Gregory, 58, 234
Stokesay, 20, 344
Stone, 188
Stoneleigh, 166, 192
Stoney Stanton, 116
Stonham Aspall, 106
Stottesdon, 192
Stourton, 21

Stow, 164
Stowell, 214
Stowe-Nine-Churches, 290
Stowlangtoft, 212, 220, 263, 268
Stratford-on-Avon, 209, 272
Stratford-sub-Castle, 234
Strelley, 282
Strensham, 184, 256, 300, 343
Stretton Sugwas, 116
Strumpshaw, 42
Studham, 170, 195
Studland, 129, 168
Studley, 284
Sudbury, 204
Suffield, 246, 250
Surfleet, 94
Surlingham, 197, 304
Sutton Benger, 341
Sutton Bingham, 215
Sutton Coldfield, 287
Swaffham, 42, 149
Swaffham Prior, 28
Swafield, 250
Swalcliffe, 209
Swanton Morley, 43
Swaton, 174
Swimbridge, 83, 184, 206, 235, 242
Swinbrook, 292, 308, 332

Tackley, 52
Talaton, 242
Talland, 223
Tandridge, 28
Tangmere, 81, 135
Tannington, 220
Tarrant Crawford, 214
Tarring Neville, 81
Taunton, 34, 201
Tawstock, 184, 240, 288, 344, 354
Teigh, 180
Telscombe, 81
Tenterden, 55
Terrington St. Clement, 42, 105, 176,
    352
Tetney, 55
Teversal, 182
Tewkesbury, 65, 156, 157, 310, 314
Thaxted, 23, 176, 184, 352
Theberton, 51
Theddlethorpe, 124
Theydon Garnon, 44, 275, 276

Thirsk, 204
Thompson, 243
Thorncombe, 308
Thornham, 250
Thornham Parva, 132, 334
Thornhill, 280, 318
Thornton-le-Dale, 25
Thorpe-le-Soken, 44
Thorpe Malsor, 89
Thorpe Salvin, 116, 194
Thrapston, 89
Threekingham, 89
Tibenham, 41, 344
Tichborne, 133
Tickencote, 166
Tickhill, 62
Tidenham, 195
Tideswell, 53
Tilbrook, 244
Tilbury-juxta-Clare, 44
Tilney All Saints, 149
Tilty, 127, 174
Timberscombe, 242
Tinwell, 48
Titchmarsh, 52, 57
Tiverton, 311
Tivetshall St. Margaret, 276
Toftrees, 188
Toller Fratrum, 189
Tollesbury, 102
Tong, 268, 283, 286, 292
Torbryan, 38, 184, 256
Torpenhow, 166
Tortington, 81, 166
Tortworth, 53
Totnes, 38, 244
Trimingham, 250
Trimley, 28
Trotton, 214, 308
Trull, 184, 225, 232, 316, 354
Trumpington, 301
Trunch, 44, 149, 206, 250
Truro, 98, 162
Tunstead, 250
Tunworth, 349
Turvey, 120
Tutbury, 115
Tysoe, 196

Udimore, 135
Uffculme, 242

Uffington, Berks, 129, 170, 345
Uffington, Lincs, 94
Ufford, 41, 204, 220, 354
Ugborough, 256
Ugley, 44
Ulcombe, 28, 308
Ulpha, 20
Upminster, 102
Upper Hardres, 55
Upper Slaughter, 52
Upton, Buckinghamshire, 308
Upton, Norfolk, 197, 247, 250
Upton St. Leonards, 53
Upwell, 149

Waberthwaite, 20
Wadenhoe, 48
Wakerley, 94, 166
Walberswick, 42
Walcott, 41, 43
Waldringfield, 44
Walpole St. Peter, 132, 142, 176, 250,
    352
Walsham-le-Willows, 149
Walsoken, 168, 200
Waltham-on-the-Wolds, 94
Wansford, 192
Wanstead, 297
Warbleton, 208, 304, 344
Warblington, 28
Warboys, 89
Ware, 196
Warfield, 260
Warkton, 57, 298
Warlingham, 212
Warmington, 89, 170
Warndon, 62
Warnford, 128
Warwick, 279, 284, 312
Watchet, 146, 345
Water Stratford, 116
Wath, 208
Watton, 349
Weare, 32
Wedmore, 32, 212, 344
Weeke, 338
Weekley, 94
Weeley, 44
Welford, Berkshire, 51
    Northamptonshire, 124
Well, 204

Wellingborough, 185, 322
Wellingham, 250
Wellington, 292
Wellow, 120, 145, 184
Wells, 31, 32, 76, 104, 108, 127, 145,
    162, 163, 170, 272, 311, 314
Wembury, 20
Wendens Ambo, 184
Wenhaston, 209
West Alvington, 38
West Camel, 263
West Challow, 112
West Chiltington, 216, 331
West Drayton, 201, 337
West Grinstead, 112, 308
West Haddon, 192
Westhall, 200, 252
West Hanningfield, 81
West Hendred, 345
West Horsley, 212
Westleigh, 345
Westley Waterless, 301, 308
Westmill, 23
Westminster—see London
West Ogwell, 182
Weston, Lincolnshire, 170
Weston, Suffolk, 200
Weston Favell, 342
Weston Longville, 250
Weston-super-Mare, 235
Weston Turville, 188
Weston Zoyland, 32, 145, 333
West Tanfield, 25, 284
West Tarring, 83
West Walton, 48, 68, 118, 170
Westwood, 58
Wetherden, 149
Weybread, 51
Whaddon, 206
Whalley, 272
Wharram-le-Street, 64
Whatton, 282
Wheatfield, 180
Whissendine, 70
Whiston, 57
Whitby, 182
Whitchurch, Hampshire, 308
Whitchurch, Oxfordshire, 23
Whittlesey, 94
Wickhamford, 20, 296
Wickham St. Paul, 44

Wickmere, 51
Wick St. Lawrence, 235
Wickwar, 53, 344
Widecombe, 36, 256
Widford, 354
Wiggenhall St Germans, 218, 354
Wiggenhall St. Mary the Virgin, 218, 250, 354
Wighill, 116
Wighton, 176
Wilby, Northamptonshire, 96
Wilby, Suffolk, 42, 220
Willand, 242
Willen, 178
Willingale, 28
Wilton, 218
Wimborne, 104, 137, 344
Wimborne St. Giles, 70, 178
Wimbotsham, 220
Winchcombe, 52, 102, 124, 342
Winchelsea, 174, 283
Winchester, 162, 195, 266, 272, 281, 302, 310, 334
Windrush, 115
Windsor, 156, 176, 264, 272, 310
Winford, 34
Wing, 132, 165
Wingfield, 268, 280, 283
Wingham, 84
Winscombe, 32, 318
Winterborne Tomson, 129, 130, 182
Winterton, 42
Winthorpe, 268
Wirksworth, 164
Wissington, 215
Witheridge, 235
Withersfield, 220
Withyham, 294

Witney, 88, 308
Wittering, 164
Witton, 146
Woking—see Old Woking
Wolborough, 174, 228, 242, 256, 354
Wolverhampton, 235
Wolverton, 180
Woodbridge, 42, 176
Wood Dalling, 41
Wood Eaton, 212
Woodton, 51
Woolland, 28
Woolpit, 110, 149, 220
Worcester, 77, 132, 272, 311
Wordwell, 220
Worlingworth, 149, 204
Worsborough, 280
Worstead, 43, 204, 243
Worth, 164, 166
Worth Matravers, 168
Wotton-under-Edge, 342
Wraxall, 34, 286
Wrington, 32
Wye, 124
Wylye, 338
Wymington, 140, 308
Wymondham, 44, 149, 334

Yapton, 81
Yarnton, 298, 316, 322, 334
Yate, 53
Yatton Keynell, 244
Yaxley, Huntingdonshire, 94
Yaxley, Suffolk, 252
Yeovil, 34, 228
York, 52, 78, 96, 127, 162, 313, 318, 354
Youlgreave, 281, 315

County Index of Places

(showing new Counties)

Bedfordshire
Dean, 94
Dunstable, 341
Eaton Bray, 120, 170, 195
Elstow, 48, 304
Harrold, 94
Leighton Buzzard, 120
Luton, 206
Milton Ernest, 346
Oakley, 260
Pertenhall, 88
Shillington, 302
Studham, 170, 195
Turvey, 120
Wymington, 140, 308

Berkshire (* now in Oxfordshire)
Aldermaston, 313
Avington, 168, 198
Binfield, 240
Dinham, 207
*Charney Bassett, 116
*Drayton, 334
*East Hendred, 170
Finchampstead, 325
Great Shefford, 51
Hurst, 240
*Long Wittenham, 112, 136
*Shellingford, 185
Shottesbrooke, 94, 174, 301
*Uffington, 129, 170, 345
Warfield, 260
Welford, 51
*West Challow, 112
*West Hendred, 345
Windsor, 156, 176, 264, 272, 310

Buckinghamshire (* now in Berkshire)
Aylesbury, 188
Bledlow, 188
Bradenham, 23
Broughton, 214
Chearsley, 185
Cheddington, 232
Clifton Reynes, 280
Dinton, 116

Dorney, 182
Drayton Beauchamp, 315
Edlesborough, 184
*Eton College, 228
Gayhurst, 70, 144, 178
Great Horwood, 140
Great Kimble, 188
Great Linford, 308
Haddenham, 68
Hanslope, 94
Hillesden, 176, 320
Ickford, 48
Ivinghoe, 129, 170, 232
*Langley Marish, 345
Little Horwood, 214
Little Kimble, 214
Little Missenden, 212
Maids Moreton, 176
North Crawley, 256
Penn, 209
Quainton, 287
Stewkley, 65, 129, 168
Stone, 188
*Upton, 308
Water Stratford, 116
Weston Turville, 188
Whaddon, 206
Willen, 178
Wing, 132, 165

Cambridgeshire
Balsham, 244, 267, 302
Bartlow, 50, 80, 209, 212
Cambridge, 64, 80, 130, 142, 156, 164,
     176, 177, 228, 267, 271, 272, 302,
     320, 342, 352, 354
Cherry Hinton, 325, 326
Conington, 80
Eltisley, 94
Ely, 22, 76, 116, 152, 162, 266, 272,
     304, 311
Fulbourn, 302
Great Shelford, 209
Haslingfield, 53, 127
Hauxton, 214
Hildersham, 280, 305

Ickleton, 83, 354
Impington, 212
Isleham, 228
Leverington, 315
March, 152
Orwell, 287
Over, 124, 232
Snailwell, 50
Soham, 53
Swaffham Prior, 28
Trumpington, 301
Westley Waterless, 301, 308
Whittlesey, 94

Cheshire
Astbury, 146, 184, 206, 228, 244
Baddiley, 182, 276
Barthomley, 53, 146
Chester, 146, 264, 272
Disley, 146
Gawsworth, 287
Lower Peover, 62
Malpas, 124, 146, 285, 288
Marton, 62
Mobberley, 146, 244
Nantwich, 264, 272
Northwich, 146
Over Peover, 281, 284
Witton, 146

Cornwall
Altarnun, 176, 188, 222
Blisland, 184, 352
Boconnoc, 20
Bodmin, 188
Breage, 212, 214
Cardinham, 222
Gunwalloe, 20, 48
Gwinear, 36
Kilkhampton, 222
Laneast, 188
Lanhydrock, 20
Lanreath, 184, 204
Lansallos, 222
Lanteglos-by-Fowey, 222
Launcells, 182, 222, 345
Launceston, 108, 188
Lelant, 284
Linkinhorne, 36, 214
Lostwithiel, 196
Morwenstow, 36

Mullion, 184, 222, 352
Mylor, 20
North Hill, 36
Padstow, 90
Pillaton, 36
Poughill, 36, 212, 223
Probus, 36
Rame, 90
Roche, 188
St. Anthony-in-Meneage, 20
St. Austell, 188
St. Cleer, 36
St. Endellion, 114
St. Enodoc, 20, 90
St. Erme, 36
St. Germans, 115
St. Just-in-Roseland, 20
St. Kew, 315
St. Levan, 38
St. Neot, 142, 315
St. Teath, 176
St. Veep, 174
St. Winnow, 20, 223
Sheviock, 90
Stoke Climsland, 36
Talland, 223
Truro, 98, 162

Cumberland (now in Cumbria)
Bewcastle, 26
Bowness, 318
Bridekirk, 188
Carlisle, 162, 244, 264, 272, 340
Gosforth, 26
Isel, 20
Millom, 20
Torpenhow, 166
Ulpha, 20
Waberthwaite, 20

Derbyshire
Ashbourne, 281, 285, 297
Ashover, 195, 285
Bakewell, 26
Chesterfield, 84, 347
Darley Dale, 28
Derby, 53, 332
Doveridge, 28
Eyam, 26
Haddon Hall, 212
Melbourne, 168

Mellor, 230
Monyash, 326
Morley, 308
Norbury, 281
Repton, 132
Sandiacre, 328
Steetley, 168
Tideswell, 53
Wirksworth, 164
Youlgreave, 281, 315

Devon
Abbotsham, 223
Alphington, 189, 254
Ashburton, 38, 142, 344
Ashton, 246, 254, 354
Atherington, 260
Awliscombe, 244
Barnstaple, 83, 340
Berry Pomeroy, 242
Bigbury, 230
Bishop's Tawton, 288
Bishopsteignton, 115
Bovey Tracey, 230, 234, 242, 261
Bradninch, 38, 242, 254
Branscombe, 332
Braunton, 83, 223, 344
Brentor, 21
Bridford, 256
Broad Clyst, 174
Buckland-in-the-Moor, 254
Burlescombe, 333
Burrington, 242
Cadbury, 315
Cadeleigh, 345
Chawleigh, 242
Chittlehampton, 36, 234
Chivelstone, 230, 254
Chudleigh, 254
Chulmleigh, 38, 242
Coldridge, 230, 242
Colebrooke, 204, 242
Combe-in-Teignhead, 223
Combe Martin, 146
Cotheridge, 345
Crediton, 208
Cullompton, 38, 142, 146, 156, 176,
   242, 311, 354
Culmstock, 340
Dartington, 230
Dartmouth, 20, 120, 234, 242

Dean Prior, 322
Dittisham, 235, 354
Doddiscombsleigh, 315
Dolton, 186
Down St. Mary, 223
Dunchideock, 242
East Allington, 230
East Budleigh, 223
East Portlemouth, 254
Exeter, 104, 127, 156, 157, 162, 270,
   271, 272
Exminster, 38
Feniton, 281
Haccombe, 281, 345
Halberton, 230
Harberton, 38, 184, 235, 242, 354
Hartland, 127, 189, 242
Hennock, 38, 254, 263
High Bickington, 223
Holcombe Rogus, 344
Holne, 230, 254
Ideford, 263
Ilfracombe, 146
Ipplepen, 30, 230, 255
Kenn, 255
Kentisbeare, 142, 242
Kenton, 38, 230, 242, 255
King's Nympton, 242, 263
Lapford, 223, 242
Little Hempston, 38
Luppitt, 189
Manaton, 255
Molland, 174, 182
Musbury, 288
North Molton, 230
Offwell, 182
Ottery St. Mary, 104, 137, 157, 228,
   334, 345
Paignton, 310
Parracombe, 181, 182
Payhembury, 242
Peter Tavy, 38
Pilton, 206, 235, 240
Pinhoe, 242, 349
Plympton St. Mary, 38
Plymtree, 242, 255, 352
Sampford Courtenay, 152
Sheepstor, 38
Shute, 297
Silverton, 36
South Milton, 189

South Molton, 235
Stoke Fleming, 308
Swimbridge, 83, 184, 206, 235, 242
Talaton, 242
Tawstock, 184, 240, 288, 344, 354
Tiverton, 311
Torbryan, 38, 184, 256
Totnes, 38, 244
Uffculme, 242
Ugborough, 256
Wembury, 20
West Alvington, 38
Westleigh, 345
West Ogwell, 182
Widecombe, 36, 256
Willand, 242
Witheridge, 235
Wolborough, 174, 228, 242, 256, 354

Dorset
Abbotsbury, 234
Affpuddle, 36
Beaminster, 36
Bere Regis, 152, 354
Blandford, 178
Bradford Abbas, 36
Cattistock, 70
Cerne Abbas, 36, 234
Chalbury, 182
Charminster, 36
Coombe Keynes, 338
Dorchester, 36
Fordington, 36, 116
Melbury Bubb, 186
Milton Abbey, 36
Piddlehinton, 36
Piddletrenthide, 36
Puddletown, 343
Sherborne, 36, 105, 156, 272
Studland, 129, 168
Tarrant Crawford, 214
Thorncombe, 308
Toller Fratrum, 189
Wimborne, 104, 137, 344
Wimborne St. Giles, 70, 178
Winterborne Tomson, 129, 130, 182
Woolland, 28
Worth Matravers, 168

Durham
Brancepeth, 234

Chester-le-Street, 96
Durham, 22, 74, 120, 162, 206, 266, 340
Escomb, 165
Jarrow (Tyne & Wear), 165
Monkwearmouth (Tyne & Wear), 165
Sedgefield, 170

Essex
Ardleigh, 108
Aythorpe Roding, 81
Bardfield Saling, 50
Barnston, 325
Birdbrook, 81
Blackmore, 81
Bradwell-juxta-Coggeshall, 182
Bradwell-on-Sea, 165
Brightlingsea, 41
Broomfield, 50
Castle Hedingham, 44, 134, 152, 326
Chignal Smealy, 44, 201
Chigwell, 304
Chipping Ongar, 102
Chrishall, 306
Colne Engaine, 322
Copford, 214
Danbury, 280
Dedham, 41
Downham, 44
Easthorpe, 135
Epping Upland, 44
Fairstead, 214
Feering, 112
Finchingfield, 23
Fryerning, 44
Gestingthorpe, 44, 152
Great Baddow, 83, 105
Great Bardfield, 244
Great Bromley, 152, 301
Great Burstead, 83
Great Canfield, 214, 322
Great Holland, 44
Great Leighs, 50
Greensted, 81, 165
Hadstock, 120
Ingatestone, 44
Lamarsh, 50
Lambourne, 180, 212
Layer Marney, 44, 212, 285
Liston, 44
Little Baddow, 212, 280

Little Maplestead, 130
Magdalen Laver, 81
Margaretting, 80, 81, 112, 316
Navestock, 81
Nazeing, 44
Newport, 208
North Weald, 44
Pentlow, 50
Rayne, 44
Rochford, 44
Saffron Walden, 176
Sandon, 44, 112
South Ockendon, 50
Stanford Rivers, 83
Stebbing, 244
Steeple Bumpstead, 297
Stock, 81
Thaxted, 23, 176, 184, 352
Theydon Garnon, 44, 275, 276
Thorpe-le-Soken, 44
Tilbury-juxta-Clare, 44
Tilty, 127, 174
Tollesbury, 102
Ugley, 44
Upminster (London Borough of
    Havering), 102
Wanstead (London Borough of
    Redbridge), 297
Weeley, 44
Wendens Ambo, 184
West Hanningfield, 81
Wickham St. Paul, 44
Willingale, 28

Gloucestershire (* now in Avon)
Ampney Crucis, 26
Bagendon, 48
Baunton, 212, 340
Bishop's Cleeve, 343
Bisley, 189
*Bitton, 53
*Bristol, 105, 157, 163, 267, 272, 342,
    343
Buckland, 340
Chedworth, 235
Chipping Campden, 53, 176, 308, 340
Cirencester, 176, 235, 340
Daglingworth, 128, 164
Deerhurst, 165, 186, 305, 314
Duntisbourne Abbots, 48
Duntisbourne Rous, 48

Eastleach Martin, 81
Eastleach Turville, 48, 116
Elkstone, 116, 126, 134, 166
Fairford, 127, 176, 321, 354
Farmington, 128
Frampton-on-Severn, 195
Gloucester, 76, 138, 142, 156, 162,
    266, 272, 314
Great Barrington, 297
Hailes, 345
Kempley, 214
Leckhampton, 88
Longborough, 52, 288
Meysey Hampton, 328
Miserden, 288
Moreton Valence, 116
North Cerney, 184, 235, 346
Northleach, 108, 176, 235, 306
Painswick, 28
Quenington, 116, 342
Ruardean, 96, 116
Sandhurst, 195
Shurdington, 88
Siddington, 116
Slimbridge, 170
Southrop, 189
Stowell, 214
Tewkesbury, 65, 156, 157, 310, 314
Tidenham, 195
*Tortworth, 53
Upper Slaughter, 52
Upton St. Leonards, 53
*Wickwar, 53, 344
Winchcombe, 52, 102, 124, 342
Windrush, 115
Wotton-under-Edge, 342
*Yate, 53

Hampshire
Avington, 70, 178
Bishop's Sutton, 345
Boarhunt, 165
Breamore, 165
Brockenhurst, 28
Catherington, 288
Chalton, 136
Christchurch (Dorset), 13, 36, 272,
    310, 334
Corhampton, 28, 165
Crondall, 301
Dummer, 263

East Meon, 65, 83, 195
Ellingham, 128, 276
Farley Chamberlayne, 180
Godshill (Isle of Wight), 23
Havant, 302
Idsworth, 215
Mattingley, 342
Minstead, 182
Newport (Isle of Wight), 234
Ringwood, 302
Romsey, 127, 334
St. Mary Bourne, 342
Selborne, 28, 322
Shorwell (Isle of Wight), 212
South Hayling, 28
Stoke Charity, 182
Tichborne, 133
Tunworth, 349
Warblington, 28
Warnford, 128
Weeke, 338
Whitchurch, 308
Winchester, 162, 195, 266, 272, 281,
    302, 310, 334
Wolverton, 180

Herefordshire (now Hereford and
    Worcester)
Aston, 116
Aymestrey, 244
Bacton, 337, 342
Bosbury, 48
Brinsop, 116
Castle Frome, 192
Dormington, 120
Eardisley, 192
Eaton Bishop, 314
Fownhope, 116
Hereford, 76, 266, 267, 270, 272, 344,
    346
Kilpeck, 115, 126, 166, 168
Ledbury, 337
Leominster, 138, 337
Madley, 313
Moccas, 168
Much Marcle, 280
Orleton, 192
Pembridge, 48
Pixley, 182
Rowlstone, 116, 166, 343
St. Margarets, 260

Stretton Sugwas, 116

Hertfordshire
Anstey, 26
Ashwell, 346
Braughing, 23, 263
Caldecote, 114
Digswell, 305, 306
Flamstead, 84, 184
Great Munden, 84
Hemel Hempstead, 83, 156
Hitchin, 84, 196
Kimpton, 170
Knebworth, 302
Little Hadham, 84
Little Hormead, 120
Little Munden, 84
Northaw, 70
Ridge, 212
St. Albans, 65, 215, 234, 288, 305,
    334, 346
Stanstead Abbots, 182
Ware, 196
Westmill, 23

Huntingdonshire (now part of
    Cambridgeshire)
Aconbury, 112
Brington, 89
Broughton, 89
Buckworth, 89
Bury, 68, 228
Conington, 53
Easton, 89
Ellington, 89
Eynesbury, 222
Great Gidding, 94
Great Paxton, 164
Great Staughton, 53, 332
Hamerton, 53
Huntingdon, 89
Keyston, 89
Kimbolton, 23, 89
Little Gidding, 178
Molesworth, 212
St. Neots, 53
Sawtry, 308
Spaldwick, 89
Tilbrook, 244
Warboys, 89
Yaxley, 94

Kent
Ash-next-Sandwich, 83
Aylesford, 23
Bapchild, 82
Barfreston, 116, 126, 128, 134, 168
Bobbing, 55
Boughton Monchelsea, 26
Boughton-under-Blean, 55
Brabourne, 74, 313
Brenzett, 81
Brook, 212, 215, 345
Brookland, 48, 82, 102, 195
Canterbury, 52, 74, 132, 162, 279,
    281, 285, 313, 352
Capel, 215
Charing, 55
Chartham, 140, 301
Chilham, 23, 297
Cliffe, 332, 338
Cobham, 306
Cowden, 81
Darenth, 134, 156, 192
Dartford, 214
Detling, 228
East Langdon, 340
East Sutton, 308
Elham, 334
Elmsted, 28
Eynsford, 82
Fairfield, 182
Farningham, 200
Faversham, 208
Goudhurst, 279, 280
Graveney, 182
Hartley, 120
Harty, 208
Hernhill, 55
Hever, 82
High Halden, 112
Hollingbourne, 342
Horsmonden, 301
Hythe, 132
Ightham, 344
Ivychurch, 55
Lenham, 234
Lullingstone, 244
Minster-in-Thanet, 135, 267, 272
Monkton, 55
Newington-on-the-Street, 55
Old Romney, 74, 82, 182
Patrixbourne, 82, 116

Rainham, 208
Ramsgate, 102
Rodmersham, 55
St. Margaret-at-Cliffe, 168
Saltwood, 208
Sandwich, 66
Seal, 55
Sellindge, 28
Selling, 314
Shoreham, 112, 244
Shorne, 200
Sittingbourne, 102
Southfleet, 200
Staplehurst, 120
Stelling, 28, 182
Tenterden, 55
Ulcombe, 28, 308
Upper Hardres, 55
Wingham, 84
Wye, 124

Lancashire
Cartmel (Cumbria), 267, 272, 344
Cartmel Fell (Cumbria), 21
Hawkshead (Cumbria), 21
Lancaster, 264
Manchester (Greater Manchester),
    266, 272
Sefton (Merseyside), 146, 244
Whalley, 272

Leicestershire
Bottesford, 94, 285, 302
Breedon-on-the-Hill, 21, 164
Garthorpe, 52
King's Norton, 178
Leicester, 326
Market Harborough, 89
Melton Mowbray, 105
Queniborough, 94
Sileby, 55
Stoke Golding, 174
Stoney Stanton, 116
Waltham-on-the-Wolds, 94

Lincolnshire (* now in Humberside)
Addlethorpe, 108, 120
Alford, 234
Asgarby, 94
Aunsby, 89
*Barnetby, 195
*Barton-on-Humber, 64, 133

Billingborough, 94
Blankney, 70
Boston, 55, 272
*Bottesford, 170
Bourne, 344
Bracebridge, 64
Brant Broughton, 94
Burgh-le-Marsh, 234
Careby, 341
Claypole, 94, 174
Coningsby, 104
Cotes-by-Stow, 184, 260
Croft, 184, 234
Donington, 94
Dry Doddington, 89
Ewerby, 89, 174
Fillingham, 208
Folkingham, 23
Frampton, 89, 344
Gedney, 105
Glentham, 208
Glentworth, 64
Gosberton, 94
Grantham, 92, 344
Great Ponton, 55, 102
Grimoldby, 124
Hackthorn, 70
Heckington, 92, 94, 108, 124, 140,
    174, 328, 330
Helpringham, 94
Heydour, 314
Holbeach, 94, 174
Huttoft, 200, 208
Leadenham, 94
Lenton, 89
Lincoln, 22, 64, 76, 108, 127, 162,
    163, 264, 272, 313
Long Sutton, 83
Louth, 92, 352
Marston, 89
Marton, 64
Moulton, 92
North Rauceby, 89
Osbournby, 222
Pickworth, 89
Quadring, 94, 105
Saltfleetby All Saints, 184
*Scartho, 64
Silk Willoughby, 94
Sleaford, 140
Snarford, 288

Somerby, 80
Somersby, 26
South Ormsby, 200
South Somercotes, 80
Spalding, 94
Stamford, 89, 94
Stow, 164
Surfleet, 94
Swaton, 174
Tetney, 55
Theddlethorpe, 124
Threekingham, 89
Uffington, 94
Weston, 170
Winthorpe, 268

Middlesex
Harefield (London Borough of
    Hillingdon), 290, 300
Hayes (London Borough of
    Hillingdon), 212
Ickenham (London Borough of
    Hillingdon), 300
London (City and Westminster), 97,
    102, 104, 118, 130, 156, 162, 163,
    177, 185, 266, 267, 272, 279, 281,
    290, 311, 340, 342, 345, 355
Pinner (London Borough of Harrow),
    322
Potters Bar (Hertfordshire), 355
West Drayton (London Borough of
    Hillingdon), 201, 337

Norfolk
Acle, 51, 197
Ashwellthorpe, 281
Aslacton, 51
Attleborough, 243, 247, 260, 334, 354
Aylsham, 41, 247, 305
Bacton, 41, 43
Banningham, 149
Barnham Broom, 243
Barton Turf, 247
Bawburgh, 51, 132
Bedingham, 51, 243
Beeston-next-Mileham, 138
Beeston Regis, 50, 247, 354
Belaugh, 41, 247
Bessingham, 51
Besthorpe, 136, 137, 138, 290, 328
Blakeney, 41, 135, 149, 352
Blofield, 41

Bradfield, 43
Breccles, 188
Brisley, 41
Burgh-next-Aylsham, 40
Burnham Deepdale, 188
Burnham Norton, 230
Carbrooke, 43
Carleton Rode, 247, 325, 333, 345
Castle Acre, 204, 232, 247
Castle Rising, 188
Cawston, 43, 149, 243, 248, 349, 352
Cley, 110, 135
Cromer, 41
Dersingham, 208, 338
Ditchingham, 41
East Dereham, 43
East Harling, 149, 316
East Ruston, 248
Edingthorpe, 51, 132, 212, 248
Elsing, 204
Emneth, 149
Erpingham, 43
Fakenham, 41
Felbrigg, 306
Feltwell St. Mary, 218
Fersfield, 280
Filby, 42, 120, 132, 247, 248
Fincham, 188
Forncett St. Peter, 51
Foulsham, 42
Framingham Earl, 51
Fritton, 248
Garboldisham, 42
Gateley, 248
Gissing, 51, 149
Gooderstone, 248
Great Bircham, 341
Great Massingham, 41
Great Snoring, 325
Great Walsingham, 218, 332, 346, 354
Great Witchingham, 200
Great Yarmouth, 342
Gresham, 200
Grimston, 41
Haddiscoe, 51
Hales, 51, 130, 132
Happisburgh, 41, 43, 197, 243
Hardley, 212
Harpley, 120, 218
Heckingham, 115, 130
Hemblington, 200, 212

Hickling, 43
Hilborough, 42, 118
Hindringham, 43
Honing, 43
Horsham St. Faith, 43, 232
Houghton St. Giles, 248
Hoveton St. Peter, 275
Hunstanton, 248
Ingham, 42
Intwood, 51
Irstead, 247, 248
Kenninghall, 276
Ketteringham, 80
King's Lynn, 142, 176, 305
Knapton, 102, 149, 354
Little Walsingham, 200, 354
Loddon, 248, 349
Ludham, 149, 247, 248, 349
Lyng, 341
Marham, 43
Matlask, 51
Mattishall, 248
Melton Constable, 323
Merton, 243
Morston, 248
Mundesley, 41
Narborough, 43
Necton, 149, 152
North Burlingham, 80, 149, 249
North Creake, 149
North Elmham, 249
Northrepps, 42
Norton Subcourse, 278
Norwich, 41, 43, 94, 149, 152, 156,
   157, 162, 214, 266, 272, 300, 316,
   334, 341
Paston, 212
Poringland, 51
Potter Heigham, 51, 132, 149, 201,
   247, 249
Pulham St. Mary the Virgin, 41, 110
Ranworth, 43, 243, 247, 249, 334, 354
Redenhall, 42
Reedham, 41
Reepham, 28
Repps, 51
Ringland, 152
Ringstead, 322
Roughton, 51
Runhall, 51
Rushall, 51

Saham Toney, 41
Salhouse, 324
Sall, 41, 118, 142, 152, 176, 204, 268,
    338, 352
Scarning, 243, 324
Scottow, 43
Sculthorpe, 188
Sharrington, 44, 152
Shelton, 176, 352
Sheringham, 218
Shernborne, 186
Shipdham, 228
Sloley, 200
Snettisham, 140, 174
South Burlingham, 145, 184, 232, 354
South Creake, 149, 184
Southrepps, 43
South Walsham, 28
South Wootton, 188
Sparham, 41
Stalham, 200
Strumpshaw, 42
Suffield, 246, 250
Surlingham, 197, 304
Swaffham, 42, 149
Swafield, 250
Swanton Morley, 43
Terrington St. Clement, 42, 105, 176,
    352
Thompson, 243
Thornham, 250
Tibenham, 41, 344
Tilney All Saints, 149
Tivetshall St. Margaret, 276
Toftrees, 188
Trimingham, 250
Trunch, 44, 149, 206, 250
Tunstead, 250
Upton, 197, 247, 250
Upwell, 149
Walcott, 41, 43
Walpole St. Peter, 132, 142, 176, 250,
    352
Walsoken, 168, 200
Watton, 349
Wellingham, 250
Weston Longville, 250
West Walton, 48, 68, 118, 170
Wickmere, 51
Wiggenhall St. Germans, 218, 354
Wiggenhall St. Mary the Virgin, 218,
    250, 354

Wighton, 176
Wilton, 218
Wimbotsham, 220
Winterton, 42
Wood Dalling, 41
Woodton, 51
Worstead, 43, 204, 243
Wymondham, 44, 149, 334

Northamptonshire (* now in
    Cambridgeshire)
Aldwincle St. Peter, 89
Ashby St. Ledgers, 244
*Barnack, 88, 115, 164
Brackley, 70, 102
Brixworth, 165
Bugbrooke, 244
Bulwick, 94
Castle Ashby, 302
*Castor, 66, 164
Church Brampton, 89, 208
Croughton, 215
Denford, 89, 124
Duston, 152
Earls Barton, 64
East Haddon, 195
Easton Maudit, 94
Easton Neston, 290
*Etton, 89
Fawsley, 285
Fotheringhay, 57
Geddington, 23
Great Brington, 285
Harpole, 192
Higham Ferrers, 94, 268, 272, 301
Irchester, 88
Kettering, 94
King's Sutton, 96
Little Billing, 186
Loddington, 89
Lowick, 57, 281
Nassington, 96
Northampton, 130, 168
Orlingbury, 70
Oundle, 94, 228
*Peakirk, 215
*Peterborough, 127, 156, 162
Polebrook, 89
Raunds, 89, 214
Ringstead, 140
Rockingham, 22

Rothersthorpe, 346
Rothwell, 64
Rushden, 94
Slapton, 212, 215
Stanford, 184, 275, 314, 342
Stowe-Nine-Churches, 290
Thorpe Malsor, 89
Thrapston, 89
Titchmarsh, 52, 57
Wadenhoe, 48
Wakerley, 94, 166
*Wansford, 192
Warkton, 57, 298
Warmington, 89, 170
Weekley, 94
Welford, 124
Wellingborough, 185, 322
West Haddon, 192
Weston Favell, 342
Whiston, 57
Wilby, 96
*Wittering, 164

Northumberland
Bamburgh, 21
Bolam, 21, 64
Brinkburn, 21
Bywell St. Andrew, 64
Chillingham, 281
Haltwhistle, 170
Hexham, 132
Newcastle (Tyne & Wear), 96
Ovingham, 64

Nottinghamshire
Averham, 52
Car Colston, 328
East Markham, 124, 185, 306
Egmanton, 185
Gamston, 52
Hawton, 328, 330
Holme, 90, 132, 185
Langar, 290
Lenton, 192
Newark, 90, 305, 311
Rolleston, 52
Scarrington, 80
Southwell, 162, 163, 171, 228
Strelley, 282
Teversal, 182
Whatton, 282

Oxfordshire
Adderbury, 88, 96, 126, 144, 328
Ardley, 48
Bampton, 88, 334
Barford St. Michael, 115
Begbroke, 48
Black Bourton, 215
Bladon, 26
Bloxham, 96
Brightwell Baldwin, 305, 308
Broadwell, 88
Burford, 311
Cassington, 129
Caversfield, 48
Chalgrove, 215
Charlton-on-Otmoor, 244
Chastleton, 20
Chinnor, 308
Chipping Norton, 106
Chiselhampton, 178
Church Handborough, 94, 116, 244
Clanfield, 127
Combe, 209
Dorchester, 90, 174, 196, 202, 304,
    313, 328
Ducklington, 140
Emmington, 48
Ewelme, 176, 204, 282, 354
Forest Hill, 341
Great Rollright, 52
Hook Norton, 52, 192
Horley, 185, 212
Idbury, 106, 324
Iffley, 66, 115, 129, 168
Kelmscott, 71
Little Faringdon, 338
Marsh Baldon, 128
Merton, 234
Minster Lovell, 226
North Leigh, 156, 209, 311, 354
Oxford, 31, 52, 57, 64, 80, 88, 96, 110,
    132, 144, 146, 156, 177, 208, 228,
    272, 302, 304, 306, 314, 316, 321,
    334, 352
Rotherfield Greys, 290
Rycote, 344
Shilton, 196
Shipton-under-Wychwood, 88
Somerton, 52, 334
South Leigh, 209
South Newington, 215

Stanton Harcourt, 52, 283, 290
Swalcliffe, 209
Swinbrook, 292, 308, 332
Tackley, 52
Wheatfield, 180
Whitchurch, 23
Widford, 354
Witney, 88, 308
Wood Eaton, 212
Yarnton, 298, 316, 322, 334

Rutland (now part of Leicestershire)
Barrowden, 90
Empingham, 94
Essendine, 71
Exton, 96, 285
Ketton, 90
Langham, 90
Little Casterton, 71
Lyddington, 26
Oakham, 174, 342
Seaton, 90
South Luffenham, 94
Stoke Dry, 144, 166, 184
Teigh, 180
Tickencote, 166
Tinwell, 48
Whissendine, 70

Shropshire (now Salop)
Alveley, 341
Aston Eyre, 116
Claverley, 215
Clee, 64
Condover, 286, 292
Edstaston, 120
Heath Chapel, 168
Holdgate, 192
Hughley, 244
Ludlow, 272, 316
Melverley, 62
Moreton Corbet, 286
Moreton Say, 343
Norton-in-Hales, 292
Pitchford, 20, 280, 284
Shawbury, 52
Shrewsbury, 180
Stokesay, 20, 344
Stottesdon, 192
Tong, 268, 283, 286,
    292

Somerset (* now in Avon)
Axbridge, 32, 344
*Banwell, 32, 184, 204, 235, 242
Barwick, 223
Batcombe, 32
*Bath, 31, 58, 106
*Bathampton, 52
*Batheaston, 34
Bishop's Hull, 223
Bishop's Lydeard, 34, 223, 234, 242
*Blagdon, 34
*Bleadon, 32, 235
Brent Knoll, 32, 145, 223, 292
*Brislington, 34
Broomfield, 225
Bruton, 32, 145
Brympton D'Evercy, 20, 71
*Cameley, 184
Carhampton, 242
Cheddar, 32
Chedzoy, 34
*Chelvey, 52
*Chew Magna, 34, 280, 283, 286
*Chew Stoke, 34
Chewton Mendip, 34, 352
*Churchill, 292
Combe Florey, 38
*Congresbury, 204
Cranmore, 32
Crewkerne, 34, 146, 176
Croscombe, 234, 244
Crowcombe, 142, 225
Culbone, 130
Curry Rivel, 142
Ditcheat, 212
*Dundry, 22, 34
Dunster, 242
East Brent, 316, 343
Enmore, 34
Evercreech, 32, 124, 145, 352
Farleigh Hungerford, 284
Glastonbury, 34
Halse, 242
Hatch Beauchamp, 34, 225
High Ham, 125, 145, 242
*Hinton Blewett, 184
Hinton St. George, 34
Huish Episcopi, 34
*Hutton, 34, 235
Ile Abbots, 34
Ilminster, 32, 176

Kilmersdon, 34
Kingsbury Episcopi, 34
Kingston St. Mary, 34
Langport, 32, 316
Leigh-on-Mendip, 32, 145, 352
*Locking, 34, 192
*Long Ashton, 283
Long Sutton, 32, 145, 232, 354
Luccombe, 23
Lullington, 192
Lympsham, 34
Lyng, 34
Mark, 32, 145
Martock, 34, 145
Mells, 32
Middlezoy, 34
Milverton, 225
Minehead, 23, 127, 242, 333
Monksilver, 125, 204, 225, 232
Montacute, 20
Moorlynch, 345
Muchelney, 34, 146
Mudford, 34
*Nailsea, 34
Nettlecombe, 200, 322, 337
North Cadbury, 20, 225
North Curry, 58
North Petherton, 34
Norton-sub-Hamdon, 34
Old Cleeve, 345
Othery, 34, 341
*Portishead, 34
*Priston, 102
*Publow, 34
*Puxton, 184
Queen Camel, 242
Rodney Stoke, 204, 234, 244
Ruishton, 34
*St. Catherines, 20
Selworthy, 22, 146, 208
Shepton Mallet, 32, 146
Somerton, 145
Spaxton, 225
Staple Fitzpaine, 34
Stogumber, 225, 344
Stogursey, 225
Stoke Pero, 48
Stoke St. Gregory, 58, 234
Sutton Bingham, 215
Taunton, 34, 201
Timberscombe, 242

Trull, 184, 225, 232, 316, 354
Watchet, 146, 345
Weare, 32
Wedmore 32, 212, 344
Wellington, 292
*Wellow, 120, 145, 184
Wells, 31, 32, 76, 104, 108, 127, 145,
    162, 163, 170, 272, 311, 314
West Camel, 263
*Weston-super-Mare, 235
Weston Zoyland, 32, 145, 333
*Wick St. Lawrence, 235
*Winford, 34
*Winscombe, 32, 318
*Wraxall, 34, 286
*Wrington, 32
Yeovil, 34, 228

Staffordshire
Brewood, 286
Checkley, 314
Elford, 283, 286
Enville, 70
Hamstall Ridware, 337
Ilam, 21, 192
Ingestre, 178
Kinver, 308
Lichfield, 298, 321
Stafford, 192
Tutbury, 115
Wolverhampton (West Midlands),
    235

Suffolk
Acton, 301, 308
Aldham, 51
Athelington, 220
Bacton, 149
Badingham, 149, 200
Barking, 145
Barnby, 346
Barningham, 220, 244
Beccles, 44, 48, 110
Blyford, 333
Blythburgh, 104, 106, 146, 176, 220,
    349, 352
Boxford, 80, 112
Boxted, 280, 298
Bradfield Combust, 214
Bramfield, 48, 132, 244, 252, 292
Bungay, 41

Bury St. Edmunds, 106, 149, 355
Cavendish, 24, 26, 106, 142
Chediston, 197
Clare, 228
Coddenham, 106, 149
Combs, 43
Cotton, 118, 149
Covehithe, 43
Cratfield, 200
Culford, 294
Dennington, 145, 220, 260, 283
Denston, 176, 220, 352
Earl Stonham, 43, 149, 208
East Bergholt, 48
Euston, 178
Eye, 42, 244, 252
Falkenham, 43
Framlingham, 41, 152, 286, 294, 342
Framsden, 40, 110, 149
Fressingfield, 110, 149, 220, 354
Fritton, 51, 130, 132, 134
Gislingham, 149
Great Ashfield, 112
Great Barton, 43
Great Wenham, 43
Grundisburgh, 149, 212
Hadleigh, 83
Hasketon, 51
Hawstead, 283
Helmingham, 42, 294
Hemley, 44
Hepworth, 204
Herringfleet, 51
Hessett, 42
Heveningham, 149
Hollesley, 43
Hopton (Diss), 149, 354
Icklingham All Saints, 208
Ilketshall St. Margaret, 51
Ixworth Thorpe, 220
Kersey, 22, 24, 110
Kessingland, 44
Lakenheath, 149, 220
Lavenham, 44, 106, 176, 352
Laxfield, 41, 200
Little Saxham, 51
Little Stonham, 42, 149
Little Waldingfield, 42
Long Melford, 106, 176, 352
Lound, 185
Mendlesham, 42, 204

Mildenhall, 43, 149
Needham Market, 152
Rattlesden, 149
Redgrave, 298
Rickinghall Inferior, 51
Rougham, 42
Rushbrooke, 276
Saxmundham, 197
Shotley, 149
Snape, 43, 200
Somerleyton, 244, 252
Southwold, 44, 102, 104, 106, 176,
   247, 252, 268, 352
Stoke-by-Nayland, 42, 120, 176
Stonham Aspall, 106
Stowlangtoft, 212, 220, 263, 268
Sudbury, 204
Tannington, 220
Theberton, 51
Thornham Parva, 132, 334
Trimley, 28
Ufford, 41, 204, 220, 354
Walberswick, 42
Waldringfield, 44
Walsham-le-Willows, 149
Wenhaston, 209
Westhall, 200, 252
Weston, 200
Wetherden, 149
Weybread, 51
Wilby, 42, 220
Wingfield, 268, 280, 283
Wissington, 215
Withersfield, 220
Woodbridge, 42, 176
Woolpit, 110, 149, 220
Wordwell, 220
Worlingworth, 149, 204
Yaxley, 252

Surrey
Alfold, 81
Bletchingley, 300
Burstow, 81
Chaldon, 215, 345
Compton, 82, 346, 347
Crowhurst, 28, 81
Dunsfold, 218
Esher, 344
Ewhurst, 112
Gatton, 344

Goldalming, 83
Hambledon, 28
Leatherhead, 131
Lingfield, 344
Merstham, 82
Newdigate, 81
Ockham, 135
Old Woking, 120
Petersham (London Borough of Richmond), 178, 300
Shere, 24, 82, 347
Stoke D'Abernon, 208, 234, 294, 301
Tandridge, 28
Warlingham, 212
West Horsley, 212

Sussex (East and West)
Amberley, 135, 166
Arundel (West), 283, 284, 286
Ashburnham (East), 294
Barnham (West), 135
Battle (East), 286
Bosham (West), 135, 164
Boxgrove (West), 81, 135, 156, 168, 311
Brede (East) 347
Brighton (East), 192
Broadwater (West), 302
Burpham (West), 135, 168
Burwash (East), 135
Bury (West), 82
Chichester (West), 166, 216, 266, 272, 334
Clayton (West), 216
Climping (West), 135, 170
Coates (West), 185
Cowfold (West), 304
Crowhurst (East), 28
East Dean (East), 81
Etchingham (East), 102
Ford (West), 81
Friston (East), 81
Hardham (West), 214, 216
Horsted Keynes (West), 82
Lewes (East), 50, 102
Lyminster (West), 145
Mayfield (East), 344
Newhaven (East), 134
New Shoreham (West), 168
Old Shoreham (West), 66, 81, 135, 166, 168

Ovingdean (East), 134
Patcham (East), 209
Piddinghoe (East), 50, 102
Playden (East), 82
Rudgwick (West), 81
Rye (East), 104
Selham (West), 166
Slindon (West), 280
Sompting (West), 64
Southease (East), 50
South Harting (West), 24
Steyning (West), 81, 168
Tangmere (West), 81, 135
Tarring Neville (East), 81
Telscombe (East), 81
Tortington (West), 81, 166
Trotton (West), 214, 308
Udimore (East), 135
Warbleton (East), 208, 304, 344
West Chiltington (West), 216, 331
West Grinstead (West), 112, 308
West Tarring (West), 83
Winchelsea (East), 174, 283
Withyham (East), 294
Worth (West), 164, 166
Tapton (West), 81

Warwickshire
Berkswell (West Midlands), 112, 126, 132
Brailes, 196
Coleshill, 192
Coventry (West Midlands), 84, 162
Curdworth, 186, 208
Knowle (West Midlands), 244
Stoneleigh, 166, 192
Stratford-on-Avon, 209, 272
Studley, 284
Sutton Coldfield (West Midlands), 287
Tysoe, 196
Warwick, 279, 284, 312

Westmorland (now in Cumbria)
Brougham (Ninekirk), 21, 178
Grasmere, 21, 152
Ravenstonedale, 180

Wiltshire
Aldbourne, 25
Avebury, 194, 260

Bishopstone, 294
Boyton, 135
Bradford-on-Avon, 166
Brinkworth, 234
Bromham, 312
Castle Combe, 25
Castle Eaton, 324
Chirton, 52
Compton Bassett, 240, 244
Dauntsey, 209
Devizes, 66, 312
Edington, 129, 176
Great Chalfield, 20, 71
Hillmarton, 244
Hullavington, 341
Lydiard Tregoze, 294, 332
Malmesbury, 108, 116
Nettleton, 58
Oaksey, 212, 214
Old Dilton, 182
Salisbury, 96, 127, 162, 163, 209, 352
Stanton Fitzwarren, 194
Steeple Ashton, 25, 176
Steeple Langford, 126, 296
Stourton, 21
Stratford-sub-Castle, 234
Sutton Benger, 341
Westwood, 58
Wylye, 338
Yatton Keynell, 244

Worcestershire (now Hereford and
    Worcester)
Badsey, 52
Besford, 260
Bredon, 345
Chaddesley Corbett, 194
Croome D'Abitot, 296
Crowle, 112
Dormston, 62
Elmley Castle, 128, 296
Evesham, 58
Great Malvern, 58, 272, 318, 345, 354
Great Witley, 180
Kempsey, 315
Little Malvern, 345
Pirton, 58
Ripple, 272
Shelsley Walsh, 345
Strensham, 184, 256, 300, 343
Warndon, 62

Wickhamford, 20, 296
Worcester, 77, 132, 272, 311

Yorkshire (now North, South, and
    West Yorkshire, and Humberside)
Adel (West), 115, 120, 166, 168
Almondbury (West), 318
Alne (North), 115
Appleton-le-Street (North), 64
Arncliffe (North), 21
Beeford (Humberside), 62
Bessingby (Humberside), 194
Beswick (Humberside), 338
Beverley (Humberside), 52, 62,
    129, 138, 146, 152, 156, 266, 272,
    273, 284, 306, 328, 337, 352
Birkin (North), 115, 168
Bishop Burton (Humberside), 25
Bossall (North), 126
Brayton (North), 115, 166
Cottingham (Humberside), 140
Cowlam (Humberside), 186
Coxwold (North), 62
Croft (North), 344
Dent (Cumbria), 25
Easby (North), 216
Edstone (North), 128
Filey (North), 102
Fishlake (South), 115, 196
Flamborough (Humberside), 102,
    260, 262, 354
Great Driffield (Humberside), 62
Grinton (North), 21
Guisborough (Cleveland), 287
Hedon (Humberside), 52, 62, 129
Hemingborough (North), 94
Hinderwell (North), 338
Holme-upon-Spalding Moor
    (Humberside), 22
Hubberholme (North), 262
Hull (Humberside), 140
Husthwaite (North), 21
Kirkburn (Humberside), 116, 166,
    186
Kirkdale (North), 128
Kirk Hammerton (North), 64, 166
Langtoft (Humberside), 186
Lastingham (North), 132
Laughton-en-le Morthen (South), 96
Liverton (North), 166
Methley (West), 284

North Grimston (North), 166, 186
Patrington (Humberside), 94, 125, 140, 174, 330
Pickering (North), 212, 214, 216, 354
Preston (Humberside), 62
Reighton (North), 186
Riccall (North), 116
Ripon (North), 162, 266, 272
Romaldkirk (now Durham), 25
Royston (South), 144
Rudston (Humberside), 26
Sancton (Humberside), 62
Skelton (North), 118, 127, 170, 325
Stillingfleet (North), 116, 120
Thirsk (North), 204
Thornhill (West), 280, 318
Thornton-le-Dale (North), 25
Thorpe Salvin (South), 116, 194
Tickhill (South), 62
Wath (North), 208
Well (North), 204
West Tanfield (North), 25, 284
Wharram-le-Street (North), 64
Whitby (North), 182
Wighill (North), 116
Worsborough (South), 280
York (North), 52, 78, 96, 127, 162, 313, 318, 354

Wales
Bettws Newydd, Monmouth (Gwent), 260
Derwen, Denbigh (Clwyd), 260
Gresford, Denbigh (Clwyd), 52, 53, 146
Llananno, Radnor (Powys), 260
Llanegryn, Merioneth (Gwynedd), 260
Llaneilian, Anglesey (Gwynedd), 260
Llanengan, Carnarvon (Gwynedd), 260
Llanfilo, Brecknock (Powys), 260
Llangwm, Denbigh (Clwyd), 260
Llangwm Uchaf, Monmouth (Gwent), 260
Llanrwst, Denbigh (Gwynedd), 260
Llanwnog, Montgomery (Powys), 260
Montgomery, Montgomery (Powys), 260
Old Radnor, Radnor (Powys), 342
Patricio, Brecknock (Powys), 260
Ruthin, Denbigh (Clwyd), 146
St. David's, Pembroke (Dyfed), 146, 270